Becoming Victoria

Becoming Victoria

Lynne Vallone

Yale University Press
New Haven and London

For information about this and other Yale University Press publications, please contact:
U.S. Office: sales.press@yale.edu   www.yale.edu/yup
Europe Office: sales@yaleup.co.uk   www.yaleup.co.uk

Set in Walbaum MT by Northern Phototypesetting Ltd, Bolton, Lancs
Printed in China through Worldprint

Library of Congress Cataloging-in-Publication Data

Vallone, Lynne.
Becoming Victoria / Victoria Vallone.
p. cm.
Includes index
ISBN 0-300-08950-3 (cloth)
1. Victoria, Queen of Great Britain, 1819-1901—Childhood and youth. 2. Great Britain—
History—George IV, 1820-1830—Biography. 3. Great Britain—History—William IV,
1830-1837—Biography. 4. Great Britain—History—Victoria, 1837-1901—Biography.
5. Queens—Great Britain—Biography. I. Title.
DA555.V34 2001 941.08'092—dc21 00-068561 CIP

A catalogue record for this book is available from the British Library.

2 4 6 8 10 9 7 5 3 1

For Max and Rosalie

Contents

List of Illustrations   ix
Acknowledgements   xi
Preface   xv

Chapter One
The Baby in the Palace, 1819–1827
1

Chapter Two
The Little Princess Enters Education Land, 1828–1832
40

Chapter Three
Private and Public Princess, 1832–1834
75

Chapter Four
The Importance of Being Victoria, 1835
122

Chapter Five
'The Fair White Rose of Perfect Womanhood', 1836–1837
168

Notes   202
Bibliography   241
Index   246

Illustrations

All illustrations unless otherwise specified are courtesy of the Royal Collection © HM Queen Elizabeth II.

1. Kate Greenaway, *Queen Victoria's Jubilee Garland*, engraved by Edmund Evans. London: George Routledge and Sons, 1887. De Grummond Children's Literature Collection, University of Southern Mississippi. — xiv

2. Paul Johann Georg Fischer, watercolour of Princess Victoria as an infant, 1819. — 4

3. William Skelton, engraving after Sir William Beechey portrait of Edward, Duke of Kent, 1815. © The British Museum. — 5

4. Lady Elizabeth Heathcote, drawing of Princess Victoria, 1822. Philip Mould, Historical Portraits, Ltd., London. — 10

5. Princess Victoria's blonde lace dress, 1831–32. Museum of London. — 13

6. Princess Victoria, self-portrait drawing, 1827. — 16

7. Princess Victoria, drawing of 'An Armenion', 1827. — 17

8. Princess Victoria, drawing of Baroness Lehzen, 1836. — 24

9. William Behnes, marble bust of Princess Victoria, 1829. — 32

10. M. U. Sears, engraving of Princess Victoria as a fashion plate. Published by the *Young Ladies' Library*, 1829. — 34

11. Richard Lane, drawing of Princess Victoria, 1829. Lithographed by Richard James Lane. Printed by C. Hullmandel, London. Published by J. Dickinson, London, 1829. — 35

12. H. H. Emmerson, illustration of 'The Princess and Her Pets' from *The May Blossom: or the Princess and Her People*, by Marion M. Wingrave, London: Frederick Warne and Co., 1881. De Grummond Children's Literature Collection, University of Southern Mississippi. — 36

13. Frontispiece to *The Fairies' Favourite; or the Story of Queen Victoria Told for Children*, by T. Mullett Ellis. London: Ash Partners Ltd, 1897. Department of Special Collections, the University of Chicago Library. — 38

14. *Princess Victoria* after John Hayter, 1833, lithographed by William Sharp. Published by J. Dickinson, London, 1833. © The British Museum. — 41

15. Princess Victoria, drawing as illustration for her composition 'Sophia and Adolphus', 1829. The Royal Archives. © HM Queen Elizabeth II. — 51

16. After Westall, 1830, engraving of *Her Majesty the Queen at the Age of Eleven Years*. © The British Museum. — 61

17. Engraving of *Her Highness the Princess Victoria in her Pony Phaeton*, drawn by J. Doyle. Printed by J. Doyle and William Fowler, 1829. © The British Museum. 69

18. 'The Princess Visiting a Cotton Mill', from Mrs O. F. Walton, *Pictures and Stories from Queen Victoria's Life*, 1901. The Renier Collection of Children's Books. © V&A Picture Library. 77

19. Princess Victoria, watercolour of *La Sylphide*, 1834. 83

20. Anon., Dash (dog) in trousers. 89

21. Princess Victoria, drawing of 'Sister Victoire', 1837. 90

22. *Queen Victoria's Journal*, entry for 26 April 1834. The Royal Archives. © HM Queen Elizabeth II. 94

23. Princess Victoria, watercolour of 'Guilia Grisi as Anna Bolena', 1834. 96

24. Princess Victoria, self-portrait drawing, 1834. 99

25. Princess Victoria, drawing of Lady Catherine Jenkinson, 1836. 99

26. Princess Victoria, watercolour map of Europe, n.d. 101

27. Queen Victoria, drawing of Leopold I, 1839. 103

28. Princess Victoria, drawing of Eliza at her toilette, 1834. 105

29. After Sir George Hayter, *The Princess (later Queen) Victoria*, engraved by James Bromley. Printed by Lahee, London. Published by Colnaghi, Son and Co., London, 1833. Mezzotint. 110

30. After Sir George Hayter, *The Duchess of Kent and Princess (later Queen) Victoria*, lithographed by Richard James Lane. Printed by Graf and Soret, London, 1834. 112

31. After Beechey, engraving by William Skelton, *The Duchess of Kent and Princess Victoria*, 1820. © The British Museum. 113

32. J. Wedderburn, watercolour illustrating *Tom Thumb*, n.d. 118

33. H. H. Emmerson, illustration of 'The Princess Gardening' from *The May Blossom: or the Princess and Her People*, by Marion M. Wingrave, London: Frederick Warne and Co., 1881. De Grummond Children's Literature Collection, University of Southern Mississippi. 123

34. Princess Victoria, drawing of Fanny Kemble as Lady Macbeth, *c.* 1833. 127

35. Princess Victoria, drawing of 'Amazons at War', 1833. 137

36. Princess Victoria, watercolour of 'The Bravo', 1835. 138

37. After Henry Collen, *Princess Victoria*, 1836, engraved by T. Woolnoth, published in 1837. © The British Museum. 143

38. Princess Victoria, self-portrait drawing, 8 November 1835. The Royal Archives. © HM Queen Elizabeth II. 161

39. Anon., Princess Victoria with autograph, published by R. A. Charlton, n.d. © The British Museum. 169

40. Anon., Queen Victoria as a blooming rose, presented with *Novelty*, vol. 3, September 1837, lithographed by William Clark. © The British Museum. 171

41. Richard Lane, coloured drawing of Queen Victoria, June 1837. © The British Museum. 173

42. Princess Victoria, drawing of 'Don Fernando', 1836. 179

43. Princess Victoria's velvet dress, 1835–37. Museum of London. 185

44. Princess Victoria, watercolour of gypsy woman and children, 1836. 190

45. Henry Tanworth Wells, *Victoria Regina: Victoria Receiving News of Her Accession*, 1880. Oil on canvas. Tate Britain, London. 197

46. M. Bowley illustration of 'The Duchess of Kent and Princess Victoria', from *Royal Children of English History* by E. Nesbit, New York: Mershon Company, 1900. 201

Acknowledgements

In a transcontinental undertaking of this magnitude and duration, one is bound to accumulate many debts of gratitude. This project has been indelibly marked by the generosity and goodwill of many people and granting institutions which I would like to thank, however inadequately, here.

I would first like to thank Her Majesty Queen Elizabeth II for her gracious permission to cite and reproduce materials from the Royal Archives and the Royal Library at Windsor Castle. Through their attentiveness, expertise and many acts of kindness, Lady Sheila de Bellaigue, Registrar of the Royal Archives, and her wonderful staff created a most congenial atmosphere for research. My happy memories of working in the Royal Archives and the friendships that I formed there will last a lifetime. For their assistance, thanks are also due to Miss Bridget Wright, Bibliographer, Royal Library, and Mrs Prudence Sutcliffe, Assistant Curator, Print Room, Royal Library. In obtaining images for this book, I would also like to acknowledge the efficient assistance of the staff at the Victoria and Albert Picture Library, British Museum Photographs Department and Blythe House, Mr Philip Mould and Miss Lottie Bailey of Historical Portraits Ltd.

A number of people aided me in my searches for children's books about Queen Victoria. I would like to thank Tessa Chester, curator of the Renier Children's Book Collection of the Victoria and Albert Museum; Dee Jones, curator of the de Grummond Children's Literature Collection at the University of Southern Mississippi, and Rita Smith, curator of the Baldwin Library of Historical Children's Literature at the University of Florida, for their cheerful and expert assistance. I am also grateful to Gordon McMullan of Kings College,

University of London, and Kimberly Reynolds of Roehampton Institute, for affording me opportunities during the writing of this book to present portions of my research to faculty and graduate students at these institutions.

Closer to home, this project and I have been well nurtured by a network of colleagues and institutions in Texas. I would like to thank my Dean, Woodrow Jones, Jr, and my department head, J. Lawrence Mitchell, for their unflagging support of my work over the years, and for this project in particular. The reductions in teaching that I was granted from the Department of English greatly assisted my completion of this project. A College of Liberal Arts Faculty Development Leave for the Autumn 1997 semester allowed me to relocate to Windsor and concentrate solely on Queen Victoria's girlhood. I also gratefully acknowledge the receipt of a Faculty Fellowship from the College of Liberal Arts which funded yet another trip to the Royal Archives. Jeffrey N. Cox, former director of the Interdisciplinary Group for Historical Study at Texas A&M University (now the Center for Humanities Research), and James Rosenheim, current director of the CHR, have provided much-appreciated course relief, research-sharing opportunities, and friendship.

I would also like to express my gratitude for a number of research grants that assisted me in making trips to England: the Children's Literature Association Research Grant; the South Central Modern Language Association International Travel Grant; and, at Texas A&M University, the Women's Studies Program Faculty Research Fellowship; the Mini-Grant Program; the Scholarly and Creative Enhancement Grant Program; and the International Research Travel Assistance Grant Program.

This book could not have been written without the unceasing generosity and warm hospitality of Geoffrey and Barbara Clemens. Their friendship has been the greatest gift I have received in writing this project. Gordon McMullan's door was always open to me and I gratefully acknowledge his friendship and recall with pleasure the many wonderful meals we've shared together. My esteemed colleague in Children's Literature Studies, Peter Hunt, and his lovely, lively family, have been ever-welcoming to me and mine.

A number of dear friends have graced me with their wisdom, humour and care: Mary Bucholtz, Giovanna del Negro, Susan Egenolf, Marian Eide,

Kate Kelly, Pamela Matthews, Claudia Nelson, Lissa Paul, Larry Reynolds, Jim Rosenheim, and Susan Stabile. John and Phyllis Vallone, loving model parents, have always provided just what is most needed. Charles Grench, former Editor-in-chief at Yale University Press, was a friend to the project at the beginning, and Robert Baldock, who has seen the book to its conclusion, has proven to be both a crack editor and a swank lunch companion.

Closest to home, *in* my home to be exact, live two whose good humour, bravery, and sense of adventure I acknowledge with delight. With nary a whimper, my children, Max and Rosalie Vallone Marchitello, picked up, packed up, and with admirable aplomb, moved to Windsor. Their struggles and triumphs in the classrooms, playing fields, social clubs, riding rings, and countryside of England have provided enduring memories of a unique, sweet interlude in our family's life. I am grateful every day for the privilege of sharing their girlhood and boyhood. This book is dedicated to them.

And for Howard Marchitello, husband and visionary, my depth-less gratitude *con amore per sempre.*

1. Kate Greenaway, *Queen Victoria's Jubilee Garland*, engraved by Edmund Evans.

Preface

If Victoria has been a good queen, as well as a good wife, a good mother,
and a good woman, this is due, under God, to the training she had in
childhood and girlhood. (Ill. 1)

'The Girlhood of Queen Victoria' (1880)[1]

Queen Victoria has never been remembered for her youth, but for her seem-
ingly never ending old age: her years of mourning, her black dress, her dour
expression, her iconic stature. One might wonder, 'Was she *ever* a girl?' – yet
Victoria was a young queen and once popularly called 'the rose of England'.
Now at the centenary of her death, it is time to reassess the early years of
England's durable queen. This study of Queen Victoria's girlhood is not
meant to compete with the many excellent large-scale biographies of
Queen Victoria such as Monica Charlot's *Victoria: The Young Queen* (1991),
Cecil Woodham-Smith's *Queen Victoria: Her Life and Times, 1819–1861*
(1972), and Elizabeth Longford's *Queen Victoria: Born to Succeed* (1964).
Nor is this book solely a work of literary and cultural criticism of Queen
Victoria as a figurehead and cultural marker of an age.[2] Rather, *Becoming
Victoria* is a study of girlhood, and combines biographical with cultural
criticism, focusing on the youth of Princess Victoria by way of her own
words and works found in her letters, stories, drawings, educational materials, and journals. *Becoming Victoria* also tells the story of children's books:
those that Princess Victoria read, those she attempted to copy, and those that
helped create the cultural climate and social mores in which she was raised.
The book locates the young Victoria within the complex and often conflicting

contexts of Georgian children's literature, conventional child-rearing practices, domestic and familial intrigues, and the frequently turbulent political climate of the period. Eventually, Queen Victoria's life itself — especially her girlhood — was transformed into fiction for a later generation, and thus in biographies of the Queen written for girls, the elderly sovereign was reanimated as a pattern girl for young readers to emulate.[3]

The desire for identification between sovereign and young subject is the motivation behind the assertion of the *Girl's Own Paper* quoted above. As queen, Victoria 'belonged' to her subjects, yet the rhetorical strategy of 'The Girlhood of Queen Victoria' emphasizes a unique conflation of girlish queen and queenly girl. Every girl, this sentiment seems to argue, can become a queen. The inverse is also true: the Queen is 'every' girl, or 'any' girl. In his 1864 biographical sketch of Queen Victoria, *Famous Girls Who Have Become Illustrious Women*, John Darton argues, 'The Queen, indeed, never appears so queenly, so true a woman, as when surrounded by her children.'[4] To be *the Queen* is to commit by one's very existence acts of authority and privilege 'unnatural' for a woman but required by the job of sovereign. This empowerment is both actual, and perhaps more important, metaphorical in meaning. The Queen can never not be 'the Queen'; *the Girl*, however, holds a tentative social position from which she may easily fall (through immodest behaviour, for example) and out of which she must grow. In these early books, Victoria's life, therefore, is retold as a 'good' story for girls, and by that I mean an 'appropriate' and inspiring story of a 'natural' woman's life — leading from daughter to wife and then mother — so that the Queen's unusual life and troubled gender position is always read through the lens of domestic containment rather than political power.[5]

Not surprisingly, even biographies of women for adult readers, once they began to be written at all, were primarily the stories of interior or domestic life. In *Telling Women's Lives*, Linda Wagner-Martin comments that

> the writing of women's lives is problematic in part because so few women have had the kind of success that attracts notice. Women's biography is more often based on private events because few women — even women like Eleanor Roosevelt — live public lives. Harder to discover, private events may be ones kept secret by the subject (such as sexual abuse,

dislike for parents, dislike by parents, or other unfortunate childhood or adolescent happenings) or those regarded as unimportant by society.[6]

Certainly this statement holds true for Queen Victoria's early life, which was simultaneously retiring and public and which contained a great deal of primarily sublimated familial tension (especially once she became a young adult). Most significantly, Queen Victoria's childhood and girlhood have been 'secret' to the extent that many aspects of this time of her life have been considered unimportant by scholars and biographers. In defending the need for the lives of people other than socially prominent white men to be told in biographies for young people, Geraldine DeLuca argues that 'women and minority scholars also need the courage to step back from the values of their own traditional academic training and risk the ridicule of pursuing their own questions about shadowy figures that have not achieved the academy's respect'.[7] Although I applaud this sentiment in general, what DeLuca ignores is that it is not only the 'shadowy figures' that are passed over, but the st(age) of life of the individual – even, in the case of Queen Victoria, of a globally famous one – that is undervalued by the scholarly community and society at large. *Becoming Victoria* attempts to redress this imbalance by bringing a fresh look at Victoria's 'age' to a scholarly and a general audience.

> Biography is too important to become a playground for fantasies, however ingenious ....
>
> Elizabeth Longford[8]

I take the force of Lady Longford's comment on the seriousness of the biographical enterprise. However, Longford's pronouncement on the proper form of biography reveals a profoundly utopian conception of the role of the biographer as objective 'historian' rather than 'fanciful' writer. We may *desire* biographies to deliver direct access to unmediated lives, but that biographers 'fantasize' their subjects seems hardly debatable. For me, the fact that every biography tells the story of its author as well as its subject is one of its chief pleasures. In nineteenth-century biographies of famous women written for a young female audience, certainly, the 'fantasy' of female

subordination and 'miniaturization' – even in books and articles purportedly celebrating female achievement and distinction – is fully in play.[9] If
the function of biography is in part the indulging of voyeuristic appetite,
and the biographer the means of satisfying that hunger, then nineteenth-
century biographies for girls – or role model anthologies, in Alison Booth's
phrase – were written to present 'nourishing' histories about inspirational,
often young, moral exemplars.[10]

Certainly, this book about Queen Victoria's childhood and girlhood
reveals my own interests in preserving the unique 'voice' of girlhood.
Becoming Victoria takes the always fascinating childhood and girlhood of
Queen Victoria as its subject, unlike comprehensive biographies in which
the brief discussion of childhood generally functions as a necessary plot
device setting up the 'real' life found in adulthood and monarchy. Unlike
the nineteenth-century apologias for Victoria's life found in role model
anthologies and children's biographies of the Queen, my intentions in helping to uncover the early years of Princess Victoria were not didactic in
design. Nor are there new scandals to be revealed, multiple indiscretions,
vast political intrigue. This is the story of the girl who, by an accident of
birth, lent her name to an Age and influenced the identity of an empire.
Although Victoria's fate must certainly colour any account of her early
years, in this study, Princess is promoted over Queen. The girlhood of
Queen Victoria, which occupied only a brief period, may now, from the vantage point of the twenty-first century and upon the centenary of her death,
seem very remote. Yet it is my hope that in bringing forward the documents
of her youth, the 'any girl' qualities of Princess Victoria that the *Girl's Own
Paper* took pains to delineate have surfaced in ways hitherto unremarked.

I will end these prefatory comments by invoking the Henry Collen painting of Victoria that serves as the cover image of this book. As I discuss in
greater detail in Chapter Four, this painting occasioned an exchange between
Victoria and her sister Feodore wherein the particulars of Victoria's facial
expression were debated. Victoria concludes that her painted mouth does not
well represent her actual mouth because she had posed with lips pressed
together (rather than parted, her usual expression) 'as it is thought more
becoming. ...'[11] It is through Victoria's 'open mouth', however, that this study
locates the 'becoming' qualities in the girlhood of the Queen.

Chapter One

The Baby in the Palace

1819–1827

You now try to go to the Round Pond, but nurses
hate it, because they are not really manly, and
they make you look the other way, at the Big
Penny and the Baby's Palace.

J. M. Barrie, *Peter Pan in Kensington Gardens*
(*1906*)

Almost one hundred years after her birth in 1819, as novelist and playwright J. M. Barrie slyly points out, Queen Victoria's image might have
called to mind pocket change rather than pomp and glory, and the place of
her birth was merely an architectural backdrop to promenade and play.
From this perspective, the old queen signifies little to Edwardian children.
In *Peter Pan in Kensington Gardens*, the narrator compresses the widely
known facts and fancies of Victoria's life at Kensington Palace from birth to
accession – her solitude, love of dolls, the Archbishop of Canterbury's audience with the newly made queen, and her public coronation – into a child's
version of Victoria's life-story: 'She was the most celebrated baby of the
Gardens, and lived in the palace all alone, with ever so many dolls, so people
rang the bell and up she got out of her bed, though it was past six o'clock,
and she lighted a candle and opened the door in her nightdress, and then
they all cried with great rejoicings, "Hail, Queen of England!"'[1] Barrie's
commentary on Victoria's status as either baby on the throne or coin of the

realm, made within the context of a story celebrating endless boyhood, highlights for Barrie, and for us, the mysterious power of both icon and child. Today, as in the past, parents, schools, and society in general attempt the impossible when they desire to know and to fix, in an absolute way, the ever-inscrutable 'Child'. How much more difficult it might be to capture a child from the past whose life-span has labelled an age, and whose supposed character has inflected a cultural personality. 'Victorian' means many things – proper, pompous, and proud are a few apt adjectives – but these are descriptors of age, not of youth. Rarely does 'Victorian' refer to the girlish, playful, or clever. Before the 'door' that Barrie considers a boundary was crossed, before the crowning of the girl-sovereign, Queen Victoria was, indeed, just a baby in the palace.

The events that led to Victoria's unlikely residence in Kensington Palace were set in motion well before she was born, with the failures of parturition and the domestic tragedies of George III's descendants. Not surprisingly, the miserable marriage between George III's heir (the Prince Regent and future George IV) and his first cousin Caroline of Brunswick, produced but one child – Princess Charlotte, Heiress Presumptive to the throne. Her death in 1817 at the age of twenty-one after delivering a stillborn boy dashed the hopes of both the Regent and the nation that a young queen would eventually be crowned. With the death of Charlotte and her child, George IV's line became extinct, and it was up to the next son of George III, William (later William IV), to wear the crown and beget heirs to the throne. Ironically, of King William's twelve children only the two daughters of gentle Queen Adelaide were legitimate, yet they were also sickly and died in infancy. The third surviving son, Edward, Duke of Kent, married somewhat late in life, and fathered a healthy child, Alexandrina Victoria, in 1819.[2] His death eight months later, before there was any chance for a son to supersede his daughter in the line of succession, enhanced the likelihood that Princess Victoria would one day claim the throne.

This brief sketch of Victoria's family history offers a backdrop to the story of an unlikely queen: *if* Princess Charlotte or her son had lived, *if* the Regent had fathered another (legitimate) child, *if* one of Adelaide's daughters had survived, or *if* the Duke of Kent had left Victoria's mother pregnant with a son before he died, Victoria would not have become queen and British history would have been irrevocably altered.

Babyhood

Kensington Palace was a venerable old building by the time the Kents came to live in it. Originally Nottingham House, the structure was purchased by William III in 1689 and enlarged by Christopher Wren and William Kent. Acres of beautiful gardens surrounded the boxy palace which was well situated in what were then the 'intensely rural' outskirts of London.[3] The palace was close to the bustle of town, but essentially functioned as a quiet country retreat. Although draughty, plagued by insects, and somewhat derelict, Kensington Palace was a symbolically important location for a wandering son of George III to call home, if only temporarily. For economy's sake, the debt-ridden Duke of Kent had been living in Brussels and then the town of Amorbach. The impending birth of a royal infant, however, was strong inducement to return to his native land, 'in order to render the Child [the Duchess] bears, *virtually* as well as *legally English*',[4] though he was not especially welcomed by the other members of the Royal Family already ensconced in the palace or nearby. Indeed he was informed, in no uncertain terms, 'not to expect *a cordial reception*'.[5]

Although it first necessitated borrowing additional funds and then a long and arduous trip from Amorbach to London for the heavily pregnant Duchess of Kent, Victoria was born in Kensington Palace at 4 a.m. on 24 May 1819, a robust English daughter. This fact was highly pleasing to her parents, and often remarked upon as testimony of Victoria's appropriateness as queen, even given her German relations. Victoria was later urged to emphasize her English birth to counteract criticism of the Germanness of her mother (she was the widow of the Prince of Leiningen and the sister of Princess Charlotte's husband, Leopold) and the House of Hanover generally. (Once affianced to Victoria, Albert of Saxe-Coburg-Gotha, her first cousin, suffered similar criticism from the press.) Although the Duke of Kent is often credited with the prophetic proclamation that his infant daughter would one day be queen, just after her birth he wrote in response to a friend who had expressed the wish that this child would one day be crowned, and the regret that she wasn't a son: 'But the fact is I see no reason to wish the case [the child's sex] otherwise, except as far as private inclination might dictate; for while I have 3 brothers senior to myself, and one

2. Paul Johann Georg Fischer, watercolour of Princess Victoria as an infant, 1819.

possessing every reasonable prospect of having a family, I should deem it the height of presumption to believe it probable that a future heir to the Crown of England would spring from me.'[6]

No one could have been less concerned about her place in the line of succession than the infant Victoria, and by all accounts she continued to be a promising and lively baby soon very fat on a diet of her mother's milk. (She was weaned in early December.)[7] In a letter written to her mother soon after Victoria's birth, the Duchess of Kent expressed her satisfaction with Victoria's large appetite and her surprise at the eyebrows raised in response to her decision to breast-feed the infant princess: 'I am so very happy that I can breast feed her so well, I would have been desparate (*sic*) to see my little darling on someone else's breast. . . . Everybody is most astonished that I am

3. William Skelton's portrait of Edward, Duke of Kent, 1815.

breast-feeding; people of the mondaine (*sic*) world are really very unhappy, how much genuine joie de vivre do they miss.'⁸ By 1840, however, this story of Queen Victoria's earliest days had been revised to emphasize the Duchess's doting care and the start to Victoria's pleasing 'middle-class' upbringing. The anonymous 'lady' author of *Anecdotes, Personal Traits, and Characteristic Sketches of Victoria the First* notes that the identity of Victoria's wet nurse was of great interest to the public: 'It was very speedily announced that the Royal Duchess intended to suckle the infant Princess herself, and this expression of maternal tenderness so unusual to royalty, was received with the highest satisfaction by the English people, who rejoiced to find that their future Queen was not likely to be reared amidst the cold forms of etiquette, but under the free and uncontrolled influence of the affections of the heart.'[9] Of course, at the time of her birth it was not entirely certain that Victoria would ever become queen, as the comment above implies. Nevertheless, the young Princess was afforded all of the dignities befitting of a highly placed royal child. Her first official portrait, an August 1819 watercolour by Paul Johann Georg Fischer, depicts a plump baby sporting a large Scotch bonnet with equanimity. (A length of the still-bright tartan ribbon worn by Princess Victoria on 2 November 1819 remains preserved in the Royal Archives. Prince Albert's note accompanying it indicates that the Fischer painting was sent to the grandmother Victoria shared with him.) The resemblance between the infant and the Duke of Kent in this picture was surely meant to flatter the fond father (Ill. 2 and Ill. 3). All due care was taken to ensure that the little princess remained in good health. She was successfully vaccinated for smallpox at ten weeks of age (and later in 1827 and 1835).

'Drina', as Victoria was called as a very young child, was the only baby living in Kensington Palace, although she was not the only royal infant of consequence. In the spring of 1819, *The Times* reported the arrival of no fewer than four additions to the Royal Family. The Duchesses of Cambridge and Cumberland gave birth to princes, and the Duchesses of Clarence and Kent delivered princesses: George Cambridge who would one day be considered a good match for Victoria; Charlotte Clarence, who would have preceded Victoria in the line of succession, and who lived for one day only; and George Cumberland, future King of Hanover. (The second Clarence daughter, Elizabeth, was born in 1820 and lived for three months.) Victoria was never to know any of these cousins very well. After her husband's death, when Victoria was less than a year old, the Duchess of Kent kept her young daughter close beside her within a small circle of intimates: her half-sister Feodore, twelve years her senior; her governess Louise Lehzen (hired as Feodore's governess and retained as Victoria's governess in 1824); her Aunt Sophia (daughter of George III); and the Conroy family (John Conroy was equerry to the Duke of Kent and became a close adviser to the Duchess after his death).

The significance of the loss of her father when she was an infant cannot be underestimated when judging Victoria's character and growth into a woman; she would seek male companionship and attention for the rest of her life. Victoria's extreme gratitude for the 'disinterested kindnesses' of Lord Melbourne, her first Prime Minister, attests to this fact. Charlot comments: 'Melbourne's devotion to [Queen Victoria] was fatherly, her fascination with him was similar to that of a student of philosophy with a guru.'[10] While the Duke was not particularly popular within the Royal Family, or perhaps outside it (he was a military man who had developed a reputation for cruelty to his men and who was incapable of staying out of debt), after dismissing his mistress of twenty-seven years, Madame de St Laurent with real regret, he nevertheless willingly accepted his 'duty' to the succession and married a suitable bride. The newly wed couple appear to have been happy enough together, and great joy was evinced at Victoria's birth. She was baptized by the Archbishop of Canterbury in the Cupola Room, the grandest room in Kensington Palace (restored to its early eighteenth-century splendour in 1991) at one month of age. The baptismal font had been brought from the Tower of London for the occasion. Victoria's christening was a stressful occasion for the Kents, as the Prince Regent was in bad temper and refused to allow the baby to be baptized with traditional second names such as 'Charlotte' or 'Augusta' as her parents desired – 'Alexandrina' was for her godfather *in absentia*, the Tsar Alexander of Russia.[11] The King's suggestions for a substitute name lacked creativity (let her take her mother's name, he said), and the baby was duly baptized 'Alexandrina Victoria'.

After the baptism, still plagued by debts, the Kent family was forced to vacate Kensington Palace. They chose to relocate to Sidmouth, Devonshire where households were cheaper to run. There the little family lived peacefully (if not entirely frugally) until the Duke of Kent took ill with a cold – caught, conventional wisdom asserts, because he was too interested in playing with baby Victoria to heed advice and attend to his wet boots.[12] This indisposition progressed into a serious pneumonia-like illness and within two weeks of suffering from pain, fever, and repeated bleedings, he was dead.[13]

Not only was the Duchess shocked and distressed by this unexpected second widowhood (her private letters make it clear that though she had met him just once before their marriage, she was sincerely fond of her husband), but she knew that she was now awkwardly placed as the widowed

German mother of an important child of the English Royal Family. Some of the Duchess's anxieties stemmed from her limited command of the English language, though she tried to lessen the effects of the language barrier by taking English lessons as soon as she was married. The Duchess's isolation was enhanced by her lack of friends in England and in the Royal Family, save for the Duchess of Clarence who had sent warm condolences during Edward Kent's illness and after his death.[14] The Duchess chose to turn for guidance to a male adviser, John Conroy, an Irishman who had been an equerry in the employ of her husband's household. Conroy's self-interest in regard to the Duchess and her daughter became obvious from the moment the Duke's life appeared to be in danger. In the letters the Duchess of Kent wrote to her friend Pauline von Tubeuf, it appears that she trusted Conroy, even as he was pushing the mortally ill Duke to name him as Victoria's guardian. That the Duchess would not allow such a frightening request to be brought before the dying Duke benefited Victoria, as this document would have assigned to Conroy greater power over her than he was ultimately able to achieve through his close alliance with the Duchess.[15] John Conroy was to play a significant role in Victoria's childhood, however, as he continued to be intimately connected with the Duchess of Kent (but not, it would seem, in a sexual relationship as sometimes rumoured) and heavily involved in Princess Victoria's education. Many of the memoranda discussing aspects of Victoria's education are in Conroy's (nearly unreadable) hand, and it is very likely that he directed most if not all of the Duchess's professional correspondence. John Conroy and the 'Kensington System' will be discussed in detail in Chapter Two.

Victoria was fatherless, but not friendless in her early years as is sometimes asserted, perhaps on the basis of Victoria's own observations made years later when reflecting on her childhood.[16] E. F. Benson provides a much-needed corrective to this vision of Victoria's 'rather melancholy' childhood, asserting that it 'would appear to have been much the same as that of any other little girl of the upper classes, who was being very carefully brought up by a lonely mother, and who had the misfortune (though in this case there was a bright lining to that) of not having any brothers'.[17] In fact, Victoria did have a brother – her half-brother Charles Leiningen who, fifteen years her senior, and the heir to the princely house of Leiningen, lived primarily in Germany rather than in England with his mother. Her sister Feodore, however, lived with Victoria and their mother at Kensington Palace until she was married in February 1828 to Prince Ernest Christian Charles of Hohenlohe-Langenburg, a handsome stranger (they had met only twice before their engagement) who was many years her senior. From extant letters between the sisters dating from their separation, it is abundantly clear that they shared a very close and loving relationship. Victoria idolized her older sister's pretty looks and manners; they wore matching dresses of white Buckinghamshire thread lace on Feodore's wedding day.[18] Although the girls were constantly together until Feodore's marriage when Victoria was nine years old, and were very frequent correspondents after that, this sororal aspect of Victoria's early youth has often been overlooked by later writers, if not by the Royal Family itself. Some of this loss of memory may be due to design: as the daughter of her mother's unhappy first marriage to a minor German prince, Feodore perhaps represented, or was perceived to represent, that foreignness or 'otherness' that the Duchess of Kent and the Royal Family were at pains to disguise in themselves. At her death in 1872, *Vanity Fair* was brusque in its dismissal of Feodore's importance: 'The less said about the Queen's German relatives the better.'[19] There are no portraits of Princess Feodore and Princess Victoria together – although a great many portraits of the young Victoria were published – which has helped to create the erroneous impression that Victoria was an only child.[20]

Feodore never appears, for example, in an 1822 series of pencil drawings of three-year-old Victoria drawn by the artist Lady Elizabeth Keith Heathcote, although she would certainly have accompanied the Duchess of Kent and Victoria on their seaside holiday at Ramsgate. Notwithstanding the absence of Feodore, these little-known drawings offer a glimpse into the daily life of the young Victoria, as they depict her clothing, toys and play-time activities with the artist's daughter, Elizabeth Anne, five months younger than the Princess. Lady Elizabeth was a student of Gainsborough, and her tiny pencil sketches, accented by lightly shaded coloured shoes and sashes, are obviously quick studies of active children probably intended as record-keeping and mementoes rather than as display pieces.[21] The Duchess of Kent and Lady Elizabeth were friends, which accounts for the access the

4. Lady Elizabeth Heathcote, drawing of Princess Victoria, 1822.

latter was given to the Princess. In the drawings, Victoria is shown to be plump, curly-headed, and happy (although one drawing shows a distressed princess pointing to her injured foot) (Ill. 4). These drawings give clues to the clothing Princess Victoria wore as a small child. Her indoor daytime wear was an off-the-shoulder dress with short puffed sleeves, an empire waist, and a sash tied in a bow. This is a fashion Victoria seems to have sported throughout her childhood: she is repeatedly depicted in such a style in portraits commissioned during the 1820s (Ill. 5). In Lady Elizabeth Heathcote's sketches Princess Victoria is often drawn wearing a pinafore over and pantalettes under the dress, and blue shoes on her little feet. She sometimes wears a necklace or a morning cap. In a drawing depicting Victoria seated on a donkey's back (a favourite way for Victoria to travel as a child), she wears a diminutive riding habit.

Less indicative of her status than her clothing, the toys that appear in the sketches — balls, books, a rabbit pull-toy, an easel and paints, shells spilling from a bucket, and dolls[22] — could be found in any middle-class home.

Although these drawings may not be particularly notable for their artistry (the character Victoria resembles any cherubic little girl), these drawings — which were not originally meant for publication or composed for flattery's sake — help to illustrate Victoria's 'normal' babyhood in a literal way. Some remnants of the material objects of Victoria's childhood can be found in a small collection of her toys currently housed in Kensington Palace.[23] A large Georgian townhouse for dolls has survived in very good shape, although it is clear that it has been enjoyed; it is of a size and simplicity that would invite play. Princess Victoria wrote to Feodore in 1829, after their first Christmas apart, to describe her gifts. Among them was a number of items to furnish the doll's house, including plates and a housekeeper doll, as well as a toy theatre.[24] In general, these toys are sturdy, typical playthings of the Georgian era. Miniature wood furniture, a toy carriage, cradle, and various dolls with handmade clothing are all items that could be found in many households. Perhaps the more delicate and expensive toys had been broken in the past, but it seems that the toys of Victoria's youth were, for the most part, practical and functional. Although she was raised simply (her diet was plain and bland, her bedtime early, and her clothing mostly unembellished) and, until she was about five years old, with great indulgence, this child's advantages were obviously legion: servants, beautiful clothes, trips to the seaside, donkey carts, royal relations.

The Royal Family was the matter of intense public interest and curiosity in the early nineteenth century that it is today: catching a glimpse of the baby princess in her carriage, or in later years riding on her donkey or strolling with Lehzen, Feodore, and an entourage of servants, was an experience many pleasure-seekers idling in Kensington Gardens hoped for. She was a friendly baby, bold in approaching strangers (except for bishops, of whom Victoria had developed an early dislike 'on account of their wigs and *aprons*', as she put it when an adult).[25] The Evangelical philanthropist and abolitionist William Wilberforce, writing to his friend Hannah More, bluestocking and reformer, reports, '"In consequence of a very civil message from the Duchess of Kent, I waited on her this morning, and found her with her fine, animated child on the floor by her side with its playthings, *of which I soon* became one"'.[26]

Also in this letter, Wilberforce tells More that the Duchess did not at this time have a fluent command of the English language.[27] This fact did not mean, however, that Princess Victoria spoke German as a child. Her mother well knew that Victoria must be perceived as entirely English, and great pains were taken to create her so. While German was 'in the air', Victoria was not taught to read or write the German language until she was seven years old. Victoria's early German exercises make it absolutely clear that she did not have a good command of that language when she first began studying it.[28] To please Albert, Victoria wrote love letters to him in German before they were married, but often broke into English in the middle of them.[29]

Victoria's beloved Uncle Leopold (her mother's brother) was also German, of course, and intimately connected to England through his first marriage to Princess Charlotte, and later, after Charlotte's death, through his 'foster father' relationship to his niece, the next princess destined to be queen. Although he enjoyed public support for a time as the grieving widower, Leopold's upkeep was costly and his popularity waned after Charlotte's death: according to the marriage settlements drawn up prior to the wedding, Leopold was to receive a pension of £50,000 a year from the Civil List for his lifetime, as well as the estate at Claremont (near Esher). (He would later use a small portion of this pension to support the Duchess of Kent.) Victoria, however, *lived* in England and for a number of years helped to keep her uncle there as well; Claremont became her second home

(*facing page*) 5. Princess Victoria's blonde lace dress, 1831–32.

and she dearly loved to visit there. Leopold was undoubtedly Victoria's favourite relative (the Hanover uncles generally kept their distance from Victoria – including the Duke of Sussex who also lived at Kensington Palace). Leopold became the only father figure the half-orphan would have. He was playful and loving with her (though as she grew older he became extremely directive and could also be manipulative), treating her like the little child she was rather than a precious, breakable object. For example, in one of the first surviving letters written by Leopold to Victoria, he gives her a pet name and reassures her that she is in his thoughts: 'It was my intention to have been with you on that day [her birthday in 1827], which has given you dear little chicken to us.'[30] Princess Victoria wrote a brief note to her uncle the following year requesting a souvenir of his trip to Paris: 'Pray don't forget to bring me a parisian toy.'[31]

Victoria adored her uncle and lavished upon him the love she would have given a fond father. Later, after his second marriage, in 1832 – to Louise, a daughter of Louis Philippe, King of the French – Victoria enthusiastically extended her affection to include this aunt whom she did not meet until their 1835 visit at Ramsgate. Victoria was most anxious to please Leopold and to become the princess he wanted her to be: beautiful, perfectly mannered and attired, clever, demure, accomplished, and social. In a very telling comment, and in fact sounding very 'modern', Leopold once suggested to Victoria in 1836 that aristocrats are akin to stage actors, and that their *job* (Leopold called his work as king 'business', and Victoria picked up this terminology once she became queen) was to *perform* royalty for the people. The Duchess of Kent, Victoria, and their entourage were on an autumn trip to Ramsgate in 1836 and multitudinous addresses were given to them by various groups and corporations as they travelled. Victoria found so much attention rather irksome, but it is at this point that Leopold describes her role as he sees it: 'I am happy to find that everybody is very civil, and I recommend though it is a little troublesome to be very attentive in returning their civilities. Unfortunately, high personages are a little like stage actors – they must always make efforts to please their public.'[32] As a child, Victoria was well practised in the art of performance: she was often on display as she grew up, and she was rarely, if ever, alone, so that as a 'good girl' one can surmise that she was required to repress many of her angry feelings. (That she often failed in this 'duty', at least by her mother's and governess's standards, is made clear in her 'Behaviour Books' discussed below.) Victoria's emotionalism comes out most strongly in her letters, not in terms of anger but through the transformation of her strong feelings – perhaps negative ones – into gushing sentiments, and drawings depicting gesture and emotion. She also loved to dress up in costume, though no amateur theatricals were allowed in Kensington Palace.

Drawing and painting were considered appropriate feminine accomplishments in the early nineteenth century, and these were activities that Victoria enjoyed very much from the time she was quite young and could scribble, into her old age. She was also an inveterate doodler (bits of blotting paper survive and are covered with little sketches of the heads of horses and ladies). Victoria clearly had a talent for drawing and watercolours, as even her earliest preserved artistic efforts demonstrate. The most remarkable aspect of Victoria's miniature album from 1827, a present from Lehzen, is her delight in dramatic scenes and gesture where her subjects are 'caught in the act'. The eight-year-old's pencil drawings include representations of a mother and child, a man kneeling, groupings of people, horseback riders, a self-portrait (Ill. 6), and 'an race horse'. She does not confine her artwork to objects and people she knows; one of the drawings depicts 'An Armenion', which is perhaps an attempt to illustrate a lesson in history or geography through a depiction of native costume (Ill. 7).

In addition to her love of drawing, like her uncle, mother, and most children, the Princess Victoria was also fond of animals – especially dogs and horses. Even while Leopold was lecturing the Princess on how to behave, or correcting through their correspondence some fault of hers, he would often 'sweeten' his criticism with a humorous story about one of his dogs: after warning her not to eat so fast, he writes, 'Dächsi is my constant and faithful companion looking generally into the fire and thinking about the affairs of Europe. He has however declined going into the Council, from motives of modesty, thinking himself not qualified [–] a deficiency in his french pronunciation arising from his having been educated in Italy.'[33] Some of Victoria's favourite pets who were painted into the record of her early years include Fanny, a black and tan terrier (shown in a Richard Westall painting: see Ill. 16, on p. 61) and Dash, a King Charles spaniel (playfully

6. Princess Victoria, self-portrait drawing, 1827.

snatching a glove in George Hayter's painting of 1833: see Ill. 29, p. 110).[34] The Kensington Palace menagerie generally included caged birds, the tamest of which the Princess would tease. In a letter from 1828, Feodore reminded Victoria how she used to torment the canaries when she was little.[35] One of the short stories the eight-year-old Victoria wrote while in Ramsgate in the autumn of 1827 is about a little girl, Ellen Stonbridge, who asks her mother if she can purchase some 'linetts'. Her mother gives permission to buy a bird if she will 'take care of it and may clean the cage'.[36] In the absence of many playmates, the affection that children often feel for animals, and the vulnerabilities of dependent creatures, helped to promote sympathy and sensitivity in Victoria and made pets natural companions for her (although it is doubtful that Victoria ever cleaned a bird's cage).

Victoria's world was populated not only with animal friends, but also with a variety of dolls. As a small girl, Victoria had baby dolls, and dress-up dolls (of the kind that a child could make clothes for), and paper dolls that Lehzen or her sister would paint in watercolour for her. These paper dolls range in size from a tiny 1¼ inch tall doll of one of Feodore's children, to the

7. Princess Victoria, drawing of 'An Armenion', 1827.

'adult' dolls of approximately 8 inches in height. These dolls are all painted in full colour, with great detail and care given to the fashions each lady wears. Victoria's paper dolls, as well as those of Victoire Conroy, survive in the Royal Archives today (the Conroy dolls were saved probably because one of the dolls was painted by Victoria). Also carefully preserved in Kensington Palace is a baby doll that had suffered a severe accident and lost its head. Responding to Victoria's report of this tragedy with sympathy, Feodore writes, 'I hope [baby] is almost recovered and that this serious bruise has had no influence on its general health, and that it is not the less in favour for having been beheaded for a short while.'[37] The callous Princess ignores her old favourite and replies, 'Lehzen mended the baby, and I put her by, as a relick; but notwithstanding this, I have got a lovely baby, which is called Clara.'[38] Victoria's first letters to her sister after Feodore's marriage in 1828 are full of news of the 'babies'. The babies sometimes wrote to Feodore themselves with the help of their 'mother's' guiding hand.[39] But a child's fickleness prevails even here: by 1829 Victoria writes to Feodore that 'Your nieces, the Babies, are pensioners, not because they are broken, but because I am tired of playing with them.'[40] The 'pensioners' are not entirely forgotten by the Princess, however, as one emerges from her retreat to travel to Malvern in 1830 where, Victoria reports to Feodore, 'I gave my big doll a tea-party as well as two of Victoire's.'[41]

In addition to dolls that a child could actually play with and manipulate, Queen Victoria is well known for having had as a child and teenager a collection of Dutch peg dolls numbering just over 130. These dolls range in size from 3 inches to 9 inches in height and are uniform in their facial features; what distinguishes each is her costume. Most represent aristocrats of Victoria's own day or characters from the stage. Intricate handwork and careful attention to the details of costume were necessary to dress these tiny dolls. Baroness Lehzen made most of them, but Victoria helped with some of the sewing of their clothes. In her discussion of the doll collection, Frances H. Low remarks that the Princess Victoria was 'an expert with her knitting needles'. Queen Victoria refutes this claim in the annotations she made on her presentation copy of Low's book: 'No. Bss. Lehzen did the minute work.'[42] These dolls were primarily for display purposes and Victoria would take some on her travels and 'arrange them' as a means of getting settled in at the various country houses and castles she visited on her grand tours.

The summer and early autumn months were travel times for the wealthy. Many families would go to resorts by the sea or to the mountains of the west and the north, for the health benefits conferred by the bracing fresh air. When Victoria was very young, the Duchess of Kent tended to take her to the seaside at Ramsgate or Broadstairs, or the hills of Malvern. In later years, the family also travelled throughout Wales and in the Midlands. Victoria and Albert, of course, had homes on the Isle of Wight and in the Highlands. As the amateur drawings of the young Princess discussed above indicate, these early trips were relatively private affairs, undertaken without attracting much attention or generating much fanfare. This policy was to change dramatically after the death of George IV when it became clear that Victoria was next in line to the throne after William IV. The commodification of the Princess began in earnest in the 1830s; until this time Victoria and her mother led a secluded, sedate, and private life.

But, to return to the infant princess, all was not entirely calm within Kensington Palace, as the baby in the palace was at times difficult to manage and prone to tantrums. The Duchess wrote to her friend Pauline von Tubeuf that the eight-month-old princess was 'a greater darling than ever, but … beginning to show symptoms of wanting to get her own little way'.[43] Queen Victoria herself remembers, from the vantage point of middle age in 1872, her days as a wilful child who was used to having her pleasures granted: 'Up to my 5th year I had been very much indulged by every one, and set pretty well *all* at defiance'.[44] It seems entirely likely that Victoria was a spoiled and excessively petted child. Although it can be construed as manipulative, parents often hold up an older sibling as a pattern for the younger one to copy – perhaps in desperation for some cooperation from the recalcitrant child – and this certainly held true for Victoria. In an undated letter young Princess Victoria writes to her mother, 'I wish you many happy returns of dear Feodora's birth-day, and hope that she may have a merry day. I am very anxious to be your comfort like dear Feodora.'[45] One can almost hear the Duchess's voice imploring Victoria to 'act more like your sister'. Victoria desired her mother's approval: in her earliest extant letter, dated 1825, six-year-old Victoria writes in baby script, 'My Dear Mamma I love you Victoria.'[46] A flower had been attached to this missive; the stem remains.

The Duchess of Kent was devoted to her daughter, the monarchy, and her own crucial connections to it through her progeny: her reason for living in England, an inhospitable foreign country, as a poor relation to a powerful family, was solely for Victoria's benefit as the future queen. Victoria's status as heiress presumptive was officially acknowledged in 1830 after the death of George IV, and provisions for a Regency – in case King William died before Victoria had reached her majority at the age of eighteen – were debated and adopted by Parliament. The Duchess of Kent, to her great pleasure, was named sole Regent (though she was to be aided by a Council of Regency). In her biography of the Duchess of Kent, Dorothy Margaret Stuart argues that the Duchess's five-year Regency of Leiningen-Dachsburg-Hadenburg, after the death of her first husband, was important training for her role as the heiress presumptive's mother and adviser: '[The Duchess of Kent] held for five years a position of responsibility and authority, and that she had enjoyed the experience can hardly be doubted; otherwise she would not have sought its renewal on the larger stage of England.'[47]

There is no doubt that the Duchess had a formal and exacting influence on Victoria's life. In the letter between the Duchess and Pauline quoted above, the Duchess goes on to tell her friend, who had once overseen Feodore's education, that although her baby is wilful, 'I am already beginning to train her, which I am sure you will think wise!'[48] Princess Victoria was brought up in accordance with the child-rearing theories of the day, such as those advocated by Miss Elizabeth Appleton in her manual *Early Education; or, The Management of Children Considered With a View to Their Future Character* (2nd edn 1821). This work was dedicated to the Duchess of Kent. In her dedication, however, Appleton makes no apologies for the egalitarianism of her regime: '[the volume] has been written, not so much with a view to the forming of their characters to greatness, as to goodness; to accomplishment as to virtue; and is, in consequence, fitted equally to the inferior ranks, as to the most exalted personages of the empire'.[49] Appleton's three maxims for forming infant characters were '1) regulating the passions, 2)securing morality, and 3) establishing a sound religion'.[50] The Duchess of Kent took these maxims as laws in the upbringing of her princess.

Besides the typical tussles of wills to be expected between any parent and child, there is no evidence that the early relationship between Victoria and her mother was in any way 'troubled' (as it would increasingly become when Victoria became a young adult), but letters and documents indicate that the Duchess's expectations for her daughter's behaviour were high and that Victoria's relationships with her sister and her governess were neither constrained nor characterized by stiff convention. One example of the formality that existed between mother and daughter can be seen in the means by which the Lutheran duchess (her daughter Princess Feodore had been married in a Lutheran ceremony led by Dr Kuper of the Royal German Chapel)[51] raised her princess in the Church of England. The Duchess was understandably concerned with Victoria's religious education which was developed, in part, through morning and evening prayers copied out for Victoria to read. In a small leather-bound book of prayers dated 1826, the Morning Prayer for 24 May 1826 (Victoria's seventh birthday) copied in the Duchess of Kent's hand, includes the words: 'Let me show, by my good conduct to dear Mamma, how grateful I am for all that she does for me! – Let me enjoy the season of my youth, by Thy Grace. Bless my dear Mamma, all my dear relations & friend's [sic] as well as myself. . . .'⁵²

One result of the constant background moralizing in Victoria's early life is her mimicking of this tone in creative writing so that in her stories she controls – rather than receives – punishment or reward for bad or good conduct. Victoria's juvenilia offer important insights into the inner life of a child – who happened to be destined for enduring fame. Through these stories we see how Victoria attempted to make sense of her world by writing herself into it or by crafting it anew through narrative choices. She both reflects her teaching when writing imitatively and diverges from it when indulging in the melodrama she so loved to watch on stage. In some of her earliest stories, the interior behavioural monitor she was expected to develop becomes externalized as Victoria speaks the conventional rhetoric of her mother and governess. For example, in another of the 1827 Ramsgate stories, the main character of the unfinished narrative is a spoiled little girl, 'An'. An is the antithesis of the obedient child Victoria was expected to become; An's mother's permissiveness guarantees her daughter's unsuitability for society. This short story functions as a cautionary tale of the kind that Victoria would have been concurrently reading in annuals of moral stories for the young such as *The New Year's Gift and Juvenile Souvenir* for 1829.⁵³ Directed toward parents, the preface to this volume states,

> The leading aim of the Tales and Sketches, of which the *New Year's Gift* is composed, has been, undoubtedly, the *amusement* of the juvenile reader; but, as the minds of children receive decided impressions of either good or evil from all that passes under their observation, it has been deemed expedient that each story should inculcate some moral truth. With this view ... the extravagances of those apocryphal personages – giants, ghosts, and fairies – have been entirely banished from [the editor's] pages, as tending not only to enervate the infant mind, and unfit it for the reception of more wholesome nutrient, but also to increase the superstitious terrors of childhood. . . . [T]he Writers of the *New Year's Gift* have been induced to confine their narratives exclusively to the romance of history, and of real life.⁵⁴

Victoria's story, which plays with the tradition of the moral tale found in *New Year's Gift*, is worthy of printing in full (the spelling and mistakes are Victoria's as a seven-year-old):

> An or the naughty girl.
> Little An was pretty naughty greedy and disobedeent. nobody like to be near her for she was so unpleasant.
> One day her Father gave a party and many fine people came; and little [A]n was allowed to come into the room. As soon as sombody adresd her she turned her back and gave no answer. As her dear Father wished to please her, so she was allowed to dine with her Papa; her Mother (who was her favourite) gave her what ever she asked for and gave her seet-meats in provusion. Ane sat between Lady D- and her Mamma; poor Old Lay D- was so plagued by An that she said to her Mother 'Mam your daughter is very ill-behaving and toublesome.' Mrs G- who was the Mother of An flushed for anger. Indeed Mam I must beg your leave to go with my darlin little Ane dear. She goes and leaves the rom with An with a plate full of sweet-meats in her hand.[55]

In Victoria's truncated story, the punishment which should take place fails to occur. It is not clear what happens to An, but as a good reader of moral tales, Victoria knew that her mother and daughter characters deserved to be humbled for their failures in discipline, diet, and social convention. The moral tale for children is predicated upon error, punishment, and, most importantly, the *recognition* of the wrongdoing and a professed *resolution* to change. Significantly, the 'naughty girl', as Victoria calls her character, may be unpleasant company, but within the story she never loses favour with her parents or her mother's protection, even in the face of others' disapproval; her 'naughtiness' is never recognized by An herself. The child Victoria could not be 'An' (although she was often called 'naughty'), but she *could* indulge her anti-moral tale by writing An into existence and then neglect-ing to follow her story to its 'natural' conclusion. In this way, an unrepen-tant and uncorrected An could continue to be indulged and eat sweetmeats without fear of reprisal or judgement, a most delicious fantasy for any little girl, perhaps especially one as closely scrutinized as Princess Victoria.

Naughty and Nice

Two important changes had occurred in Victoria's life by her fifth birthday that would affect the way that her personal and intellectual life would be led: a governess, Louise Lehzen, who had originally come to the family to teach Feodore, and a tutor, the Reverend George Davys, were assigned to monitor the Princess's education and behaviour. Victoria's nursery days were over, and her training as a princess would begin. As a member of the Royal Family, of course, even allowing for the retired life she led at Kensington Palace, Victoria could hardly have been unaware of England's rigid class system and her own exalted social position within it. She was taught from her earliest years to be grateful for her advantages which came directly from God. Victoria's evening prayer for her eighth birthday (24 May 1827) begins, 'Most Gracious God, who by Thy wise providence has appointed to mankind their several stations and offices in this life, I acknowledge Thy Wisdom and Goodness in this and all Thy other dispensations; desiring in all things to pay a ready and cheerful submission to Thy holy Will.'[56] And yet, Victoria's *unwillingness* to submit is one of her strongest characteristics. When a young child, this defiance was outwardly shown, but as she grew up, her refusal to acquiesce turned inward, as she began to hold herself apart from her mother. Louise Lehzen became her confidante and closest friend and held this position until Victoria's first Prime Minister, Lord Melbourne, took over in 1837.

Lehzen, as she was called by Princess Victoria (she was made Baroness Lehzen in 1827 by George IV), spoke impeccable English and was a handsome, proper woman (although she had the disconcerting habit of chewing caraway seeds in company) when in 1824 she became arguably the most important person in Victoria's life (Ill. 8). Lehzen's theory of education and child-rearing was to provide at all times a good example of decorum for her young charge to follow.[57] In 1872 Victoria wrote, 'At 5 years old, Miss Lehzen was placed about me, and though she was most kind, she was very firm and I had a proper respect for her. I was naturally very passionate, but always most contrite afterwards.'[58] As one of the many biographies of Queen Victoria written for children and published to celebrate the Diamond Jubilee or to mourn her death notes, '[Victoria]

8. Princess Victoria, drawing of Baroness Lehzen, 1836.

had a time to learn, and a time to play; for although she was a Princess, and would some day be a Queen, she must learn to obey, and do her best to grow up a wise and good woman.'[59] Teaching Victoria to obey was Lehzen's province. She became Victoria's constant companion as she played and studied; developing the strong-willed little girl into a well-mannered young lady was her first concern. Overseeing or keeping the 'Behaviour Books' in which Victoria's conduct was listed at very frequent intervals throughout the day was also within Lehzen's purview. The Behaviour Books were first kept in 1830 when Victoria was eleven years old. The earliest dated book is the least formal of the four preserved and may have served as a kind of prototype for the later books (the second is rather confusingly called 'First Good Behaviour Book' although it post-dates the original). This continual recording of Victoria's behaviour may have been an effective method of emphasizing her failings and successes if the book was referred to at the end of the day, or was presented to the Duchess of Kent.

The 'First Good Behaviour Book' (31 October 1831 until 22 March 1832) was a paper-bound copybook. It looks as if Victoria wrote the comments herself at first and then perhaps Lehzen copied them over. The need for the Behaviour Books, if the record itself speaks for anything, is clear as Princess Victoria appears to be relatively ill-behaved with some regularity. She often calls herself 'good', but there are also multiple instances of 'naughty with Mamma', 'very exceedingly naughty', and 'rather naughty and peevish' in later 1831 and early 1832.[60] This book is also used as a kind of memorandum book by the Princess: she notes a few birthdays, her riding lessons, and an abbreviation 'k.l' which most likely stands for the 'kicking lessons' (a lesson in keeping your seat for the advanced rider) that Victoria enjoyed at Fozzard's Riding School. Although good lessons are praised, many comments refer to Victoria's attitude or conduct towards Lehzen: for example, 'rather impertinent to Lehzen' (morning of 31 October), 'very illbehaved and impertinent to Lehzen' (morning of 1 November), and 'Naughty and vulgar' (afternoon of 1 November). The Princess's behaviour is generally described as 'good', but there are a number of notes of extreme behaviour where Victoria's penchant for underlining as emphasis, continued throughout her life, is indulged. For example, on the morning of 21 August 1832 at Beaumaris, Victoria writes that she was *very very very* terribly NAUGHTY' (the 'verys' are underlined three times and the 'naughty' four).[61] Someone had clearly expressed disapproval, which Princess Victoria then obligingly, or perhaps grudgingly, duly recorded. In her journal for the same day, however, Victoria does not indicate that anything out of the ordinary had occurred, simply 'I worked and did several things during the morning.'[62] One wonders what the 'several things' might have included. And, on the afternoon of 24 September 1832, Victoria reported that she was 'VERY VERY VERY VERY HORRIBLY NAUGHTY!!!!!' (Every word is underlined four times), while her journal blandly remarks, 'The heat was intollerable.'[63] Cross-checking between such unpublished materials demonstrates the degree to which Victoria herself edited her early diary, and the extent to which her every action was scrutinized. There is nothing in the early journal to put off or excite the journal's 'extra' audience (governess and mother). Victoria is sometimes praised for a 'good lesson', but at times she is 'odd', 'foolish', or just garden-variety 'naughty' (without the hyperbole attached). The Behaviour Books are fascinating documents as they allow a glimpse into the specific methods of Victoria's upbringing and education. In general, surveillance, monitoring, and correction together created the climate in which Victoria began her formal education.

In addition to Lehzen, Victoria's tutor, the Reverend George Davys, began to oversee her education in 1823 at the request of the Duchess of Kent who had been reading with him to improve her English. Davys was a mild man, patient and kind. In 1827 he came to live in Kensington Palace and stayed until Victoria became queen. Davys maintained his position with the family even when Victoria accumulated many different masters, and was rewarded for his devotion and loyalty with succeeding promotions within the Church. He was made Dean of Chester in 1831, and eventually became Bishop of Peterborough in 1839. As a gesture of respect to him, Davys's daughter Mary Ann, four years older than the Queen, was selected to become a member of the new queen's Royal Household. The fact that Mary Ann Davys was a commoner posed a protocol problem for the Queen, as the hierarchy of the Queen's intimates was rigidly set. For example, the Ladies of the Bedchamber, in the 'first circle', were composed of members of the peerage (through marriage or independently); in the second circle were the 'Bedchamber Women', all married to lords or viscounts; and the third circle, 'Maids of Honour', included unmarried women of aristocratic families.[64] Miss Mary Ann Davys fitted none of these categories, so a new title was made just for her: 'Resident Woman of the Bedchamber'.[65]

The Reverend Davys's first task with the very active four-year-old was to teach her to read. Victoria remembers her resentment when about seven years old at being sent out driving with her maternal grandmother, the Dowager Duchess of Saxe-Coburg-Saalfeld who was visiting the Kents, because 'like most children of that age, I preferred running about'.[66] Victoria turned out to be a reluctant reader and a defiant pupil. Davys was able to achieve success with his recalcitrant royal when he instituted a somewhat unusual reading method which incorporated her inability to sit still with her native curiosity: Davys put cards with nouns printed on them in front of the objects named all around the room where they worked.

Victoria learned to associate the words with the corresponding objects, and was eventually able to place the cards correctly. She was thus first initiated into word recognition and the beginnings of literacy. A revealing anecdote about the character of the very young Victoria and Davys's first encounter with his royal pupil is offered in his journal (a few entries were published in *V.R.I: Her Life and Empire*, by the Marquis of Lorne, one of Victoria's sons-in-law): the Duchess of Kent was most anxious that her daughter perform well during this first visit, and to encourage her she offered a treat to Victoria if she said a good lesson. 'However,' Davys comments, 'the Princess asked for the reward before she began the lesson.'[67] Davys's journal extracts make delightful reading as they highlight the charming – because natural – antics of the four-year-old: she doesn't want to write the letters Davys requests (if it's 'h' one day, she wants 'o' and if the next day she is indulged with the previously desired 'o', she asks for 'h', etc.) Davys marvels, '"She seems to have a will of her own."'[68] When she misbehaves in the nursery she tells Davys about it, but when he asks her to spell 'bad' as part of her lesson, she '"imagined that the word was intended to be applied to herself (which it was not), and she cried".'[69] Victoria was not a timid little girl, but she was a sensitive and emotional one. These qualities remained with the Queen throughout her life.

As she grew up, Victoria's emotional and aesthetic sensibilities were perhaps most indulged by trips to the theatre for plays, opera, and ballet (she began to go regularly in 1831, though her first visit was in 1829). Here her creative imagination was stimulated. Her excitement is evident in her many drawings and paintings as a child and in her teens illustrating the stage productions she had enjoyed. That Victoria's love of narrative as a child was developed in the theatre – once she was allowed to attend – rather than through books is not entirely surprising, given that the Princess's reading material was carefully selected to reflect the best children's literature of the previous generation (approved 'classics' from authors such as Maria Edgeworth, Mrs Trimmer, Dr Aikin and Mrs Barbauld, and Charles Lamb). This didactic literature emphasized Enlightenment ideals such as reason and the pursuit of knowledge rather than fantasy or adventure – in other words (from the *New Year's Gift* 1829), 'the romance of history, and of real life'.[70] Miss Appleton warns,

In the first six or eight years of life, every thing should tend to use which is offered to the senses and the faculties; every thing that children hear, see, or learn, should be for use. Every tale they read, or that is read to them, should have a moral; and that which the mother may purchase in which she cannot find one, should be committed without ceremony to the flames.[71]

The poetry of Victoria's youth was similarly didactic (Cowper's poetry was ubiquitous in Georgian nurseries), and, at times, somewhat dreary as well. One of Victoria's gifts from her mother for her eighth birthday was a small embossed leather book of hand-copied poems, the clasp engraved with the date and the initial V. The first poem, in the Duchess's hand, is entitled 'The way to be happy'. It begins, 'How pleasant it is, at the end of the day/ No follies to have to repent;/ But reflect on the past, and be able to say,/ That my time has been properly spent.'[72] Under 'Poetry' in the bound 'List of Books Read by the Princess Victoria' for 1826, we see that Victoria read, among other books, *Poetry Without Fiction; by a Mother.* Fancy, even in poetry, was discouraged. She was introduced to John Gay's fables in 1827, but even these imaginative tales are primarily concerned with imparting moral lessons. Lehzen relates how she would read improving literature to the young princess as she was being dressed, both for Victoria's pleasure and as a means to preserve decorum in front of the servants: 'I began early, while Mrs. Brock was dressing you to read aloud to Your Majesty those little stories written by mothers for little children. I did so to prevent Your Majesty from getting into the habit of talking with the servants, and to talk before them to me, which I thought ought to be avoided; besides Your Majesty *liked* to be read to.'[73]

One of the first books Victoria owned, so identified because of the large initial V inked on the cover that could only have been written by a very young child, is called *Chronology of the Kings of England.* This tiny book composed in rhyme is intended for beginning readers and includes a crude woodcut illustration of each sovereign and a short verse with dates and brief commentary to help children memorize the chronology. Elizabeth I's verse, for example, reads 'Eliza's reign, so golden to/the State,/Begins in fifteen hundred/fifty-eight.' The book ends with George IV, reigning monarch, thus: 'In eighteen hundred twenty,/George the Fourth,/The regal robes adorn'd:/O what his worth!'[74] Although memorization was an important aspect of childhood education in the Georgian period (and through the Victorian period as well), Victoria's need to know her royal ancestors was especially acute and began especially early. The Princess could not have been quite so ignorant of her potential future station as legend would have it. Princess Victoria would certainly have known, as this mnemonic book helps to demonstrate, how the succession unfolded.

At first, Mr Davys was Victoria's primary master, although by 1825 she also had tutors for French (Monsieur Grandineau), and writing, geography, and arithmetic (Mr Steward). There were behaviour books of a sort for Victoria's lessons as well, beginning in December 1826 and ending in May 1832.[75] These sturdy books about the 'Daily State of the Princess Victoria's Studies', were leather-bound and printed with the days of the week (Monday to Saturday), Masters, Hours of Attendance, Course of Study, and Remarks. The 'Daily State' books were formal documents chronicled by Lehzen that could be distributed and used as evidence of Princess Victoria's proper education. The paper-bound Behaviour Books of the early 1830s, by contrast, were a more private venue for commentary on the progress of Victoria's education in conduct becoming to a princess. For the week ending 3 December 1825, when Victoria was six years old, she had two lessons per week in moral stories and geography, writing and arithmetic, religion and history, French, natural history and poetry, and repetition of the lessons on Saturday. Her knowledge was 'good' generally, but 'very good' in one religion and history class, one French lesson, and one natural history and poetry hour. She was 'indifferent' in her morning lessons on moral stories and grammar with Mr Davys on Wednesday.

It is not difficult to imagine or identify with Princess Victoria's 'indifference' or, indeed, naughtiness, in attending to her lessons, when some of the particulars of the curriculum are known. In a copybook of English grammar and orthography, Princess Victoria's dictation attempts (with her mistakes corrected in red and tallied) reveal the stultifying didactic precepts Princess Victoria was forced to listen to (and encouraged to absorb). For example, one paragraph from 1827 concerns a reading on clever children. Here is a partial transcription of an example of Victoria's dictation:

'We read of chelder who ware estemed podegies on account of thier progress in lirning; but they ware only cheldren of extraordinary industry, their cehf merit was that of insessant applecaion, added to grarate dosility; they all had an unbounded respect for their tehers, consequetly a swetness of temper, and an active obedience; ...' All in all, Princess Victoria makes 23 mistakes.[76]

Although it may seem that the Princess was overworked as a six-year-old, she generally attended lessons only two hours out of the day.[77] The rest of her time would have been spent reading, preparing for lessons, riding or walking in Kensington Gardens, and playing. Alison Plowden comments, in her biography of Queen Victoria, that although the Queen would bemoan the monotony of her childhood, her sedate life at the palace 'sounds quite a sensible regime for a young child — a quiet, regular life with plenty of fresh air and exercise — and these earliest years seem to have been happy ones, if a little lonely'.[78] Her few companions would have been Feodore (until her marriage), Lehzen, attendants, and Victoire Conroy and her sister Jane who were very frequent visitors. Dorothy Margaret Stuart comments that the two girls who shared a common name also 'shared walks, dancing lessons, riding lessons, visits to the theatre and to the seaside; but they did not share their dolls, for the Princess always kept a firm grasp on her flounced and feathered family, and Victoire's father declared mockingly that she took after her grandmother, Queen Charlotte'.[79] It does not appear, from the evidence preserved, that the Conroy daughters were favourites of Victoria's since she rarely mentions them with affection in her journals or letters, and her hatred for John Conroy is not only legendary but an accurate description of her feelings, as is made very clear in confidential letters she wrote in 1835, in response to her mother's pressure to accept him as her eventual Private Secretary.[80] Victoire was foisted upon Victoria as a companion of her mother's choosing; Victoria never enjoyed the companionship of a bosom friend as did her cousin Princess Charlotte with Mercer Elphinstone.[81] However, Victoria often wrote to her Aunt Sophia, an intimate of the Conroy family, about Victoire, her siblings and parents: she knew this would please the old lady, indicating that she was astute about personalities and politics from a very young age.[82]

First Images

Without the assistance of photography in delineating young Victoria's face and figure, it is necessary to guess at Victoria's appearance in her childhood. However, since it was such a well-documented childhood, there is an abundance of information about her early years, including comments on her face and figure. She had fair skin, blue eyes, and wavy, blonde hair that would later turn to a medium brown. Her eyes, easily caricatured, were slightly protruding and her chin was slightly recessed. She was a petite child who grew into a tiny adult – not 4 feet 9 inches tall, as some allege, but 4 feet 11 inches or so until she developed the typical curvature of the spine of an old woman and lost two inches in height. Victoria was probably the victim of osteoporosis (bone thinning) due to a lack of calcium in her diet and the physical stresses caused by her nine pregnancies. Uncle Leopold was obsessed by Victoria's small stature and often urged the child to grow, making jokes that do not entirely mask his anxiety over her size: 'By all the information I can collect it seems that you are growing very much. I hope you will persist in so laudable a measure and outgrow your mother, which even you may do with a little exertion.'[83] She was a fat baby, chubby toddler, and plump little girl, but she became a slender teenager as her surviving clothing attests. The 'Grecian style' white marble bust of Victoria sculpted by William Behnes in 1829 when Victoria was ten has been called an excellent likeness.[84] This sculpture has been continually on display in the Private Apartments of Windsor Castle (Ill. 9). As a three-dimensional object, this bust offers the clearest glimpse of Princess Victoria as a child. A copy was engraved as the frontispiece for the 1829 *Juvenile Forget Me Not*, a typical annual gift-book miscellany; the first article was a tribute to Princess Victoria written by William Kennedy. In Victoria's copy this poem has been cut out very roughly – the poem may have been mounted in a keepsake of some kind, or it may have been removed for modesty's sake.[85] Though physically unprepossessing, in her girlhood years Princess Victoria developed a forceful personality and a will of iron, as Albert noted at their second meeting in 1839 after a separation of three years when he described Victoria as 'not much grown, but she has acquired much greater firmness.'[86]

9. William Behnes, marble bust of Princess Victoria, 1829.

Victoria's form and feet were small, but her appetite was quite large. The admonishing Leopold also weighs in with commentary on the twelve-year-old's eating habits in an 1832 letter: 'If I was to give an opinion I should say that a certain little Princess eats primo frequently a little too *much* and almost always a little *too fast*. Eating fast is particularly unwholesome, and should therefore be avoided as much as possible, because it lays the foundation of many a disease.'[87] As she grew into a young adult, Princess Victoria took this advice to heart: she often boasted within her journal how little she ate. Certainly Victoria was made to feel self-conscious about her height and eating habits and was taught, like any middle- or upper-class girl, that her appearance would influence others' perceptions of her. Neatness and cleanliness were considered twin aspects of moral behaviour. As a child she was expected to sit up straight and work on her posture (although she did not lie on 'the board' to straighten her spine as did Feodore).[88] She began to wear earrings at the age of thirteen, and she was proud of her long and shiny hair until it was cut off after an illness when she was fifteen. The 'natural' appearance of the infant and young princess gave way to the artifice of the lady as Victoria became a teenager. Her hair was elaborately dressed each morning (she often wore fashionable hairpieces). This passive morning chore she generally spent listening to Lehzen read improving literature or, when she became an older teen, the newspapers, which she relished as a sign of independence.

Was Princess Victoria 'pretty'? After her first few years on the throne, the Queen was not known for her outward attractiveness. Paintings of the monarch can hardly be trusted for objectivity (although certain facial features are repeated so often or corroborated by photography that they can be relied upon) and Victoria often appears dour, anxious, or grief-stricken in her photographs; as sovereign she rarely smiled. This last fact, however, has a history. First, it was not the fashion of the nineteenth century to smile when photographed, and the photographic plates required an extended time for exposure, which encouraged smiles to appear forced or as grimaces; and secondly, Victoria felt that her smile showed a great expanse of gums and that she looked more attractive and more dignified – she was the Queen of England, after all – with her mouth closed. She had often been told, when a child, to close her mouth, as she had a tendency to let it hang open. In a letter to Feodore, Princess Victoria reveals her pride in an 1835 portrait by Henry Collen, due, in part, to her satisfaction at the look of her closed mouth (see Ill. 37).[89]

Frequent comments made about the young Queen Victoria were that she was 'dignified', 'confident', and 'at ease'. Charles Greville, who had not

10. M. U. Sears, engraving of Princess Victoria as a fashion plate.

always been kind in his words about the Princess, wrote about Victoria's first Privy Council that she behaved 'with perfect calmness and self-possession, but at the same time with a graceful modesty and propriety particularly interesting and ingratiating'.[90] The combination of her childhood training and temperament is admirably revealed in the mannered beauty displayed by the young queen.

The images of Princess Victoria shown to the world ranged from a 'Grecian seal' of a classically draped infant whose relationship to the late Duke of Kent is again emphasized; to a baby fashion plate published for the Young Ladies' Library in 1829 (Ill. 10); to the profile of a heavy-lidded and

11. Richard Lane, drawing of Princess Victoria, 1829.

romanticized princess wearing a low neckline and long gloves drawn and lithographed by Richard Lane in 1829 (Ill. 11). This image of the Princess became very famous: in a number of biographies of Queen Victoria written for children to celebrate her anniversaries or as tributes after her death, the young princess is shown wearing this dress (see Ill. 12). Numerous engravings of Princess Victoria's portraits were published in 1829. Her image is a familiar one in prints dating from about this time, as the number and variety of reproductions increased. (It was not until 1832 that she emerged from the seclusion of Kensington Palace for general public display to the delight of the throngs of people who followed the royal carriages and gathered to

listen to the addresses paid to the Duchess of Kent in order to glimpse the Princess.) By 1830 it was obvious that Victoria was next in line to the throne. The indifferent health of William IV, and his fluctuating popularity, made the young Victoria an interesting subject indeed. Her image began to be used as 'shorthand' for youth, feminine beauty, and proper childhood behaviour (as the frontispiece to the children's annual certainly attests).

Although the 'real' child Victoria was little known beyond a small circle of people, her childhood was seized upon in later years and credited as being the impetus for the Queen's simple, domestic and ordinary virtues.[91] By focusing on the early years of the ageing Queen, perhaps her inevitable death could somehow be magically forestalled. For these reasons, during her lifetime (especially in the Jubilee years 1887 and 1897) and just after her death, she was often celebrated as a good child (or as a mother raising good children). These nostalgic reassessments of Victoria showcase the fact that the qualities of a loving daughter – obedience, piety, and modesty – turn out to be the exact specifications needed to make a good queen. (When trying to entice Wendy to come to Never Land as storyteller to the Lost Boys, Peter Pan tells her that what they need most is '"a nice motherly person"'. The gratified girl replies, '"Oh dear, but that is exactly what I think I am."')[92] That Victoria's *own* experience of childhood and character *when* a child is overlooked in the fulfilment of expectations such as those Peter sets out for Wendy is immaterial to the image-making process. Even if there were no such princess as the perfected Victoria, she could always be invented – and was, in picture books, paeans to the Royal Family, and poetical tributes.

In *The May Blossom; or The Princess and Her People* (1881), a picture book written by Marion Wingrave and illustrated by H. H. Emmerson, Princess Victoria is 'reanimated' in her Richard Lane dress in the grounds of Kensington Palace (Ill. 12), and her home adventures – described in verse – are interspersed with brief meditations on the positive and negative qualities of adults: 'gossiping people', 'patriotic people', 'fashionable people', and 'church-going people', for example. The Dedication reads in part, 'To

(*facing page*) 12. H. H. Emmerson, illustrtion of 'The Princess and Her Pets' from *The May Blossom: or the Princess and Her People*, by Marion M. Wingrave.

"She was so pretty and so pink that the Fairies came to see her."—*Chapter I.*

13. Frontispiece to *The Fairies' Favourite; or the Story of Queen Victoria Told for Children,* by T. Mullett Ellis.

the sweet little children/We dedicate this book,/In which, we trust, with pleasure/The darling ones may look:/Learning from the Child-Princess/All good and noble ways – /A royal little maiden,/In these her childhood's days. . . .'[95] Victoria was certainly queen, so this meant that she must have first lived the life of a fairytale princess. This conflation of fancy

and fact is made literal, in effect, in the picture book *The Fairies' Favourite,
or the Story of Queen Victoria told for Children* published on
Commemoration Day 1897 by T. Mullett Ellis and dedicated to 'the
350,000 children of OUR MOTHER'. In this text Victoria is cast as a folk-
tale heroine, superlative in her beauty and goodness, loved and protected by
fairies and other creatures (Ill. 13). The little book opens conventionally
with 'once upon a time' and then relates the story of the Princess's trouble-
strewn path to the throne. It is only through the intervention of guardian
fairies that the Princess is able to outwit the evil 'Grumbleland' (a very
thinly disguised portrait of Victoria's uncle, the Duke of Cumberland, who,
legend has it, tried to poison the infant Victoria)[94] to become the triumphant girl monarch, 'the first Queen of the People'.[95] But it would take only
a few years for the didactic image of the populist girl heroine to change to
J. M. Barrie's irreverent 'modernist' take on Queen Victoria as a 'big penny'.
This tension – between experiencing the innocence of childhood, on the
one hand, and fulfilling these cultural expectations, on the other – only
intensified as Princess Victoria grew up and her future prospects became
certain. And it was especially within the girlish almost-queen's highly dis-
ciplined educational programme that these competing desires of nation
and nurture were played out.

Chapter Two

The Little Princess Enters Education Land[1]

1828–1832

> The first habit, therefore, to be formed in every human body, and still more in the offspring and heir of royalty, is that of patience, and even cheerfulness, under postponed and restricted gratification.
>
> Hannah More, *Hints Towards Forming the Character of a Young Princess* (1805)

I Will Be Good

Children are generally educated according to the accepted standards and values of the previous generation, which often renders educational innovation difficult. So it was for Princess Victoria when in 1828 the time for a more formal educational training arrived. One link between the past and Princess Victoria's educational future was the figure of Hannah More, the indomitable reformer, author, patron, and Evangelical. A half-generation before Victoria's birth, More had included in her reforming gaze not only the masses of illiterate cottagers she was educating in her Sunday Schools and the readers of the religious tracts she was avidly penning and editing, but also a rather more singular worthy cause. Her *Hints Towards Forming*

14. *Princess Victoria* after John Hayter, 1833.

the Character of a Young Princess (1805) was written for the moral and instructional needs of just one child, Victoria's doomed cousin, Princess Charlotte.[2] More's *Hints*, although designed for an entirely different princess – but certainly published to attract upper-class mothers, and not specifically noted as a model for Victoria's education anywhere that I have found – are remarkably in tune with the training Victoria received and the girl she became (Ill. 14). For example, More advocates learning Latin but not Greek (although various tributes to the Queen assert otherwise, Victoria never studied Greek), the pre-eminence of the modern languages French and German over Italian (Victoria's knowledge of Italian was quite tentative and her study of it was begun as a result of her own strong interest in opera), the subordination of traditionally feminine studies – 'what are called the fine arts' – in favour of more intellectual pursuits (although Princess Victoria was schooled in drawing and, later, singing, these accomplishments were a source of pleasure for her and not viewed as the centrepieces of her education as they might have been fifty years earlier).[3] Owing to her respect for the intellectual capabilities of the female sex in general, and of the future female sovereign in particular, More offered an enlarged view of female education in *Hints*. Yet she was no radical, and made clear distinctions between an appropriate education for a princess and that of a prince. The former would have less opportunity for 'observation' as a means of 'improvement' and should therefore glean most of her information and behavioural models from published sources: '[The Princess] must then, in a greater degree, depend on the information which books afford, opened and illustrated by her preceptor.'[4] The young Victoria was indeed highly dependent on books for her knowledge of the world of politics (for which she read multivolume works of history such as Russell's *History of Modern Europe*) and of family life (which Maria Edgeworth's moral tales provided). To 'experience' the deeds and characters of great men, Victoria read the Sully, Clarendon, and Rollin that More recommended.[5] All of these authors would be well represented in any school; the library of the Enfield school which the Keats boys, for example, attended early in the century, was comprised primarily of these texts.[6]

Princess Victoria was familiar with Hannah More's works, as some of them were given to her as gifts: a Mr Choveaux presented *Sacred Dramas* to the young princess in 1826, and *Memoirs of the Life and Correspondence of Mrs. Hannah More* was given to her by her state governess, the Duchess of Northumberland, in 1835.[7] She also owned the fifth edition of *Hints* itself, printed in 1819. The two-volume set was given to Victoria by her mother in 1835, and contains a tiny sheet of folded paper inserted at the preface where 'on the death of Princess Charlotte' is written (this edition may have been published as one of the many tributes to Charlotte after her death in 1817).[8] It is tempting to guess that these books first belonged to the Duchess of Kent and that she later gave them to Victoria in the troubled year 1835 as a pointed remark about her behaviour. This supposition is endorsed by the report of a 'munificent subscription' made by the Duchess in 1830 to a fund dedicated to the erection of a monument to Hannah More.

Anecdotal evidence supports the view that the Duchess's largesse was due to her gratitude to More for her *Hints Towards Forming the Character of a Young Princess*. 'The Duchess had carefully studied this valuable work, and had drawn from it much useful information, and many practical "hints towards forming the character" of her precious charge. . . .'[9]

The primary focus of More's book was not curricular, but the creation of a well-trained, 'womanly' future sovereign (Charlotte was heiress presumptive from her very birth since no brother superseded her right to the crown) — and in one aspect of this goal in particular, her advice seems to have been heeded by Victoria: 'But above all,' More intones, 'there should be a constant, but imperceptible habit of turning the mind to a love of TRUTH in all its forms and aspects.'[10] That Victoria loved 'truth' — or perhaps more accurately, loved *precision* in all things — can be verified in part by the many lists she kept (of her Christmas presents, for example, or the names of the guests at her mother's evening entertainments, or the records of the dolls she owned), the careful descriptions of the plots of the ballets and operas she enjoyed, and by her delicate watercolours of costumed dancers and actresses. Indeed, in a long letter to the Bishops of London and Lincoln, her mother writes that 'Her adherence to Truth is of so marked a character, that I feel no apprehension of that bulwark being broke down, by any circumstance.'[11] One of the many apocryphal stories about the young Victoria and her honesty begins with the Princess's misbehaviour during a lesson. This ill conduct was mentioned by Lehzen to the Duchess of Kent at the lesson's conclusion. Victoria does not let this remark pass, however, without confessing to her mother that she was naughty not once, but *twice*. In her biography of Victoria, Elizabeth Longford relates the anecdote a little differently, and finds it illustrative of Victoria's character: 'One morning as her tutor was about to begin her reading lesson he asked the Duchess if [Victoria] had been good. "Yes, she has been good this morning," the Duchess replied, "but yesterday there was a little storm." Drina chimed in. "Two storms — one at dressing and one at washing." This engaging mixture of self-deprecation and complacency remained with Queen Victoria to the end of her life.'[12]

These variations on Victoria's truth-telling cannot be verified, but the constant repetition in biographies and sketches of the character of the

Queen helps to outline a desirable national character, much like that of George Washington and the cherry tree. That the future sovereign reportedly does not succumb to that most 'female' of frailties – artful dissembling for self-preservation's sake – is notable here. It is clear from the Behaviour Books that Victoria's conduct was very carefully accounted for and, like any child, she *was* ill-behaved more than once during some of her lessons, so the story is indeed plausible. Its symbolic meaning, of course, is more important than its literal truth, as Victoria's honesty can serve as a model for Britain's youth to emulate, yet also stand for the uprightness and moral superiority of Britain itself. Only honesty – not the misbehaviour that preceded it – signifies in these stories of the childhood foibles of prominent figureheads, although in Victoria's story there are no appropriate morals to be gleaned from it as there are in Washington's. In the month of February, American schoolchildren continue to draw pictures of cherry trees and axes, and housewives to make cherry pies to commemorate the birth of the first American President and the virtually concomitant 'birth' of the American ideal of honesty. Victoria's story of the two naughty episodes has not achieved the same level of apocryphal lore as young Washington's 'I cannot tell a lie'; this status is reserved for the watershed moment in Victoria's child life when she 'learned' that she was no ordinary princess, but the future Queen of England. In a memorandum written by the Duchess of Kent to the Bishops of London and Lincoln, she makes it clear that she wants this knowledge to come to Victoria's attention by accident rather than 'art'. A notation to this memo states: '[Victoria's awareness of her station] occurred on the 11th [of March 1830] in looking over "Howlett's Tables".'[13]

This event took place just after her formal examinations by the Bishops of London and Lincoln (discussed below), but the anecdote survives in a number of competing versions. The essential and consistent facts of the story are these: the Princess Victoria was unaware of her eventual station until she discovered a genealogical table of English sovereigns placed in one of her books. She considered this table and remarked to Lehzen, 'I see I am nearer to the throne than I thought' and, most importantly, makes a solemn gesture with her finger upraised and vows, 'I will be good.' The dubious nature of some aspects of this story bear consideration: it is doubtful that

Victoria could really have been ignorant of her position in regard to the throne, or that she would have made such a pious statement, which sounds as if it could have come from an Evangelical children's book, or that she had never read such a table before (the chronology of English sovereigns was taught to her). Louise Lehzen's version of the event is that it was *her* idea to bring the issue of Victoria's place in the Royal Family forward in this manner. In Lehzen's retelling, Victoria remarks wisely that she now understands why it is necessary for her to learn Latin although her female cousins do not.[14] George Davys's son, Canon Davys, tells another version of this drama in which his father plays the key role of informing the Princess of her future.[15] And Queen Victoria's own recollection of the event disputes its most crucial aspect: the preternaturally wise response of the child-princess who perfectly understands her duty 'to be good' for her country's sake. Victoria's annotation of Lehzen's letter (mentioned above) removes her from sounding like a pattern child, and restores her child self to the human: 'I cried much on learning it – & even deplored this contingency.'[16]

It is easily imagined that the prospect of becoming queen – however or whenever exactly it was communicated – would be extremely frightening to a young girl. Victoria may have worried that the change was imminent and that she would be separated from Lehzen and everything familiar to her while still a child. Prince Albert's annotation of the Duchess of Kent's memorandum states that 'the Queen perfectly recollects the circumstances & says the discovery made her very unhappy'.[17] The Marquis of Lorne's biography of his mother-in-law, *V.R.I. Her Life and Empire*, contradicts the story of Victoria's ignorance by stating that 'There was no doubt that every care was taken to avoid premature disclosures on this subject [the accession]; but Queen Victoria used to say that she had a vague idea of the state of affairs from almost her earliest years.'[18] This seems most likely, though least romantic. Finally, it doesn't matter, as the 'I will be good' comment has become an indelible mark setting Victoria apart as a legitimate and appropriate heir to the throne. Such legitimacy was at the heart of all of Victoria's training, including her diet, morning and evening prayers, regular exercise, and lessons.

The document 'Distribution of the Day 1829' offers a glimpse into the Princess's daily life through the schematic division of the hours of the day.

On Mondays, for example, the ten-year-old began her first hour-long lesson at 9.30, studying geography and natural history; the next hour was spent in a drawing lesson, and from 11.30 until 3p.m. she 'walked or played' for two and a half hours and had one hour for dinner. From three to four she made 'a Latin exercise and drawing', and from four to five she had a French lesson. The following hour was a repetition of her lessons and the final half-hour of Victoria's 'work day' was spent 'playing'. The particular lessons changed from one day to the next (except for the hours of playing and walking, which remained constant throughout the week, except for Sunday which had no prescribed activities or lessons). Other lessons in the week included music, religion, history, 'poetry by heart', German, dancing, writing, and arithmetic.[19]

One aspect of Victoria's study of the English language and composition involved writing drafts of letters to people (such as her tutor or Victoire Conroy) she might naturally address in a letter. Mr Davys would then correct the epistle. In a short letter dated 4 November 1828, the Princess writes to Mr Davys about a book she is currently reading and on which she desires his opinion: 'I should like to know what Kidnapers means in that book called "Evenings at home or the Juvenile Budget opned." I should like to know if you aprove of this book which I am reading now with great pleasure except a few dul stories.'[20] Mr Davys corrects not only Victoria's spelling mistakes, but also perceived errors in style, so that 'except a few dul stories' is changed, and in red ink is inserted 'although there are in it'. Victoria's opinion of the Aikins' nursery classic (a collection of six volumes of stories, poems, and dialogues published in 1792–96 by a brother and sister) is diluted by this change so that her own lack of pleasure in the 'dul' stories becomes more distanced from her frank opinion through the objective comment that dull stories exist. Victoria's relationship to these stories is downplayed, but her request for Davys's assessment remains (notice that Victoria does not indicate whether Davys's approbation would change her own opinion in any way).

As a result of the Duchess of Kent's disapproval of novels, much of Victoria's childhood reading could be categorized as 'dull'. For example, 'The Storm', from *American Stories for Little Boys and Girls* (1831) by author and editor Mary Russell Mitford, although it sounds promising and contains an interior story about a shipwreck, is primarily the tale of four children kept indoors (except for the eldest boy) by a winter storm.[21] This situation affords the children the opportunity to fall into errors of logic, behaviour, and sentiment, which their gentle mother then corrects. Says Jane to her mother after her laziness has been spotlighted, "'You always make me feel ashamed of myself, mother, when I am not obedient; and I am sure I often think I will govern my temper better.'"[22] Even the inner story of the shipwreck, which held some suspense for the readers (and listeners to the story within the frame tale) ends rather anticlimatically: the survivors spend only one night on a forbidding island before they are rescued. Miss Appleton argues that the excitement elicited by narrative is a powerful, corrupting influence on children and that any good mother would ban such offending books. The 'injurious' author, as Appleton terms it, 'lifts the veil, which should never be withdrawn before childhood, from plot, intrigue, scandal, slander, satire, finished vice, levity, and folly of a world they know not, nor ought to know. . . .'[23] Proper reading should be bland, she suggests: 'Very quiet scenes are sufficient for simple minds, and little or no plot is required, or indeed given, by plain writers who address them.'[24] According to the rationalist writers for children, the best fiction, like the most wholesome food — like good little girls themselves — should be modest, unadorned, and unremarkable.

Victoria's relationship with books was continually mediated by others through criticism of certain genres or titles offered by her mother, or mother-substitutes such as Miss Appleton and Hannah More, as well as through the gifts of books she received where the giver is implicated as the 'author' of the gift. Interestingly, Sir John Conroy's selections were among the most 'literary' presented to Princess Victoria. He gave her the two-volume set of the Lambs' *Tales from Shakespeare* (in 1826) and *Pittman's School Shakespeare* in 1831 as well as *The Rambler* and *Rassilas* [*sic*] in 1834.[25] But Victoria also mediated for others. She sent some of her books from early childhood — perhaps her favourites — to her sister as an aid to her nieces' and nephews' progress in learning English. Their first language was German and they spoke French with their mother. Victoria was keen that the children also learn their aunt's tongue, and to that end she sent them Mrs Trimmer's *Fabulous Histories*, the *Frank* and *Early Lessons* of Maria Edgeworth, and the *Cries of London* (an illustrated book of London street sellers and their wares – such as muffins, fruit, chestnuts, and ballads – and the sellers' advertising 'cries'), among other volumes.

Child Author

The clearest examples of the constitution of Victoria's literacy – the effects of her reading – can be found in the manifestations of her own writing style. In her creative writing, Princess Victoria emulated the 'plain style' preferred by moralist educators such as Miss Appleton, but many of her tales – even those most derivative of authors of children's books – were inflected by a dramatic sensibility uniquely her own, as is demonstrated by the story of 'An', the moral tale mentioned earlier that defies readers's expectations of punishment. Another example of an early story from 1827 is the following very short, untitled composition. Victoria's use of vague pronoun references allows for different interpretations of this tale of charity and pride. By the end of the tale, either the heroine of the story and the author have converged into one conflated, reformed character, or the unnamed parental voice intervenes in the child's unsuccessful attempt to combat her character flaw. In either case, a lack of distinction between character and child author or the crucial mediation afforded by the controlling adult, emphasizes the struggle between internal and external monitors played out in fiction and in life:

> One fine morning a little Girl went out to walk and she met a very poor man to whom she gave something and he was very thankful and when he went she was sorry that she could give him no more bread. I was delighted to see my little girl so good perhaps to much so for my darling child grew proud. *I wished to conquer her feelings* but Alas it was in vain. Perhaps I did not try in the right way. Come here my dear I hope you will med. She did indede mend. Finis. (My emphasis)[26]

Perhaps the best example of Victoria as a child author can be found in a tale she wrote at the age of ten and a half on 11 October 1829 when the Kents were on a late summer/early autumn tour of the West Midlands. On the way to and from Great Malvern, their destination, Victoria visited Oxford, Stratford, Kenilworth, Birmingham, Worcester, Gloucester, Bath, Salisbury and Portsmouth.[27] This trip would have been the first taken by Victoria without her sister Feodore, and so she may have felt lonely and pursued an amusement that could be had by a single child. Writing stories was such a pursuit.

Victoria's self-constructed vision of the dutiful child in a loving family is titled 'Sophia and Adolphus: in the Style of Miss Edgeworth's Harry and Lucy'. While the names of her main characters were very common in the Royal Family — Victoria had an Aunt Sophia and an Uncle Adolphus (the Duke of Cambridge) — it is interesting to note that Sophia and Adolphus were also the names of two of William IV's illegitimate FitzClarence children, from whose presence Victoria was barred.

Victoria's story 'Sophia and Adolphus' attests to the impression that Maria Edgeworth's works made on Victoria's development as both daughter and monarch. The story is dedicated to Victoria's governess: 'My dearest Lehzen, I have taken the liberty to dedicate to you, this book hoping to entertain you. I am my dearest Lehzen, your very affectionate frind, Victoria.'[28] The story exists in two copies in paper-cover exercise books and is written in Victoria's large, round, baby script; one version is in pencil, the other, a much abbreviated version, is in ink. Besides length, there are not many differences between the two, and each is dated 11 October 1829. Clues on the title page of the ink version, however, lead me to believe that its probable *raison d'être* was as a rewrite of the first attempt: ink was more permanent than pencil (Victoria was taught to ink over her pencilled writings in her Behaviour Books and eventually her journal), its dedication to Lehzen is more formal ('My dear Baroness ... I am my dearest friend your's very affectionately'), the original 'frind' is corrected to 'friend', and the Princess claims greater authority for herself in this version by removing the self-proclaimed imitation of Edgeworth.[29] It cannot be determined exactly why the story was written in the first place — was it a task devised by her mother or tutors? — but the careful and detailed illustration that accompanies the story, as well as the inscription, point to an independent project undertaken to please Victoria's most beloved adult friend and constant companion.[30] Whether written for pleasure or not, Victoria's composition self-consciously inherits and imitates the rationalist discourse on child-rearing and education made popular in the late eighteenth/early nineteenth centuries by the author-educator Maria Edgeworth, whose volumes could be found on any middle-class girl's schoolroom shelf. (In addition to *Early Lessons* and *Frank*, Victoria owned all six volumes of *The Parent's Assistant*, *Harry and Lucy Concluded* (4 vols) and a volume entitled *Edgeworth's Little Plays*.)

Victoria's pencil drawing of a family tableau introduces the main characters and acts as a 'frontispiece', telling its own story of Victoria's construction of girlhood (Ill. 15). The four-member family is enjoying an evening talking together (the lit chandelier offers this clue), while Sophia is doing some kind of needlework; everyone looks pleased (even the pets seem to be smiling). Princess Victoria illustrates the rational, domestic bliss of a close-knit family of taste and manners: there are paintings on the wall, a shelf of books, decorative furniture (characterized by the heart-shaped side chairs the children sit on and the carved feet of the mother's armchair) and beloved, beribboned pets. The children are framed by their parents. The mother is seated next to Sophia and is the very picture of elegance and sweetness: she holds something in her demurely crossed hands, wears a frilled cap and side curls which match her ruffled skirt, and her dainty foot rests upon a tiny footstool. The father (who somewhat resembles Victoria's favourite, Uncle Leopold) leans over Adolphus and puts his arm around his son's chair, smiling downwards. Sophia's position highlights her leading role in the narrative: every human and animal figure except for Sophia herself is in profile or at an oblique angle to the viewer; Sophia, by contrast, looks directly at the viewer. In addition, the trajectories of all glances (except for that of the puppy in the basket) – including the viewer's – converge upon Sophia. This drawing is obviously not one of Victoria's finished compositions, but a sketch meant to suggest, one conjectures, the most vital aspect of the story – the family relationship – and Sophia's place of prominence within it.

Education – specifically, scientific inquiry – within the domestic milieu was the goal of Maria Edgeworth's 'Harry and Lucy' tales, and so it is not surprising that Victoria's creative attempt features a pair of children and their rational parents.[31] In her literary biography of Maria Edgeworth,

15. Princess Victoria, drawing as illustration for her 'Sophia and Adolphus', 1829.

Marilyn Butler describes the purpose of the earliest 'Harry and Lucy' stories as 'frankly educational: the children ask a great many questions and their parents supply the answers, in well-judged phrases calculated to make brick-making, or many another process, intelligible to the very young'.[32] As author, Victoria 'manufactures' a child's-eye view of family life by appropriating Edgeworth's narrative method and trajectory. In some respects, Victoria follows quite closely the plot-line of the first volume of *Harry and Lucy Concluded* in particular: her characters take a trip to stay with friends – Sir Henry and Lady Eustace – just as Harry and Lucy vacation with Sir Rupert and Lady Digby. Victoria's story is fascinating in part because it is the tale of an 'ordinary' family written by a most unusual child whose life bore very little resemblance to that of the middle-class Harry and Lucy. It is worth noting, however, that the values expressed by Victoria's characters are decidedly 'middle-class': charity, neighbourliness, literary appreciation, economy. An example of such prim morality can be found in the brief dialogue between Sophia and her mother about the value of some new acquaintances. Sophia prefers the company of the talented Smith girls to the vicar's children, but her mother remonstrates that these entertaining girls fail to read improving literature:

> ... but did you not like better the vicar's children than his sister in law's? Perhaps mamma, said Sophia but Miss Maria plays on the pianoforte and sings and dances and speaks french and Miss Louisa does not. Certainly my dear, Miss Maria does all that but then she never reads good books she always reads novels which cannot impress on her mind any good knowledge of geography or history. I should not like if my own daughter Sophia was to make fashionable and affected acquaintances, but simple well informed girls like Miss Louisa and Miss Mary.[33]

Although the ten-year-old fatherless heiress presumptive to the throne of England, Victoria imagined and perhaps identified with or even yearned for the family life described in Edgeworth's fiction – to the extent that she is able to produce a reasonably 'Edgeworthian' tale.[34] The childhood she created in her own story possibly corresponded to a desire for such a middle-class, intact family of her own. Victoria's 'family romance', then, concerned not mistaken birth and noble parents, but the stable home life of father–mother–sister–brother. Victoria was certainly missing Feodore at this point. Most of Victoria's evenings, which she would later describe in detail in her teenage journals, were spent surrounded by her mother's friends, at the very least the hated Conroy family and Victoria's Aunt Sophia (the somewhat reclusive daughter of George III who bore an illegitimate child by her father's equerry and who became an ally of the Duchess of Kent), if not an entire entourage of glittering people. After entry upon entry listing the number of people in Victoria's household or those who had open access to her, an understated description of a family 'evening at home' with her visiting half-brother Charles of Leiningen and two Württemberg cousins is quite startling and poignant: 'At 7 we dined together. I staid up till 1/4 past 9. It was a very pleasant and amusing evening. Mamma playing on the piano, my cousins and Charles looking at prints &c.'[55]

In 'Sophia and Adolphus', therefore, the young Victoria constructs a fictional childhood that has become familiar to her through reading rather than direct experience. Victoria's story includes a steam engine and a cotton manufactory (although the children are eager to see these examples of industry, various events conspire against the outings – which obviates her need to describe machinery); the children also go to a 'laboratory' to watch an experiment in ice-cream making – all stock Edgeworth elements in the 'Harry and Lucy' tales.[36] In discussing nineteenth-century child diarists, Carolyn Steedman writes that 'all children who write are forced into some kind of premeditated choice in the presentation of ideas' – played out nicely here in Victoria's case as fiction modelled on a writer favoured by *adults* as well as by children.[37] Victoria, however, is *not* only 'explicitly invest[ed] in rational discourse' as Elizabeth Kowaleski-Wallace argues about Edgeworth:[38] interestingly, this child is well versed in the discourse of drama as well as that of the moral tale.[39] In describing her playgoing to the absent Feodore in 1829, Victoria indicated her preference for the melodramatic over the historical, 'I was four times at the play: first at Drury-Lane to see Charles the 12th of Sweden; the three last times at Covent Garden, where I saw the Sublime and Beautiful, Oberon, and Ivanhoe. I liked the Sublime and Beautiful best of all, then Ivanhoe, then Oberon, and last of all Charles the 12th of Sweden.'[40]

Victoria's story includes many moments of pathos: Sophia's family is very charitable and routinely helps poor 'widdows' in distress, sometimes as a result of Sophia's somatic pleading ('At supper her father remarked the traces of tears on her cheeks').[41] The greatest melodramatic turn occurs when Sophia predicts that Adolphus will be drowned if he goes ice skating:

It was a fine cold winter's morning when Adolphus knocked at his sister's door. Come ... in ... Adolphus said Sophia out of her room quite lazily. I am going to scate with the Master Hamletons. Oh! Adolphus said Sophia as she threw her snowy white arms about her brother's neck. don't go, you will be drowned, you will be drowned! Never fear, dear Sophia, make your curls as quietly as if I was by your side; good bye, good bye.[42]

This comically histrionic but loving exchange between siblings owes more to the romance tradition (not on any approved reading lists) than to Edgeworthian ideals. In the chapter on 'Books' in *Practical Education*, the Edgeworths openly disdain 'sentimental stories and books of mere entertainment', especially for girls: 'This species of reading cultivates what is called the heart prematurely, lowers the tone of the mind, and induces indifference for those common pleasures and occupations which, however trivial in themselves, constitute by far the greatest portion of our daily happiness.'[43]

The tragedies of orphans and half-orphans (like Victoria herself) abound in the story. Lady Eustace, the family's Lincolnshire hostess and mother of Mary, has an unfortunate accident – she 'falls on her head' and 'expired after a few hours at the cottage', much to her husband's 'griafe'.[44] Alas for the ill-fated and clumsy Eustace family! as 'About a few weeks after [his wife's death] Sir Henry fell from his horse and died two days after saying in his will that Sophia and Adolphus's mother where to take care of his little girls until they where married.'[45] As a result of these untimely deaths, Sophia becomes a kind of foster sister/tutor to Mary Eustace: 'She taught her to read, and to wright; to talk french; to walk straight; to hold up her head and to make neat courtesies.'[46]

Highly tutored herself, Victoria repeatedly creates a situation in her narrative where the girl is put into the powerful position of extending philanthropic largesse and offering educational expertise. Mitzi Myers describes Georgian women writers of educative tales such as Maria Edgeworth as 'reimagin[ing] their own childhood and invent[ing] the future childhoods of their gender in more satisfying forms than unmediated realities proffer[ed]'.[47] For Victoria, the 'more satisfying childhood reality' *she* constructs includes both the happy domestic family pictured in her illustration and powerful autonomous roles for girls as instructors and monitors. While Harry is the older and superior sibling in *Harry and Lucy* – Lucy is called

'Mrs. Quick-Quick' and must try to learn the patience and doggedness of her brother – Victoria's Sophia is the true heroine of the tale. The character Sophia's opinions often sound quite a lot like those of her creator: when Sophia calls Miss Debret 'a delicate, wimsical spoiled, but goodnatured girl' or describes the lodgings provided for her and Adolphus as 'two very *very* small rooms hardly to be called rooms, rather cells',[48] Victoria's voice when irritated (as can be heard in the journals) is audible. In a few years' time, Princess Victoria herself would travel, unpack her dolls and personal items, repack them, visit multitudes of important Whig families previously unknown to her, and essentially live on display for months at a time.

The story ends abruptly in the middle of a history of Greece that Sophia is reading to the bedridden Adolphus who had indeed fallen through the ice while saving a young boy. Edgeworth's Harry is also a hero and receives a 'severe strain' for his efforts:[49] he saves a child from a fire and is badly burned as a result. The dauntless Harry is primarily concerned with the extent of the fire damage to the roof he has designed. When told he must be confined to bed he merely asks, '"How long, Sir?" ... in an intrepid tone'.[50] Lucy is a great comfort to her injured brother, as is Sophia to Adolphus. Not surprisingly, Edgeworth in her fiction often narrates sibling relationships: as the eldest of twenty-two children, Maria had extensive experience with children and shared with her father and various stepmothers a belief in the superiority of educating children at home, and the benefits of communal inquiry. In Edgeworth's tales, the role of the sister to the brother is one of gentle subordination. While Lucy is shown to be intelligent and active, her acquisition of information and experience is generally keyed either to feminine faults or to her brother's greater claim to her time or attention. Lucy and her mother have a conversation in which Lucy realizes that the greatest use of her scientific learning is to help her become a 'better' (less nosy, more helpful, self-controlled) woman:

'Mamma, this is another advantage of having a taste for things of this sort [scientific inquiry]; they help us to turn the mind from what you call foolish curiosity.'

'Yes, Lucy, they will often assist you in managing your own thoughts and your own mind,' said her mother. 'This is one of the great benefits which women derive from cultivating their understandings, and the best use they can make of a taste for literature and science.'

'Mamma,' resumed Lucy, after some pause, 'I am very glad that you let me *go on* with Harry. I am sure it has been the cause of great pleasure to me. Even on the journey, it was so pleasant to be interested in the same things. But above all, during Harry's illness, it was the greatest happiness to feel that he liked to have me with him always, reading and talking to him, and being interested in the sorts of things which he liked best.'[51]

Victoria's Sophia similarly attends to *her* brother's needs by entertaining him during his convalescence. Victoria's heroine, however, never concedes domination to her brother. In the conclusion to Victoria's story, once again, all eyes are on Sophia as she controls the action by performing a selfless deed. As a young author, Victoria highlights child heroism, untimely deaths, and charitable impulses, in order to construct a unique form of female acculturation filtered through the lens of Edgeworthian themes, but ultimately illuminating the distinct imagination of a girl negotiating family fortunes and failures through storytelling.

Victoria's creative writing, like that of all children, reveals her preoccupations and artistic ambitions (imitating a well-known author or trying out a new genre), and helps to flesh out her childhood character. Most young children are 'artistic': that is, imaginative, confident in most situations, dreamy. This artistic aspect of Victoria's childhood self has not been fully explored to date, and yet it seems crucial to understanding the Victoria who was, and the queen she became. For a few years at least (and it is not surprising that the bulk of Victoria's surviving stories date from her ninth to twelfth years, before adolescent anxieties and erosion of self-esteem had set in) Victoria remade her world through fiction. It is possible that there were other stories written and since lost, but this is not very likely as even materials of apparently complete inconsequence — an unused book for sums, for example — have been dutifully saved. A remark the Baroness Lehzen made about her young charge is worth repeating here: in a letter written to the Queen in 1867, Lehzen reminisces about her Kensington years and comments, 'It was a real pleasure to listen to Your Majesty's childlike talk, when Your Majesty asked:

"May I tell a story?" "The dear Child's" mind lay open for me, listening to those beautiful stories.'⁵² It is fortunate that some of the youthful openness of mind that Lehzen appreciated is available in these preserved fragments of fiction.

The Princess not only translated instructional and moral lessons into tales, but personal events also reappear as stories. For example, in an undated story (internal evidence as well as the large, messy penmanship suggest a date of 1829) Victoria briefly reimagines late seventeenth- or early eighteenth-century Sweden, the setting for one of the first plays she had ever seen. In her recitation for Feodore of her attendance at the theatre, mentioned above, *Charles the 12th of Sweden* is her least favourite play of the four; however, it seems that this historical moment (she was tested on it in January 1835) piqued Victoria's interest. Accompanying the opening 'playlet' is the following note: 'Ernestine was the daughter of a Swedish father who lived in the time of Charles the 12th of Sweden.'⁵³ Victoria's 'The Maid of Sweden', although just a fragment, ably (and, to adults, quite humorously) begins to dramatize a story complete with appropriate rural dialect, patriotic sentiment, and rising action. The opening one-scene act begins *in medias res*, as Ernestine enters 'saing' 'Father a man brang some letters from my brother Fritz.' The farmer replies, 'Well then bring 'em in.' Soon Gustavus enters (his relationship to the farmer and his daughter is unclear) with bad news:

G. I have bad news to tell you Ernestine.
E. What! Bad news and how tell us quick.
G. The enemy have taken some castles and I am afraid will hurt your
    father's garden. (Father starting up)
[F.] My garden.

Gustavus is a brave young man, and immediately springs to action to save the farmer's garden: 'Without delay let us send to our nabours and tell 'em to make ready for me in armer.' The next and final act opens with twenty young men ready for battle, 'at their head Gustavus'. In the spirit of Shakespeare's Henry V, Gustavus rallies the intrepid company: 'My brave friends we must arrange this house for a place of refuge; and make a rampart.'⁵⁴ Act II (and the entire drama) ends here. Perhaps Victoria's regimented days – with study, playtime, walks, meals, bedtime, and so on all highly pre-scribed – often precluded her ability to finish the stories she began for her own amusement.

Additional finished tales (much briefer than 'Sophia and Adolphus') survive in another marbled-paper copybook. These are undated, but the unlined pages, messy pencil orthography and style suggest a possible date of 1828 or 1829. The first story, called 'Dame Raver', consists of an intro-duction and two chapters. This story has a modest premise: the widowed Dame Raver lives in a little cottage with her daughter, son-in-law, and two granddaughters. Her upper-class 'double' is the widowed Lady Merton. The two meet when a storm forces Lady Merton to abandon her open car-riage and take shelter with the kindly Dame Raver. The second chapter pri-marily concerns the visit of some old friends of Lady Merton's who had been away for four years. Mrs Heller recites the story of their journey to Madras in 1825 in some detail, but the rest of the trip is encapsulated quite succinctly:

> My husband left me after we had been a month there. One year passed without any thing of importance happning. But the second year my son fell ill but after 2 months illness recovered [and] received a letter of rec-comendation from Mr. B- to an old Bramin at Elord wither my son wished to go. But he was prevented from going by his still delicate state of health. Many other things not worth mentioning happened. Thank you said Lady Merton. Your daughters Elizabeth and Mary are charm-ing girls.[55]

The reason for Colonel Heller's four-year absence is obscure, but the family is reunited in England and all visit Lady Merton. Mrs Heller remembers Dame Raver, as she had been the children's nurse when they were young. All of the ladies travel to Dame Raver's cottage the following day and 'made her quite happy'.[56] The end of the tale is proclaimed at this point.

Victoria's story is quite an accomplished effort for a young child. The plot is very neatly concluded by the union of the different, seemingly unre-lated, families in the final pleasing visit to Dame Raver. Victoria here describes the crucial bonds of female relationships sustained through telling stories and caretaking, and offers a sentimental gloss on the relationship between the lady of the manor and the grateful cottager. The lives of the two upper-class women, Lady Merton and Mrs Heller, are tied to the worthy Dame Raver by her service to them: she shelters Lady Merton from the storm, and had cared for Mrs Heller's children in their infancy. Victoria also includes details about the Hellers' sea voyage to India. These are minor facts, to be sure – native produce and drink found on identified islands ('Madera' and 'St. Helina') along the way ('Madera' wine, dates, and oranges), for the most part – but even these tiny details bespeak Victoria's 'active' girls' education where social systems as well as geography are digested and transformed into fiction.

The companion finished piece to 'Dame Raver' is called 'Emely and Hariet, or the twine sisters'. This piece of prose is somewhat longer than 'Dame Raver' and its six brief chapters take the twins from childhood to adulthood. Like Sophia and Adolphus, Emely and Hariet come from an intact family. They are the daughters of Farmer Sanden, a polite man whose farm was situated on the 'lovly banks of the Eden'.[57] The story opens with the tantalizing offer of an improving trip for the girls: 'My love said [Farmer Sanden] to Mrs. Sanden I have just got a letter from your sister Margret and she invites Emely & harriet to go to France with her. Mrs. S. I shall be happy to consent. Farmer S. And I also.'[58] The children travel with their aunt to London, then to 'the tower' and from there to 'Callais' by a steam packet. Their ultimate destination is Paris, where the three would live in a little house for a month.

In the second chapter the twins sightsee at the Tuileries and the Louvre. But after only a fortnight's holiday, all merrymaking comes to an end with the unwelcome news that Mr Sanden is no more: 'Emely and Harriet were shocked and greaved.' By the time they all arrived back home, Mrs Sanden had already vacated the farm and was now living in a 'small cottage just on the banks of the Eden'. The farmer's widow's reduced circumstances ironically prove to be the family's gain, for they are taken up by a wealthy family as a pet project. It happens in this way: Harriet sees a carriage out front as she is 'sauntering about in the parlour'. Four ladies get out of the carriage and inquire after her and her sister. One of the ladies – Miss Selena Digby – asks Mrs Sanden if the girls would be allowed to live with her at her parents' home. Mrs Sanden refuses this request, but allows the twins to go to the Digby home for three hours a day. Harriet and Emely are taught French, music, embroidery, and drawing by Lord Digby's daughters.[59] Soon afterwards, the girls are sent to boarding school. 'After they had been 2 months there they received a bridal cake and gloves and letter from Miss Digby from whom the things came saing that their mother had married her brother mr. Digby. What was their astonishment.'[60] What indeed.

The girls return to school – now twelve years old and 'very accomplished agreable and good girls' they are, too – and the new Mrs Digby has two additional children in quick succession. Her fortunes continue to rise as well, since her new brother-in-law conveniently falls off his horse and dies (a common accident in Victoria's stories), transforming Mr and Mrs Digby into Lord and Lady Digby by his demise. By Chapter Five, Emely and Harriet are eighteen years old. Harriet is the first to marry. Her suitor is a Mr Gorden – 'a simple, clever, dull and affectionate man'. Harriet is not in love with Mr Gorden but desires the approval of her betters and so accepts him: 'She did not wish [marriage to him] pertictularyly but as it pleased Miss Selena & old Mrs Gorden she consented.' After marrying off one of her heroines in a decidedly unromantic manner, Victoria includes a little detail about the wedding presents given to the left-behind Emely: £4 each from the bride and groom in a 'little brawn pocketbook'. In the final chapter 'old Lady Digby' dies and Emely marries Mr Frankland. In a manner reminiscent of 'Dame Raver', the opening and end of the story are brought together by coincidental circumstances when Emely discovers that her married home is to be the very farm on the banks of the Eden where she had been born. As it turns out, Mr Frankland is the 'neveu by a sister' of Farmer Sandens, and as the latter died without male issue, the ownership of the farm now devolves to him.

Here again, Victoria draws her tale to a close by returning to its beginning. Emely's fortunes have improved through her marriage, changing her status from farmer's daughter to squire's wife, mistress of the similarly 'very much improved' property. This fairytale plot of the quick rise from obscurity to prominence (Cinderella marries the prince, which makes her stepsisters her subjects; the miller's daughter in 'Rumpelstiltskin' becomes queen) resembles Victoria's own transformation: from one day to the next

16. After Westall, 1830, engraving of *Her Majesty the Queen at the Age of Eleven Years*. Princess Victoria sketching with Fanny (dog).

she is 'magically' changed from protected and powerless daughter of the house to the Supreme Ruler of the British Isles. The story the child Victoria narrates in 'Emely and Hariet' tells of rather more modest advancements in social standing – more Fanny Price than Little Lord Fauntleroy – through practical marriages and improved estates. The drama of Victoria's own exalted life cannot be found in her writing, but the 'excitement' of family relationships, travel, death, moral truths, and childhood agency all combine to create a charming and evocative fictive world. Unfortunately, Victoria did not continue writing stories into adulthood, yet she would become a best-selling author of two volumes of memoirs: *Leaves from Our Life in the Highlands* (1868)and *More Leaves* (1883). She was once asked in 1888 to allow her juvenile poetry to be copied. In her annoyed response, written in a note to her private secretary, Sir Henry Ponsonby, she dismisses this request and, more importantly, shows her amnesia. These early stories and her own lively imagination seem entirely forgotten as Victoria snaps: 'Really what will people not say & invent! Never cld. the Queen in her whole life write *one line* of *poetry* serious or comic or make a Rhyme even!'[61] I did not find any verses written by the Princess, but the creative spirit that suffuses her delightful tales and drawings deserves to be recalled when remembering and remarking on the Queen. Princess Victoria's drawing master, Richard Westall's 1830 'mannered' portrait of the Princess sketching or writing outdoors promotes a bucolic gloss on her life that is more picturesque than factual. Princess Victoria would not have been left to wander alone with her pencil, writing pad, and canine companion to sketch or write freely. As an attempt to capture Victoria's lived girlhood, Westall's painting fails. However, the disjunction between the girl Victoria and her transformation into artistic subject points to the larger public concern with image and symbol. The illustration of a carefree but industrious child set against tamed nature (a Grecian urn upon a wall suggests a garden nearby) comfortingly signals normative English girlhood while at the same time Princess Victoria's actual interests in drawing and writing are highlighted (Ill. 16).[62]

The Politics of Education Land

Although designed to emulate, for the most part, any upper-class English girl's training, Victoria's entrance into 'Education Land' was not without political consequence, as the Duchess of Kent was highly ambitious for her daughter and for herself. Encouraged by John Conroy, the Duchess's behaviour in relation to Victoria was motivated by two burning desires: the nation's approbation and continued control over her under-age daughter (rather than losing her to the influence of the court). The Duchess desired not only the somewhat intangible general acceptance of her crucial role in raising the child who by 1829 appeared to be heiress presumptive to the throne and by 1830 was universally accepted as such, but also approval of her methods for doing so. The Duchess's specific requirements from the government were additional moneys to be used to support Victoria in grander style than had been previously possible given the widow's straitened circumstances, and formal designation as Regent in the case of William IV's death before Victoria reached her majority at the age of eighteen.

George IV's failing health, and the prospect of a sole member (the future William IV) of the Royal Family in the way of Victoria's eventual accession, prompted the need for outside assessment of Victoria's educational progress in the spring of 1830. The Duchess was ready; she had been preparing for this moment for her entire English life. As the Distribution of the Day, reports from her masters, lists of books read, lesson books, and other materials make clear, Victoria's education was very carefully crafted and remarked upon. These were the ammunition in the Duchess's arsenal of evidence of the Princess's correct upbringing (all of the above documents were sent to the Bishops before Victoria's examination). It must be noted that, barring the case of Princess Charlotte (whose education was also scrutinized), there had not been an heiress to the throne since the Stuarts, so the Duchess of Kent, as sole parent of Victoria, had a heavy burden to bear in raising her. 'At the present moment, no concern can be more momentous, or in which the consequences, the interests of the Country can be more at stake, than the education of it's [sic] future Sovereign,' she wrote in a 'most confidential' letter to the Bishops of London and Lincoln on 1 March 1830.[63] (Of course, if her child had been a prince, the author of his education would not have been his mother, but a male adviser or guardian.) The Duchess of Kent's foreignness and inability to mix well with the factionalized Royal Family did not help matters either; her vulnerability and loneliness is one reason why Sir John Conroy was able to play such a significant role in Victoria's childhood. Victoria had to be educated as a *female* aristocrat, but also as the future queen. The Duchess directly addresses this difficulty in the letter quoted above in which she outlines the history of Victoria's early education: '... I allowed no attempt to be made, to push The Princess intellectually beyond Her years: – on this point, I was firm, – satisfied, as far as my poor judgement could direct me, that it was the safest and surest course, although not the most brilliant.'[64] She also indicates the peculiar circumstances she finds herself in as lone parent responsible for educating the heiress to the throne:

> Had the subject been a Prince, the case would have been different, as then, the established plan adopted in such cases, would have been pursued. But here, I must take care, that the course of study is not adapted alone to the Sex, but that it shall be conducted on a large and liberal system, rather than to the circumstances of The Princess, for until lately, Her station was doubtful.[65]

Victoria was uniquely positioned, yet it was necessary that her training reflected this singularity and simultaneously adhered to every expectation of female decorum – and be recognized as doing so. To this end, the Duchess of Kent (with Sir John Conroy's assistance) put on a goodly bit of 'private' theatre (anticipating and requiring, in fact, that the production eventually become 'public') when in the spring of 1830 as the Princess approached her eleventh birthday, she was tested by outside examiners – the Bishops of London and Lincoln and the Archbishop of Canterbury – on her knowledge in her various subjects. The primary purpose of the Duchess's letter to the clerics was to request their assistance in three ways: to assess the quality of Victoria's education to date, to test her progress, and to offer suggestions for any changes to be made in her instruction for the future. In seeking the approval of highly respected and (politically) disinterested parties, the Duchess of Kent hoped to call attention to her fulfilment of her duty to her daughter and adopted country.

Before this important examination, the Duchess of Kent asked for progress updates from Victoria's different masters. And in every case, perhaps not surprisingly, the Princess was reported to be performing very well in her subjects. In history and in geography, Davys called her 'better informed ... than most young persons of the same age'. Although Victoria was learning about the world in these lessons, much of her political knowledge came from Leopold, who routinely discussed world affairs with his young niece in their correspondence. On 13 December 1831, when Victoria was twelve years old, he wrote, 'Here I am much troubled by business, the state of affairs with Holland is however particularly irksome, we are neither at peace nor at war, with nearly all the bad effects of the latter.'[66] In an earlier letter Leopold describes his travels around Europe to the nine-year-old, and asks Victoria to trace them on her globe in order to personalize and increase her knowledge of geography.[67]

Victoria's ability in reciting poetry was praised in particular, and her nominal Latin admitted: 'We are not far advanced in Latin, but, I think the Princess would be able to undergo an examination in those parts which she has read.'[68] Her German master praised her 'soft and distinct' pronunciation and indicated that her vocabulary was about 1,500 words.[69] The Arithmetic and Writing Master, Mr Steward, found the Princess's abilities in mathematics to be great ('[she has a] peculiar talent for Arithmetic'); however, if one reads between the lines, his assessment of her progress in writing was perhaps more qualified: 'If The Princess endeavours to imitate Her writing examples, Her success is certain.'[70] Her desire to imitate proper orthography must have been erratic; the young Victoria's handwriting was often messy. For obvious political reasons it would have been difficult for any of the masters to give such an exalted student a negative report, so any suggestion of less than perfect progress is notable. Although copious evidence suggests that Victoria was an able student with an active mind, not a plodding or unimaginative one as biographers sometimes suggest, it is impossible to gauge Victoria's 'intelligence' from this distance. The Duchess's fears about Victoria's lack of concentration were gently assuaged by Davys before the examination: 'During the last year, the Princess has made considerable progress. That absence of mind which Your Royal Highness had, for some time, so much lamented in the Princess, has been in a great measure corrected by the improving understanding of Her Highness; and there is now much reason to believe that the powers of exertion will every day be growing stronger. . . .'[71] In any event, all parties connected with this examination were participating in a highly unusual educational experiment – the training of a female future sovereign.

After receiving the reports she most wanted to hear – and given the extreme political timeliness of a positive assessment of the heiress to the throne – the Duchess would have felt that Victoria was ready to be examined. In the letter requesting the examination, the Duchess describes Victoria in a glowing manner: 'the general bent of her character, is strength of intellect, capable of receiving with ease information, – and with a peculiar readiness in coming to a very just and benignant decision, on any point Her opinion is asked on'. This final description of Victoria can also be read as meaning that she was an opinionated and strong-willed child.

Regardless of the Duchess of Kent's view, the experiment yielded positive results: the examination was an unqualified success for the Duchess, as well as for Victoria. After perusing the many documents submitted to them, the Bishops found the course of Victoria's education to be entirely appropriate as to the subjects studied and their arrangement. After the examination itself, the clergymen were pleased to report that Victoria had acquitted herself very well in the subjects of scripture, history, chronology of English history, religion, geography, use of globes, arithmetic, and Latin grammar. Her drawings were also praised. In short, the Bishops could find nothing to alter in the Princess's intellectual training, and urged that the current plan should be continued.[72] The Duchess lost no time in expanding the circle of intimates involved in adjudicating the Princess's education, as the very day after this letter had been received, the Duchess sent another 'most confidential' letter – this time to the Archbishop of Canterbury. He was given, by 'confidential servant' (Conroy), all of the information relating to Victoria's studies that the Bishops had received, plus their letter of assessment with the Duchess's covering letter.

The request was the same: judge Victoria and judge me, as 'I wish to proceed on sure grounds to fulfill the only object I have in life, the bringing up properly, this singularly situated and precious child!'[73] In response, the Archbishop, in a private conversation with the Duchess, agreed with the Bishops of London and Lincoln that Victoria's education was entirely satisfactory. He also suggested that copies of the documents pursuant to Victoria's education be sent to him for safe keeping and later exposure 'for the purpose of satisfying the public and all parties concerned that her Highness had been brought up in all respects with the greatest judgement & care'.[74]

The Archbishop himself personally examined the Princess on 1 May. (In the leather-bound volumes that track the Princess's education lesson by lesson and day by day in terms of the subject and Victoria's aptitude for that lesson, the Archbishop's 'excellent' stands out in a sea of 'goods'.) His report is perhaps the most detailed of the three, relating, for example,

> She was then questioned in history – and appears very well versed in the chronology and accession of the Kings and Queens of England [which puts to rest the suggestion that Victoria would not have at least suspected her eventual role in this well-known chronology] and acquainted with many particulars both of ancient and French history. I asked her opinion on several points, & especially on the character of the English Sovereigns, on which she appeared to have thought for herself, and for a young person of her age to have formed a just estimate.[75]

Victoria's confidence in her own thinking is highlighted here. The Archbishop finds no fault with her Latin and in general considers Victoria to have shown 'great intelligence'. No changes in her educational programme are requested: 'I am of the opinion no change could be made for the better.'[76] By July 1830, after the death of George IV, Victoria had become the heiress presumptive to the throne, and the 'confidential' correspondence between the Duchess and the three clerics was released to the government by the Archbishop of Canterbury; Victoria's 'hidden' public girlhood began in earnest at this point.[77]

The Duchess of Kent wrote an 1830 birthday letter to her eleven-year-old daughter, as was her habit, but, now that the examination and the realization (of her future station) had been successfully surmounted, this letter for the first time purposefully foregrounds Victoria's position as an extra incentive to be good:

> I have that confidence in you, my dearest child, – that should it be the will of Providence (which is still uncertain for the present,) – that if you be called to fill the highest Station in the Country, – you will shew yourself worthy of it; – and that you will not disappoint the hopes of your anxious Mother! – then, only then, can you be happy and make others happy.[78]

The theme of the suffering mother and the plea for self-conscious behaviour continues in her New Year's Eve letter to Victoria in 1831: 'Every eye will be on your actions and it will only be, by having religion at your heart, justice in your feelings – and knowledge in your head, that you can hope to be of use, where you be placed. So guided, under the will of God you may hope to succeed. That success, and your filial love will be your mothers [sic] reward – for a long life of unceasing anxiety for you.'[79]

The spring of her eleventh year marked the separation between childhood and young adulthood for Victoria, as these letters from her mother show. The Duchess of Kent was not able to resist reminding Victoria that she had a job to do and that 'every eye' would be watching her performance of it. Victoria was indeed under great pressure from an early age to be an exemplary girl. The Duchess of Kent told the Princess repeatedly (here in her birthday letter of 1832) that she was different from other children: 'I wish my beloved Victoria to become a *Pattern* to Others: – you possess every means for doing so, you receive the most suitable education.'[80] For her part, Victoria would write conciliatory letters to her mother such as this brief missive of 1829: 'Dearest Mamma, I must thank you for your *great kindness* to me, and I hope to repay it by being a good and obedient child to my dearest Mamma. I hope never any more to hear Mamma say "I am shocked" but to hear her say "I am pleased."'[81] It could not have been easy to be the young daughter of such an insecure mother, heir to the throne of England, *and* a 'pattern' for all youth. In this case, the stakes were rather high – the reputation of England's crown. Cecil Woodham-Smith argues that the Duchess 'always adored Victoria, but she never understood her. The Duchess was a duck who had hatched a swan.'[82] There is much to be said in favour of this view that the close relationship between the two that developed after Victoria's marriage could only exist once the Duchess's position of authority had eroded almost completely, and Victoria's tyranny was somewhat subdued by the desire to please a beloved husband.

But before this *rapprochement* could take place, years would pass when the Duchess of Kent was an irritating presence to her daughter and to the King. One area of conflict between the Duchess and the King involved finances. Raising a princess is an expensive business, and the Duchess of Kent believed – in this case, with utter reasonableness – that she deserved

17. Engraving of *Her Highness the Princess Victoria in her Pony Phaeton*, drawn by J. Doyle.

additional funds from the government. After her husband's death, the Duchess understood (and was encouraged in this understanding by her brother, Leopold) that for Victoria's sake she would have to reside permanently in England and rely on the Royal Family's largesse for her income. George IV in his Civil List was less than generous in his offering to the Duchess, and so, in desperation, she accepted Leopold's offer of £3,000 a year, and the government was satisfied that she was well taken care of. (Leopold was willing to help his sister and niece, but felt that both he and the Duchess were being mistreated by the government and the Royal Family.) Until 1831, all applications by the Duchess for a pay rise were denied.[85] Immediately after George IV's death in 1830, the Duchess applied yet again for funding from the Civil List. By this time, Leopold was no longer supported by England; in 1831 he had accepted the role of King of Belgium and was living in Brussels. In her correspondence with the Prime Minister, Lord Grey, about these matters, the Duchess implies that it is incommensurate with Victoria's eventual station as ruler of the British Isles that she be maintained by funds channelled from another country and that for this reason she has told Leopold that she no longer wants to be supported by him.[84] William IV agreed to an income of £6,000 for the Duchess. In her letter of 27 January 1831, however, the Duchess wished Lord Grey to know that these moneys represented a net gain of only £3,000 for the Princess, as Leopold's money had ceased by her command. She would not refuse the grant, but it was not sufficient for their needs or their position: 'However, to evince my duty to The King, – I shall not decline accepting the grant, – but I may say, that situated as The Princess and myself are, inferior to no member of His Majesty's family, – I do not consider the proposed grant, as altering materially our position.'[85] By the summer of 1831, however, when the Duchess was writing from the more powerful position of potential Regent, William IV recommended that she be given a greater allowance to help support his heir, and Parliament voted them an additional annual income of £10,000.

While her mother and John Conroy were snubbing the Royal Family, wrangling about money, organizing her studies, and overseeing her every movement, Victoria was studying, riding in her pony phaeton, writing, playing with her dolls, and drawing (Ill. 17). She was undoubtedly especially lonely in the years immediately following Feodore's and then Uncle Leopold's departures (in 1828 and 1831, respectively). As Feodore wrote years later about her own childhood in lines that have since become notorious: 'My only happy time was going out driving with you and Lehzen; then I could speak and look as I liked. I escaped some years of imprisonment, which you, my poor darling sister, had to endure after I was married.'[86] In 1831, the Duchess of Northumberland – Charlotte Florentia (Clive), wife of third Duke of Northumberland and daughter to the first Earl of Powis – the Duchess of Kent's choice, was appointed Victoria's state governess, and became a frequent visitor to Kensington Palace. Louise Lehzen, however, retained the Princess's heart. Victoria continued to write numerous fond letters to her sister and her uncle, and they filled her in as to their various, especially domestic, doings (although Leopold would write about politics, too). Feodore was busy giving birth to and caring for her six children in the years 1829–39 and she would often write to her younger sister about the joys and trials she was experiencing in raising her brood of small children. Leopold married again in 1832, this time to the eldest daughter of the King of the French, and regularly wrote affectionate letters to his young niece about his wife, growing family (he had three sons and eventually a daughter

– called Charlotte, the future Empress Carlota of Mexico – his first-born died as an infant), his political successes, and his indispositions. As suggested in the previous chapter, Leopold was full of good advice for Victoria, and he continued his father/mentor relationship with her across the miles.

Victoria's childhood, therefore, though lacking in freedom and autonomy in the extreme, was certainly not devoid of entertainment. In 1829, just after her tenth birthday, the King had organized a juvenile ball to coincide with the visit of the child-queen of Portugal, Donna Maria Da Gloria. In this delightful venue, Victoria was able to show off her graceful dancing – here performed in public for the first time with her partners Lord Fitzalan, Prince William of Saxe-Weimar, young Prince Esterhazy, and the sons of Lords De la Warr and Jersey.[87] The slim and vivacious princess, elegantly but simply dressed, was highly admired and contrasted favourably with the portly child-queen of Portugal. As Monica Charlot remarks, 'Even at ten [Donna Maria] was podgier than Victoria and indubitably less childlike.'[88]

The Duchess of Kent's firm ideas about raising daughters and her uncompromising position on feminine decorum (which included retaining 'childlikeness' for Victoria as long as possible), informed by Hannah More's precepts and those of conduct literature and inflected by the current age, resulted in Victoria's seclusion and restricted circle of acquaintances in her childhood years, particularly until her thirteenth year. In a fascinating memorandum of the Duchess's written in 1831 about a conversation she had had with the Duchess of Northumberland (for whom it is intended is not clear, but the most likely recipient would have been Sir John Conroy), she makes her programme for Victoria crystal clear. The Duchess of Kent mentions describing Victoria's studies to the Duchess of Northumberland, their progress, and the examinations Victoria would now face every spring before they left town for holidays. But beyond her academic training, and perhaps more significantly, the Duchess had also discussed with the Duchess of Northumberland Victoria's 'moral' upbringing:

I told her how particularly anxious I was, to give Victoria a dignified sense of her great station: And that she could be of great use to me, and assist me, by her advice. Victoria is not to be fashionable, but is to acquire that equality of *dignity* that will affect all clases [*sic*]: I wish my child to be a pattern of female decorum – as to example – and *associates* – that every one may be sure of her *even* course. . . . I never did, neither will I now, associate Victoria in any way with the illigitimate [*sic*] members of the Royal family [William IV had his numerous adult illegitimate FitzClarence children at court]: – With the King they die; did I not keep this line how would it be possible to teach Victoria the difference betwen Vice and Virtue.

The Duchess ends her memorandum with an added note: 'I made also the remark that I like secrecy in all who are about me. . . .'[89] Secrecy, isolation, determination, and regularity are the hallmarks of what became known as 'the Kensington System' of education. The Duchess of Kent, with Sir John Conroy, devised this system in order to raise Victoria as the future sovereign by training her in academic studies, and in the ways of correct female behaviour, as well as by limiting her affective relationships to a very few persons. This last method would ensure their control over her, especially as a regency was not out of the question given the King's age and state of health. In 1831 the Duchess was highly gratified to be awarded the role of Regent by the new Whig Parliament, in the event of King William's death before Victoria turned eighteen. The 'Conroyal' dyad had hoped that a regency would be in place until Victoria turned twenty-one, but this was not to be. Like a prince, at eighteen years of age Victoria would gain her majority and her right to rule alone from that moment. Nevertheless, the Regency Bill was an enormous success for the Duchess. As Monica Charlot relates in her biography of Victoria, the Duchess of Kent wept upon receiving the news that Parliament was considering her as potential Regent: '[she] proclaimed that this was really her first happy day since she lost the Duke of Kent'.[90] Her hard work in constructing Victoria as a perfect queen-in-waiting, and herself as the child-queen's dutiful and wise mother, had certainly paid off. The Lord Chancellor, who introduced the Bill on 15 November, supported the Duchess of Kent with high praise for the '"[discharge of] her duty in the education of her illustrious offspring – and I speak upon the subject not from vague report, but from accurate information – "' and concluded, '"Looking at the past, it is evident we cannot find a better guardian for the time to come."'[91]

The Duchess saw herself as essentially a loner, and desired Victoria to follow the same lonely path. She avowedly avoided developing partisan feelings (although statements to this effect were perhaps counteracted by her arranging to stay with the most important Whig families when travelling). As the Duchess comments in the above memorandum: 'I am on very friendly footing with their Majesties but I will never allow any one else to meddle in my affairs: I am on very good terms with all the family: But being all divided among themselves politically and *often personally*: – my object is to avoid for myself and Victoria any coalitions in their concerns – to remain friend [*sic*] with all. – '[92] This paints a rosier picture than is accurate. The Duchess was *not* on good terms with the Royal Family in general. They were a factious and contentious group, certainly, and the Kents were not allies with anyone of any importance among them. Even as the Duchess was receiving the approbation of Parliament, the King was becoming angrier with their reserve and Victoria's isolation. King William was not pleased with his sister-in-law, though he did not take this dislike out on his niece, of whom he was genuinely fond. But the Duchess was so provoking! She refused to acknowledge his children with Mrs Jordan, and had kept Princess Victoria away from his coronation. This last incidence of severe disrespect was blamed on the Princess's fatigue, but in reality the Duchess was outraged that Victoria's uncles were to precede Victoria in the coronation procession. As the heir to the throne, the Duchess of Kent argued, her daughter should immediately follow the new King. When her desires went unsatisfied, the Duchess took her toy (Victoria) and went home. The snub was not ignored in the press, and at first the Duchess was excoriated for her conduct; however, retractions were printed which revised this antagonistic view to understand the decision as appropriate, given the 'delicate' state of the Princess's health. Whatever the precise reason for the Duchess's behaviour, any illness or indisposition of Victoria's was a fiction. Agnes Strickland relates that the Princess was unable to attend the coronation due to a fall from a pony, but Victoria flatly denies this explanation.[93]

A power struggle over Victoria ensued. The Duchess's need to control Victoria's image at every step required that she not be linked with the decadence and moral sloppiness of the House of Hanover, although this need had the effect of precipitating the King's wrath. Such game-playing helped to support speculations that the Princess was frail and sickly. A letter to *The Times* in 1831 refuted a report that Princess Victoria was unable to walk or stand and had to be wheeled in the drawing-room assembly for the Queen's birthday. (The author of the letter implies that it is the Duke of Cumberland who was responsible for spreading this rumour): 'I am happy in being able to say that Her Highness enjoys excellent health, and may God avert all danger from so valuable a life.'[94] In a move engineered to wrest control over his heir, William decided that Victoria's name had to be changed from the foreign-sounding 'Alexandrina Victoria' to something more suitably 'English'. His decision was a double insult to the Duchess, as her husband had helped to choose the baby's first name as a compliment to his ally, the Tsar Alexander, and the second was a tribute to her own. The Duchess was not at all pleased at this impending Act of Parliament, but she agreed that Victoria's name could be changed to 'Charlotte Victoria'. She admitted that 'the Country will like it'.[95] The matter was debated in Parliament on the same day in 1831 as the Duchess's allowance was voted upon (3 August) but was finally dropped; Victoria was allowed to retain her birth names and 'the Country' became used to and ultimately felt affection for, the sound of her un-English name. Due to her mother's efforts, the young Victoria was something of a cipher in the court, while the mystery surrounding her would begin to be dispelled in the public's eye as the Duchess and Sir John Conroy initiated the next important phase of Victoria's life: the systematic Royal Progresses through Victoria's eventual kingdom.

Chapter Three

Private and Public Princess

1832–1834

I stayed on and saw a temple & my name in stars
& a crown.[1]

Princess Victoria, *1832*

The Travel Journals

On 31 July 1832, the thirteen-year-old Princess was given a small gift from her mother to be used during their forthcoming trip to Wales. Although the octavo-size blank journal half bound in red morocco leather was not an expensive or, seemingly, a particularly notable gift, Victoria's dedication to it initiated what became an obsession for life-writing that endured until two weeks before her death at the age of eighty-one. The journals of this period offer a glimpse of the monarch-in-making.

Victoria autographed her book – 'This book, mamma gave me, that I might write the journal of my journey to Wales in it'[2] – and, most likely prompted by her mother or Lehzen, began recording the events of her trip early that next morning as they set off from Kensington Palace without fanfare. The drama surrounding the trip had taken place before the carriage left the grounds: in King William's mind, the trip had an air of insubordination and forwardness about it, and he attempted to quash the entire undertaking. Although still the King, he could not control his sister-in-law's tour of many of the major Whig estates that dotted his country, or stop the celebrations that were held in their honour wherever they went. These 'disgusting' 'Royal Progresses' seemed to him to smack of unseemly political partisanship and favour on the part of the heir apparent's mother.[3] Certainly, the Duchess of Kent had carefully planned this excursion as an elaborate means of showing off and she, with Conroy, was determined to make it a success. However, this campaign trip to Wales could be effective only if its instructive purpose was understood by all participants: Victoria needed to be educated about her country and her country needed to be educated about its future sovereign. In a letter about her friend the Duchess of Kent, who would soon visit her country house in Chester, Lady Elizabeth Belgrave pinpoints exactly both the political function and the fatigues of these journeys: 'It really is an enterprise ... for a woman by herself in a responsible situation to meet all those Addresses and Testimonials, which she does so well and manages so cleverly under the *semblance of a quiet journey, making the Princess known and securing friends for after times*' (my emphasis).[4]

It must be noted at the outset that Princess Victoria was at first a very bored, if not reluctant, diarist. It is unfortunate for both the young Princess and for posterity that the journal was *not* intended to be the repository of Victoria's private musings, but an open record for her mother's and Lehzen's perusal. The gift most certainly carried an obligation, as it was yet another tool meant to train the memory, give practice in orthography and spelling, and encourage (limited) self-reflection. A kind of passive resentment can be read in the Princess's perhaps stubbornly tedious recitations of the mundane details of their leave-taking:

> We left K.P. [Kensington Palace] at 6 minutes past 7 and went through the Lower-field gate to the right. We went on, & turned to the left by the new road to Regent's Park. The road & scenery is beautiful. 20 minutes to 9. We have just changed horses at Barnet, a very pretty little town. 5 minutes past half past 9. We have just changed horses at St. Albans. . . . We have just passed through Braunston where there is a curious spire. The Oxford canal is close to the town. 1 minute to 4. We have just changed horses at Dunchurch and it is raining. . . .[5]

Victoria must have had access to a precise timepiece and she preferred to keep her emotions in check — for whatever reasons — rather than confide

18. 'The Princess Visiting a Cotton Mill', from Mrs O. F. Walton, *Pictures and Stories from Queen Victoria's Life*, 1901.

them to the page (although she notes drunk postilions and wonders at the mysteries of the 'Ladies of Langollen', who are 'famed for their seclusion and singularity').[6]

A word about the manuscript journals is in order here: entries were first written in soft pencil and some time later inked over. (This process can be seen in the second manuscript volume only.) It is possible that some of the copying in ink was done by Lehzen in the later journals. But in the first volumes it is obvious that the childishly large (in the first few pages about four words to a line) and messy pencil writing scrawled on the unlined pages, matches the later, more controlled inkings. As a young teenager, Princess Victoria's journal handwriting was not particularly neat, but it is easy to read and did improve in style. The Queen's handwriting, by contrast, became more idiosyncratic as she aged. Princess, then Queen, Victoria wrote in her journal virtually every day of her life (barring illnesses and *accouchements*). In *The Private Lives of Victorian Women*, Valerie Sanders comments that 'Essentially, the diary requires only brief spurts of attention, and is the ideal outlet for a woman who is likely to be interrupted, or who dreads publicity.'[7] Victoria's time was rarely, if ever, completely her own, and she was trained, as a result of the tensions that surrounded her and the attentions trained on her, to keep her own counsel – even within the relatively private forum of the journal itself.[8]

Although in later years she would chafe and fret at the emotional disruption caused by her uncomfortable position between the King and her mother, the former resisting – if not forbidding – their early autumn travel away from London, and the latter insisting upon it, in 1832 Victoria seemed not unwilling to enjoy her journey and her journal began to reflect greater interest in her surroundings. The royal entourage travelled north-west through Coventry and Birmingham on their way to Powis Castle in Wales, and even their stops along the way served an important political function in Victoria's educational programme. While the horses were changed or when the group needed a meal or rest, the Princess would be taken on instructive side trips to places of interest within the economic 'heart' of England – the industrial Midlands. These visits – often to factories – were also considered a sign of royal favour bestowed upon the nearest town, the labourers and the factory owner (Ill. 18).

The engraving shown in Ill. 18, reproduced in the children's book *Pictures and Stories from Queen Victoria's Life* (1901), commemorates Victoria's excursion to a cotton mill in Belper, where the group had stopped on 23 October. In the illustration of this scene, a diminutive and demure Princess Victoria stands at the head of the well-dressed crowd and looks on as a venerable gentleman holds a spindle and explains the methods of cotton manufacture to the visiting royalty and gentry. A group of female factory workers stands behind the gentleman and observes the Princess. The caption reads, 'The poor workers appear to have been very pleased to catch a glimpse of their future sovereign.'⁹ This sentimentalized scene perfectly enacts Victoria's education through travel and the 'natural' relationship of indulgence and respect that should develop between the young royal and the lower-class workers. By visiting the factories, Victoria could be viewed by the lower class in their *own* 'awe-inspiring' setting of British mechanical triumph – of which, through their labour, they constituted an integral part – and they would thereby recognize that as future sovereign, Victoria belonged to them; for her part, Victoria claimed a kind of legitimation for her eventual position as queen through her spectatorial gaze at the labourers 'creating' an economically strong Britain for 'her'.

As a member of the Royal Family (and as future queen), Victoria's presence at different locations in England and Wales acted as a reminder of the aristocratic 'mortar' that was holding Great Britain together and upholding core British values. This cohesive function is aptly illustrated by one of the Princess's first official acts as a child dignitary: laying the cornerstone of a new school near Bangor. Like other luminaries of the past and present who lend their status to ceremonial occasions, the Duchess of Kent accepted the invitation to help celebrate the construction of a new school and receive homage in return. Victoria recalls the excursion thus: 'Then Mr. Rowland, the clergyman, gave me a small trowell [*sic*] with mortar with which I smeared the stone which was there, then I beat the stone thrice with a wooden hammer & Mamma did the same. Then Mr. Rowland read a short prayer & afterwards Mr. Saunderson read an address to Mamma which she answered. We then looked at the school girls who were a little further on & whose neat and tidy appearance pleased us very much.'¹⁰ At times, however, the education in British culture that Victoria received on this trip failed to excite her curiosity, as in the following example of another expedition to a school: on their way back to Kensington the royal party stopped at 'the great grammar school of Dr. Butler's'. Dr Butler took it upon himself to inform Victoria of his pedagogical methods which, though called 'very simple' by

Victoria, were apparently too complicated for writing down: '.... but [it] would take me too much time to explain it here'.[11]

In addition to these intangible relationships formed between princess and factory workers, princess and schoolchildren, we learn from Victoria's journal that she literally began to collect bits of industrial England on these forays into the land of 'the people'. She was given 'an oaken box with a silver top and filled with the famous Shrewsbury cakes' (2 August 1832), 'gloves of staple manufacture' (4 November 1832), 'a small gold box filled with the *smallest nails* I ever saw as a specimen of their manufactories' (6 November 1832), and a fox's brush (31 October 1832).[12] She buys for herself some 'minerals' from a boy (6 August 1832) and 'Derbyshire spar [crystalline minerals] in different little shapes and forms'(20 October 1832). Through her collection of a miniaturized England represented by these manufactured objects, Victoria became invested in a process of ownership that would be completed by her eventual accession. As a 'finishing school', Victoria's travels provided her with a 'text' to memorize (the map of England and Wales), a text to compose (her journal), and a role to play: part schoolgirl, part patroness.

The royal retinue also visited the slate quarries and Victoria enjoyed watching the complicated process of slate cutting: 'It was very curious to see the men split the slate, and others cut it, while others hung suspended by ropes and cut the slate; others again drove wedges into a piece of rock as in that manner would split off a block. Then little carts about a dozen at a time rolled down a railway by them-selves'.[13] On another excursion they visited a dairy and observed butter-making.[14]

When in Birmingham in the early stages of her trip, Victoria commented that they 'visited the manufactories which are very curious'.[15] Victoria is generally rather sparing in her descriptive commentary, but as they moved further north through coal country she is sufficiently moved by the look of the place and its people to attempt to describe the surprising nature of what she sees for the first time: the environmental and social devastation wrought by the coal industry. Still, Victoria's powers of description are not great:

The men, woemen [*sic*], children, country and houses are all black. But I can not by any description give an idea of its strange and extraordinary appearance. The country is very desolate every where; there are coals about, and the grass is quite blasted and black. I just now see an extraordinary building flaming with fire. The country continues black, engines flaming, coals, in abundance, every where, smoking and burning coal heaps, intermingled with wretched huts and carts and little ragged children.[16]

In fact, this description is very reminiscent of the discussion of the industrial Midlands found in Maria Edgeworth's 'Harry and Lucy' stories (discussed in Chapter Two).[17]

Although the journal was decidedly conceived of as an educational obligation, it became an integral part of Princess Victoria's everyday life, perhaps functioning as both an outlet and a means of stability for the young Victoria. The travel diaries are especially fascinating because of their unique qualities: written from the perspective of an adolescent stranger (to the families, homes, and locations she visited), yet one whose 'open secret' (that she would some day be Queen of England) was in continual play. The travel narrative is the story of leaving home. In the case of the relatively 'homeless' Princess Victoria, however, she travels *to* her home(land) (her country) rather than away from it: the debt-ridden Duchess of Kent was allowed to live at Kensington Palace because of her daughter, but her position within the Royal Family was uneasy and troubled, not least because of these Grand Tours and her eventual commandeering and renovation of portions of Kensington Palace for her own use, against the wishes of King William. In a land where property ownership was a primary indicator of male status and economic stability, the future Queen of England and her mother owned very, very little. Eventually, of course, all of Britain (and India) would become her 'home', and she would own land from its northern to its southern boundaries, but until that happy time (which first necessitated the death of a close relative), the young Victoria was ironically consigned to the status of rootless, perpetual visitor. Not yet the queen whose travels would breed (at times inaccurately) boastful 'Queen Victoria slept here' plaques, the Princess and her bed were never parted. To close her first ever journal entry she wrote, 'I was asleep in a minute in my own little bed which travells always with me.'[18] In this way, the travelling princess whose 'home' perhaps could be distilled down to this 'little bed', created for herself, and remarked in her journal, another form of stability and comfort, self-absorbed and self-contained.

Most crucial to Victoria's happiness when in London or away from Kensington was the presence of her beloved governess Lehzen. Victoria's journal makes clear how essential Lehzen was to her peace of mind and moment-to-moment existence. If 'dear Lehzen' were ill, for example, her indisposition would be recorded at length and her recovery cause for rejoicing: 'But I am sorry to say, that dear Lehzen was very unwell, and was unable to come to breakfast. After breakfast she was better and thought herself able to go with us [on the steam-vessel]. . . . Lehzen went down, into Mrs Smith's own cabin, and lay down on her bed. The way was very pretty, and it would have been much pleasanter to me, had dear Lehzen been well.'[19] When Victoria is ill, Lehzen stays by her side at all times while the Duchess of Kent goes about her own business. This delegation of duties, where the employee (as indeed she was, though an extremely highly placed one and a created baroness as well) remained with the sick child and the mother represented the household elsewhere, was not unusual in aristocratic families and would not have been interpreted as an abrogation of maternal duty or evidence of any want of affection on the Duchess's part. However, this state of affairs helps to explain the deep affection that Victoria had for Lehzen and the distance between mother and daughter. On 17 August 1832 the Duchess of Kent's birthday, Victoria did fall ill. This illness does not seem to have been severe, and she comments on it for two days only.[20] During this time, Lehzen worked quietly on a beautiful doll (representing 'La Sylphide', a favourite character in a popular drama Victoria had recently seen in London) while Victoria lay on the sofa (Ill. 19). The Duchess of Kent and 'the other party' (perhaps Sir John Conroy) went to the Lake of Llanberis for the entire day (18 August).

Victoria was ever-careful in her journal. She never criticized her mother or any other (important) person (although at times she would censure a drunk postilion or a clergyman's 'shocking' sermon, but even these mildly negative opinions were rare), yet Victoria's journal is certainly not a completely opaque document. The Conroy family accompanied the Kents on this trip, of course, and were included in most domestic events with the

19. Princess Victoria, watercolour of *La Sylphide*, 1834.

family – dining, attending church, riding, visiting – although they did not always share the same accommodation. Victoria's relationship to Victoire *can* be gleaned from the journal by way of a comparative analysis of Victoria's comments about the Conroys and those made about others. On 12 August Victoria rather offhandedly mentions the birthday of this constant companion (Victoire was just a few months younger than Victoria and named for her godmother, the Duchess of Kent) in a sentence primarily concerning her emotional attachment to relative strangers. At the time, Victoria was missing her cousins, Hugo and Alphonso Mensdorff (sons of the Duchess of Kent's oldest sister, Sophie) who joined them briefly in Beaumaris: 'I arranged [Victoire's] presents, and at breakfast, where the[y] all were, I again missed Hugo and Alphonso very much, and so I did the whole day.'[21] In terms of outward display, Victoria's conduct toward Sir John's daughter may not have been very warm, but it cannot be faulted. In one entry Victoria's mask slips when she reveals her understanding of Victoire's subordinate status by writing, 'I then sent for Victoire & we played together.'[22]

Victoire Conroy hovers in the journal (and as a subject of Victoria's watercolours) as a presence who is frequently noted but never analysed (in the way that her love for her governess, uncle and sister are, for example). More significantly, Victoria's *bête noire*, Sir John Conroy, similarly 'haunts' the journal. His 'special treatment' by Victoria is subtle, yet legible. For example, he is often called 'J. C.' or 'Sir J. C.', although in general abbreviations are very unusual in Victoria's journal. In *A Royal Conflict*, Katherine Hudson begins her extended exploration of the relationship between Victoria and Conroy with the arrival of the travelling party in Oxford on this trip. The Duchess of Kent and Princess Victoria had been given addresses by local dignitaries in Bangor, Conway, Anglesey, and many other places; in Oxford, at the very end of their sojourn, Sir John Conroy was recognized. While the Duchess and Princess were, in Victoria's words, 'warmly & enthousiastically' (underlined twice) received, Conroy was given the keys to the city. The Vice-Chancellor of the Divinity School of Oxford University, Dr Rowley, made an impressive and eloquent speech in Latin praising Sir John for his loyalty and service to the Duchess of Kent and her daughter. As a reward for his efforts, Dr Rowley conferred the honorary degree of Doctor of Civil Law upon Conroy. Hudson writes:

This very curious, indeed spectacular episode – which received considerable national publicity ... demonstrates how popular the Duchess of Kent and her Equerry Sir John Conroy were in the eyes of the people of England, and how no less a body than Oxford University had set the seal of approval on their education of Princess Victoria; it shows, too, in this year of 1832, the importance of the Princess as a figurehead of unity and continuity in a time of great political upheaval.[23]

Perhaps Victoria was singularly unimpressed by this honour as she notes nothing about Conroy's triumph – at first. But, then, written in very tiny hand in the entry for 8 November she marks an asterisk and writes the following in the margin, 'And Sir John got the freedom of the city of Oxford.'[24] This is a unique example of revision in the manuscript diaries. It certainly looks as if someone has suggested to Victoria that this interesting information about Conroy should not be left out of her record. This is an instance where the reader, or readers, of Victoria's journal show themselves, at least in shadow.

Although Victoria's 'troubles', in the shape of the Conroys, came along with her, when taken as a whole, life on the road offered the Princess many more opportunities for fun and amusement than her staid and regimented life at Kensington Palace. Through the 'lens' of the journal we are able to see Victoria's 'playing' as more childlike and active than the 'walking and driving' that the daily schedule from Kensington Palace would indicate. Victoria mentions playing with her dolls ('... I unpacked my dolls & settled them'),[25] 'dissected pictures',[26] billiards and blowing soap bubbles,[27] paper dolls,[28] popular games such as 'Commas' and 'Fright' (with Lady Conroy, Victoire and Lehzen),[29] cards as a game and as building material ('Victoire & me began to make a cottage of cards'),[30] engaging in foot races,[31] playing 'battle-door & shuttle cock and ball',[32] and general running about ('I wrote music, ran about the passage, & played with my dolls').[33] Society at Norris Castle on the Isle of Wight, where Victoria and the Duchess stayed in the autumn of 1831 and 1833, was very lively and Victoria enjoyed the many post-prandial ladies' parlour games such as 'The Hens and her Chickens', 'Puss in the Corner' and 'Forfeits' played before the gentlemen rejoined the ladies (Victoria notes that she is always in bed before their return).[34] The conventional picture we are given of the young Victoria is of a quiet child eating breakfast with her mother on the lawn of Kensington Palace, watering the flowers, holding another's hand, riding in a carriage – and all of these activities did help to construct the fabric of her childhood. But Victoria was also rambunctious – even as a young teenager – and allowed to run and play vigorously. And while exercise ideology of the Georgian period found in such little books as *Youthful Recreations* (*c.* 1810) 'gendered' different activities – football was considered a 'manly' exercise 'not proper for girls' – exercise for both sexes was promoted as beneficial for health:

> To prevent *bodily weakness and infirmity*, exercise is necessary; and one physician has said, that 'he did not know which was most necessary to the human frame, *food* or *motion*.' To play with *battledore* and *shuttle-cock* or with a *trap* and *ball*, is good exercise; and if we had it in our power to grant, not only the children of the affluent, but even such of the poor as are impelled by necessity to pick cotton, card wool, to spit and spin or reel all day, should have at least one hour, morning and evening, for some youthful recreation …[35]

Although Victoria would later reject the idea of transcribing the teaching method of the famous Dr Butler, whose pedagogical methods she declined to consign to her journal, she gives more effort to the rowdy Rural Sports she witnessed: 'Donkey racing, climbing up a greasy poll for a live duck at the top, jumping in sacks, running with wheel-berrows blindfolded, & chase after a pig with its tail soaped [and] the right hand hid behind. As I have a bill of the whole & the sailors names (for they were all our sailors) I shall only say that nothing could be more rediculous & amusing.'[36]

This active princess also loved speed in all the forms available to her: in the carriage, on horseback, on sailing vessels. For example, as the carriages made their way slowly through the hilly Welsh landscape, Victoria wished that they could pick up speed. When at last the road straightened, to her disgust, the pace remained the same: 'The scenery here is quite lovely, and the road is as flat as a table; we might go on very fast, but I am sorry to say, we do not.'[37] She gloried in fast riding: 'At 2 we went out riding, and cantered almost the whole way, and once even we glopped.'[38] Victoria and the royal party were often entertained by sailing trips on the yacht *Emerald* as well as excursions on Mr Ashton-Smith's steam vessel. Victoria was a good sailor, and rarely seasick (though she exaggerates years later when she boasts that she was '*never*' seasick).[39] Victoria was impressed with the steam vessel's beauty and thought that 'the machinery is quite wonderful for it's order and cleanliness',[40] but she reserves her highest praise for the *Emerald*, 'to which the Gazelle [another yacht] is not to be compared, in my eyes, at least, in point of beauty & elegance'.[41] This was written after the *Emerald*, with the enthusiastic princess on board, had soundly beaten the *Gazelle* in a race. Sailing on a barge one day Victoria comments with pleasure on a choppy sea that most would have found unsettling: '... it was so rough that it went up & down quite delightful'.[42] She was also very fond of dancing. One of the most satisfying events of this trip for Victoria – marked by underlining as emphasis – was the evening after the 'glopping' on horseback, when after dinner Victoria attended 'a *little ball*'.[43] At thirteen, Victoria was not a precocious girl pining for suitors, but an extraordinarily healthy (she was rarely ill for more than a day or two) and somewhat immature child who rather refreshingly continued to play with dolls and put together puzzles.

Another playtime activity that gave Victoria great pleasure was dressing in costumes – or, as we shall see, dressing Victoire Conroy up. The numerous references to dressing up are surprising, as wearing costumes is just one step removed from acting, an activity not sanctioned for upper-class girls of the 1830s. One might recall the horror expressed by Jane Austen's modest Fanny Price at the private theatricals held at Mansfield Park in Sir Thomas Bertram's absence. In *Mansfield Park* (1814), Fanny's 'correct' conduct in regard to the play ensures her a place in the aristocratic stratum, while her female cousin's enthusiasm for acting foreshadows her eventual expulsion and displacement from the manor. Hannah More, too, although she had had some early success as a dramatist, ultimately gave up the theatre as incompatible with her Evangelical beliefs. Her early play *The Search for Happiness* (1773) was written for schoolgirls to perform privately as an acknowledgement of their desire to act, yet also as moral antidote to the immodest dramas that might tempt them. George Rowell, in *Queen Victoria Goes to the Theatre*, notes that Princess Victoria wrote 'longingly' about her enjoyment in watching some of the adults at Chatsworth, the

Duke of Devonshire's home, put on charades. The Princess described the scene in her travel journal of 1832 and later illustrated in watercolours the vivid tableau of the final act which she could only admire from a seat in the audience.[44]

Victoria's love of costume and the garish was the natural extension of her interest in the theatre, ballet, and opera.[45] The dolls that interested her at this stage in her life were no longer the 'babies' present in her first letters to Feodore, but the tiny Dutch dolls that Lehzen would dress in elaborate costumes to commemorate the performers they had both admired. Victoria's watercolours of dancers, singers, and actresses are painstaking in their details of dress and ornament. By recreating the clothing and gestures of her favourites, Victoria could relive the exciting dramas she had watched unfold on stage. Victoria even dressed her dog Dash in trousers — a scene captured in a sketch by an anonymous artist (Ill. 20).[46] It is not surprising, then, that Victoria mentions early on in her trip to Wales that she and Victoire Conroy played at dressing-up and that this activity continued from time to time after the trip had concluded. Except for copying Taglioni's 'La Naiade' early in 1833 ('I dressed myself up as 'La Naide' as Taglioni was dressed, with corals in my hair'),[47] Victoria's choice of roles is remarkably transgressive and theatrical. This good, Protestant, English princess 'cross-dresses' in a number of ways — or has Victoire or her sister Jane do so: as a man ('... Jane went out walking under our windows dressed as a man',[48] 'After dinner Victoire was dressed up with shawls like a turk & had mustaches done with [word missing] on her face',[49] 'After dinner I dressed myself up as an old Turkish lawyer. A large green shawl turban, a white beard & a green cloak with sleeves completed the dress'),[50] a Nun ('After dinner I dressed myself up as a nun to amuse Mamma'),[51] an exotic woman ('After dinner I dressed myself as a Turkish lady. A red scarf & a white shawl made the turban with a dark blue one & a bright red one for the dress & large hanging white sleeves. I remained so for the [word missing] of the evening'),[52] and as a bandit's wife ('After dinner I dressed myself up as an Italian Brigand's wife; a colored shawl over my head a white one in front & some gold chains. . . . Then as a nun again in black & white shawls' (Ill. 21).[53] These after-dinner amusements, which were evidently sanctioned by the Duchess of Kent as she must have been part of the audience for them,

Pray Sir don't look so melancholy

20. Anon., Dash (dog) in trousers.

nevertheless cease to be mentioned in the journal after early 1834. Victoria
may have grown out of her fascination with trying on costumes and assum-
ing different identities (answering the question that if most girls dress up
to be princesses, what do princesses dress up to be?), and/or such 'childish'
playacting may have been deemed inappropriate by the Duchess of Kent.

   Certainly Victoria had a very serious role to play as heiress presumptive to the throne. This was not 'true' acting, of course, as there was no
pretence involved in fulfilling her destiny as queen, but display was all-
important. In fact, Victoria functioned as a kind of 'property' in the
Duchess of Kent's royal road show where Conroy was 'properties
master'. Early in the 1832 trip to Wales, the Kents and the entourage

21. Princess Victoria, drawing of 'Sister Victoire', 1837.

stopped at the Regent Hotel in Leamington, where people thronged below their windows in the hope of catching a glimpse of the Princess. They were often rewarded for their pains, as the Duchess required that Victoria appear at the window with some frequency. Yet, as the evening came on, Princess Victoria could no longer be seen from below as she stood by the window and waved, so the Duchess engineered, with Sir John's assistance, a lighted 'stage' for her daughter: Victoria stood upon a stool with her mother's arms around her 'for support', and Sir John was positioned close behind them, arms outstretched and holding two wax candles in his hands to illuminate the tableau of loving mother and dependent daughter.[54]

A similar moment of display occurred on the occasion of the Duchess of Kent's birthday in 1832. Victoria probably began suffering from period pains around the 17th of each month. As a means to celebrate the Duchess's birthday (17 August), she received commemorative addresses from the Bishop of Bangor and other gentlemen, and the unwell Victoria fasted and rested. But that evening she and her mother were out on the balcony to see and to be seen. Sir Richard Bulkeley had gathered his tenants together to admire the royal party: 'At 7 we were on the balcony, to see the tenants of Sir Richard Bulkley, who were drawn up before the house, in all 300, with himself.'[55] Bonfires were lit, and the Princess watched from her vantage point above the crowd.

At times, especially when Victoria was travelling from country seat to country seat or when making educational excursions, 'the people' could get a closer glimpse of the Princess. Victoria enjoyed the attention she received, which was often expressed in picturesque ways, such as fireworks ('my name in stars & a crown'). (On subsequent 'progresses' the masses of people would make her nervous and peevish.) One month after the balcony performance, the party made a day trip to Chester. They crossed the dramatic Menai Bridge where an arch of laurel and flowers had been erected[56] (Victoria was to have a lesson a few days later on the building of this structure, by Mr Hazledine, owner of the foundry where the ironwork was done)[57] and proceeded into the cathedral town of Chester. Along the way as the group went from visiting the castle prison to the cathedral, curious onlookers thronged: 'The crowd was enormous & we then procceded to the castle where the jail was; we went about the jail & viewed from a balcony the cells where the prisoners were confined. I am however happy to say, there were but few. We then went to the armory & from there in our carriages, & proceded[58] along the streets; we could not have been received better, the hurraying, all the way & our ladies with us [in] the carriages waving their handkerchiefs.'[59] Lady Elizabeth Belgrave was among the royal party and commented with satisfaction on Victoria's behaviour during the flurry of attention: 'The Princess does her part, too, perfectly and with great simplicity and good nature.'[60] Two days later, on a longer trip through Norwich, Victoria reported that 'The little charity girls strewed the way with flowers, & flags hung from the windows.'[61] They ended up in

Knutsford where 'We were most civilly received, the streets being sanded in shapes which is peculiar to this town.'[62] The trip had been a success and Victoria was, not surprisingly, a popular figure wherever she went. An account of the Kents' visit to the Eisteddfod (a festival of music and poetry dating from the twelfth century) in the *North Wales Chronicle* notes that 'At four o'clock Mr. Stubb's band struck up God Save the King and the Royal Duchess and princess, followed by a splendid train of about 50 of the fairest and noblest of the land, who had been invited to dine at Baron Hill that day, came forth from the principal entrance. . . . a scarlet cloth was placed upon the pavement and seats placed thereon for the royal visitors.' There was musical entertainment, which included the national song 'Mewn Awen Fwyn Lawen' embellished with an additional stanza praising Princess Victoria, 'of Tudor's famed Line'.[63] Victoria also notes in her journal the numerous addresses that her mother received as they journeyed back to London. Victoria's role as England's daughter is emphasized here in the many tableaux of Duchess and daughter – the latter beautifully dressed and posed – awaiting speeches of approbation. Victoria did not need special costumes or circumstance to be role-playing here; as Leopold would note in 1836, 'high personages' are like actors in performances who must strive to please their audiences.[64]

Although descriptions of her own dramatic play ceased in her journal, entries about the theatre began to proliferate in it in 1833 and 1834. Victoria ultimately transformed her journal from a travel narrative commemorating a specific journey, to a daily obligation that did not end at the return to Kensington Palace in 1832. When in London (as opposed to travelling), one of Victoria's chief pleasures was attending the theatre and opera. In emotional entries about wonderful plots and performers she enjoyed watching, Victoria expressed her intense involvement in the drama, song, and dance of the period. From the moment the Princess was first allowed to go to the theatre, she fell in love with drama. This love was anticipated by her considerable dramatic flair, as close attention to her childhood stories and love of costume confirms.

Whether Victoria possessed the 'genius of movement' from her childhood, as one rather fawning assessment of the Queen written just after her death holds, is difficult to determine, but her enormous admiration and appreciation of dance, song, costume, narrative, and acting, and the inspiration they gave her, are indisputable.[65] Truly, writing, drawing, singing, and performance animated Victoria's girlhood. About the melodrama *The Innkeeper's Daughter* she writes, '[it] is very horrible but *extremely interesting*'.[66] She thrilled to see generic mishmashes such as 'the new Romantic, Operatic, Magical, and Ballet Burletta of Lurline or the Revolt of the Naides' (1834). The Naiad Lurline, played by Mrs Honey, wore stunning costumes that the Princess was able to recount in detail: 'Her first dress was a thin white muslin very short and ornamented with 4 bunches of coral down the front. A zone of gold studded onyxes encircled her waist; bracelets of gold on her arms, very short sleeves and a sprig of corals on her forehead with long black curls hanging down. Her second dress as an amazon was also very pretty. A breast plate of silver, a petticoat of blue embroidered and fringed with silver, short sleeves and a helmet with a red plume. She looked QUITE LOVELY in both.'[67] The royal party ventured to Covent Garden to see comedies or the ballet or pantomimes a few times in 1832 (after their return home from their trip). In early 1833 Victoria attended *The Barber of Seville* at Drury Lane, and in her journal she confides that she will avoid rehearsing the plot because '[i]t is so well, known that I need not describe it'.[68] This comment highlights the almost hybrid public/private nature of Victoria's journal: her plot summaries seem to serve both as reminders to herself about what she has seen and as information to be shared with the other readers of her journal. On this occasion, however, the famous phrase that clings to the conventional picture of a dour old woman that Victoria would become made its first appearance in her girlhood journals – with one important difference: Victoria writes, 'I was *very much* amused' (Ill. 22).[69]

Victoria was an avid drama critic; she evaluated and minutely described in her journal the acting, dancing, costumes, hairstyles, and facial features of the performers, and the plots of the performances she witnessed throughout 1833 and 1834. In Victoria's journal entry for 27 April 1833 she demonstrates her keen attention to the performances she had seen by this comment about Taglioni, a celebrated dancer of the period: 'Mlle. Taglioni made her first appearance this season. She is grown very thin but danced *beautifully* so highly & *gracefully*, & each step so finished!'[70] The delighted enthusiasm Victoria felt after hearing the singer Giulia Grisi's portrayal of

Tamburini who sung likewise
beautifully; Rodrigo, M. Ivanhoff
who sung very well. Signor
Zuchelli. Desdemona, Signora
Guiletta Grisi. She sung,
acted quite beautifully! and
looked lovely. ~~Particularly~~ at

~~[crossed out line]~~

She acted and sung ~~[looked sweetly?]~~ beautifully
in the last scene; and also
~~then~~ in two trios in the 1st
second acts. When the opera
was over she was called for,
and she came on led by
Rubini. At that moment a
wreath of roses ~~[crossed out]~~ with
a small roll of paper inside
was thrown on the stage; the

22. *Queen Victoria's Journal*, entry for 26 April 1834.

...icked it up and placed it on
...er head. They were very much
applauded. We came away
directly after the opera. Lord
...chester & Lady Thereon join
...us here. We came home at a
...y to 12. I was _very_ _much_ amused
...ended ...!!!

Sunday 27th April.
I awoke at 7 and got up at 8. At
9 we breakfasted. At 10 we went
down to prayers. The D﬈ service
was performed by the Dean who
gave us likewise an excellent
sermon. It was taken from
the Epistle general of St James
1st verse. At 11 came Victoire
...ﬆ½ past 2. At ½ past 11 we
...ent out walking. At 1 we lunched.
...t ½ past 3 we went out driving for the

23. Princess Victoria, watercolour of 'Guilia Grisi as Anna Bolena', 1834.

Desdemona can almost be heard resonating off the page of her journal (Ill. 23).

As she grew older, Victoria's love for the dramatic could also be indulged – although to a lesser extent – within her leisure reading. While the great majority of the tales and stories made available to the Princess were heavily moralistic, not all the stories were dry or boring. Included in the annual *The Amulet: A Christian and Literary Rembrancer* (1832), a gift from the Duchess of Kent, is a sensational novella entitled 'The Mosspits' by Mrs S. C. Hall (editor of the *Amulet*) that Victoria may well have enjoyed reading.[71] The main characters are Agnes, a good wife, and Edward, her less intelligent.yet religious husband, and a flighty younger sister, Jessy. The last two fall under the spell of the politically and personally intemperate Harry Hinton who is involved in burning ricks and inciting tenants to rise against their landlords. The charming Harry Hinton ultimately seduces Jessy. One night, the manor house is burned and Harry, Edward, and another man are taken to jail for the crime. A mad girl – a spurned former lover of Harry's – gives evidence at the trial that Edward did not participate in the arson but rather had tried to stop it. The mad girl perceives her rival – the ruined Jessy – at the trial and creates a scene. Jessy is able to corroborate her evidence, however, and Harry is convicted and sentenced to death for his part in this crime. On hearing this pronouncement, Jessy expires at the feet of the worthy Agnes. Edward is set free. The chastened family leaves England and is reconciled to the ways of religion and virtue through the example of the godly and goodly Agnes who had kept her head throughout all the crises. The text is certainly relentlessly moral, but the story is thrilling and includes lurid and exciting scenes of class conflict, sexual predation, madness, and sudden death. Notwithstanding the details of 'The Mosspits', the preface to this 1832 edition of the annual emphasizes the didactic nature of the volume and attempts to claim that the goal of the book was more elevated than that of mere entertainment.[72]

Another sensational book included in the Princess's library was Bulwer-Lytton's novel *Godolphin* (1833). Just as she admired love scenes on stage, Victoria may have enjoyed the romantic exchange between the hero Godolphin and his lover, Constance, which ends thus: 'Words like these [of asking for forgiveness] from the lips of one in whom such tender supplication, such feminine yearnings, were not common, subdued Godolphin at once. He folded her in his arms, and kissing her passionately, whispered, "Be always thus, Constance, and you will be more to me than ever."'[73] This scene would certainly provide fodder for an active imagination. Unless they contain a dedication or autograph, it generally cannot be ascertained exactly when Princess Victoria read these more thrilling works except that it was before she became queen in 1837 (when her bookplate was altered to reflect her change in status). In the case of the novel *The Highland Smugglers* (1832), however, Victoria indicates that she bought the book while staying at Plâs Newydd, Lord Anglesey's home in North Wales, in 1832.[74] Some books in the Princess's library were decidedly unread – pages remain uncut.

Daily Life

Victoria's lessons resumed in earnest after her return to Kensington Palace on 9 November 1832 and would never again be interrupted for long periods of time until she became queen on 30 June 1837 and her studying days ended. Her formal education had not ceased entirely while she was travelling – indeed, given the number of events and educational trips she attended, it was a kind of 'working holiday' for the princess. In the journal Victoria mentions studying even during the first ten days of the trip.[75] She does not often describe the content of her lessons or say how they are superintended, but a likely supposition is that Lehzen served as 'master' during the lesson hours. In 1832 specific instruction is mentioned in Scottish history (28 August); French exercises (7 September); 'religious' lessons (20 September); 'religion, writing and arithmetic' (4 October); on a very rainy day, 'french, writing, latin & history' (5 October), history (6 and 9 October), and in preparation for their long journey from Plâs Newydd to Chester, Chatsworth, Oxford and home, she reads in her 'road-book' (11 and 13 October) and the lessons stop.

Victoria's journal provides clues to the extra intellectual education she experienced in her early teens. This additional education included artistic expression through painting and music, as well as practical skills. In the case

24. Princes Victoria, self-portrait drawing, 1834.

25. Princess Victoria, drawing of Lady Catherine Jenkinson, 1836.

of the latter, Victoria – like any middle- or upper-class girl – was learning how to keep an accounts book of income and outgoing funds. Although she would never manage a household, Victoria was trained to be responsible for her personal expenses. There would have been many occasions on this journey for Victoria to purchase various souvenirs or to practise charitable giving and, accordingly, Victoria mentions writing her accounts book on this trip.[76] Victoria also 'writes music' (copies the score so that she can later play it) from time to time. Her love of music was shared by the Duchess of Kent and it provided an opportunity for mother and daughter to spend time together in writing music and playing duets.[77] Virtually any house that Victoria visited or stayed in would have had a piano available for her use. But Victoria's paintbox and pencils, like her little bed, always travelled with her. She notes in her journal the time she spent painting (often with Victoire Conroy).[78] Without the benefit of her master, Mr Westall (whose lessons she greatly enjoyed) and his drawings to copy, Victoria was on her own is deciding on the subject matter for her artistic attempts (Ill. 24.). She often drew or painted from life (or sometimes memory) the aristocratic ladies whose visits took up a large proportion of her trip (Ill. 25). She also mentions 'painting to [her] map' on 12 October 1832. No other details are given about this map, but it may well be the same watercolour map of Western Europe preserved in the Royal Archives with Princess Victoria's other materials (Ill. 26). This brightly coloured map is charmingly (if not absolutely accurately) drawn and painted. The scale of the map offers an interesting glimpse into Victoria's position as a loyal British subject: Great Britain is much too large and looming at the edge of Europe, yet from the perspective of the future sovereign, the relative importance of Great Britain to her neighbours is appropriately depicted here.

Victoria's library included didactic travel narratives such as Mrs Hofland's *The Young Northern Traveller, or the Invalid Restored*, the story of delicate and serious Frederic Delmar, the fourteen-year-old invalid son of a widowed woman. Frederic is taken on a trip to Denmark, Sweden, and Russia by his uncle and his impressions of the lands he visits are recorded which, as Mrs Hofland herself states in the preface 'can hardly fail to be useful to [the young reading public]'.[79] In her later teens, Victoria often confessed to Leopold her desire to travel to the Continent to visit some of the places she was reading

26. Princess Victoria, watercolour map of Europe, n.d.

about, but she also makes it clear that she understands her duty is to remain in Great Britain and wait for her Uncle William to die.[80] Perhaps her map represents an attempt to 'inch' just a bit closer to Uncle Leopold — so close across the Channel in Belgium — on paper, if not in actuality.

Though they remained for the most part separated by distance, Leopold's greatest period of influence over his famous niece dates from her early and mid-teenage years (Ill. 27). The time when his advice would be viewed as meddling, and gently but firmly put aside, was not to come until Victoria reached her eighteenth year and became queen. But for now Leopold was Victoria's window on the world and arbiter of taste. He urged that she concentrate on history in her studies and 'learn human-kind's ways and manners'.[81] Perhaps more importantly, her uncle joined her mother in reminding the Princess of her eventual role and how she must mould her character in preparation for it. In her birthday letter for 1832, Leopold writes, '[b]y the dispensation of providence you are destined to fill a most eminent station, to fill it *well*, must now become your study. A good heart and a truly honorable character are amongst the most indispensable quali-fications for that position.'[82] The following year, Leopold's letter is more properly termed a sermon in which he exhorts her to be serious, forswear vanity, practise self-reflection, and weigh the importance of events and annoyances and ignore petty trifles.[83]

As royalty, Leopold generally felt rather beleaguered — even before he became the King of Belgium. The tedium of the job, the high expectations of the public, and what he believed to be the constant erosion of his politi-cal power, all served to irritate the King. His advice to his young and untried niece, therefore, was often tinged with bitterness and caution: 'Our times as I have frequently told you, are hard times for Royalty and never was there a period, when the existence of *real qualities in persons in high stations has been more imperiously called for*. It seems that in proportion as sovereign power is abridged, the pretensions and expectations of the public are raised. It becomes therefore indispensable, without diminishing the happiness of your present situation, to give every now and then a serious thought to the future.'[84] King Leopold was not above manipulating Victoria's emotions by reminding her of his great love for her, which also implied an obligation to him. After the death of his first child, a crown prince, just before her birth-

27. Queen Victoria, drawing of Leopold I, 1839.

day in 1834, Leopold tells Victoria, 'I merely write to you that you should see that even in the *most dreadful moments* of my life, I do *not* forget one, who has always given me proofs of *sympathy* and *affection*.'[85]

Leopold's importance to Victoria is also demonstrated by her active desire to please him. This somewhat abstemious relative made his views on eating and manners abundantly clear to the hungry princess, and as a result she boasts that her eating has become more seemly: she writes in 1834, 'I wish you could come here, for many reasons, but also to be an eyewitness of my extreme prudence in eating, which would astonish you.'[86] Leopold's letters often concerned health – his in particular. In the following rather incoherent comment to Victoria he includes his thoughts on the special tribulations attending one's royal station: 'And nothing is more melancholy than bad health. Persons in high station are liable to it, because they are subjected to more moral irritation and vexation than people in inferior station, thus health always suffers from it, and really makes it obligatory for them to be a little attentive.'[87] Victoria takes Leopold's sage wisdom to heart and also enjoys passing it on to her sister. In 1836, she wrote to Feodore, 'I consider [exercise] the most important part of your present regime, which will even perhaps make you grow, only think how important.'[88]

Other clues to Victoria's ardent and loyal nature can be found in the bond between the two sisters. The warm relationship between Princess Victoria and her older half-sister deepened after Feodore, Ernest, and their two eldest children (Charles and Eliza) visited the Duchess of Kent and Victoria for two months in the summer of 1834. Victoria was very impressed by her sister's gentle mothering and the intricate details of bathing and putting small children to bed (Ill. 28). In only seven years' time, Victoria would begin to put into practice with the Princess Royal some of the childcare lessons she learned by watching Feodore (through orders given to nurses, if not personally). The precocious and pretty Eliza quickly became Victoria's favourite and a darling of her journal. Victoria confides to her journal how pleased she was at the easy resumption of intimacy between herself and her sister. Feodore would often accompany Victoria to her room to watch her undress and prepare for bed like 'former times'.[89] Victoria played with the children and once dressed them up in costumes to amuse their grandmother — Charles was a 'scotch-man with bare legs and a plaid dress' and Eliza was beautiful as Taglioni in *La Sylphide*. Victoria gives a minute description of her costume just as she would in recalling a costume she had admired on stage.[90]

Victoria was ever dramatic in her grief at the leave-taking of relatives — even those she rarely wrote about unless they were visiting. Just before Feodore's visit, Victoria's Uncle Ferdinand (one of the Duchess of Kent's older brothers) left Kensington Palace after a short stay. Victoria's outpouring of emotion at the separation from this uncle perhaps seems excessive — '*Bitter* and VERY MANY were the tears I shed at parting with *so excellent* and dear an Uncle and friend. I love him SO VERY DEARLY!'[91] — until the comments are put into the context of Princess Victoria's search for father figures and relatives with whom she could forge — at least for a time — close family ties. Victoria was not particularly devoted to Uncle Ferdinand but she could pretend in her journal and to herself, that once he had come into

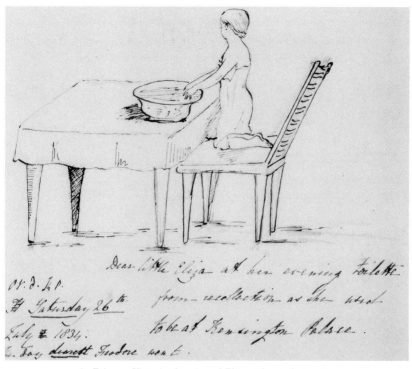

28. Princess Victoria, drawing of Eliza at her toilette, 1834.

her life, his departure signalled a significant loss. And yet, when Feodore left after her visit (a real tragedy for the fifteen-year-old), Victoria's melo-dramatic yet sincere grief at again losing her sister reflects an authentic sorrow rather than a display of emotion or temper as her reaction to her uncle's departure may well have been. The sisters exchanged caps, that inti-mate morning apparel that would serve as a physical reminder of the other, and shed bitter tears: 'I *clasped* her in my *arms* and *kissed her* and *cried* as if my *heart* would break; so did she, DEAREST Sister. We then *tore* our-selves from each other in the DEEPEST GRIEF.'[92] 'Sister's Love', a poem by Agnes Strickland (she of the 'error-riddled' biography of Queen Victoria that was recalled after publication to appease the Queen's ire), included in one of the many Christmas annuals owned by Princess Victoria, demon-strates the high emotionalism found in Georgian sentimental verse. As a sensitive and isolated young person who missed day-to-day contact with her

sister and the natural alliance it would have afforded her, Princess Victoria
may have found greater truth in the sentiments expressed by Strickland's
maudlin poem than in Strickland's later attempt at biography:

> Bright seraphs, pausing on the wing,
> Might gaze on and approve
> That beautiful and precious thing,
> An elder sister's love. . . .
>
> To lean upon a sister's breast,
> And court her ready kiss,
> Then sink, confidingly, to rest
> So pillow'd – this is bliss. . . .
>
> But when thy darkest moments come,
> And fickle friends remove,
> Thou'lt find thy dearest rest and home
> Is in a sister's love.[93]

The trip to the resort town of Tunbridge Wells to 'take the waters' for health
soon after Feodore's departure did little to comfort the lonely princess pining
for her sister's love. Any trip taken by the Princess and royal retinue was a publicity event, of course, and boring speeches of praise accompanied most public
outings. At Tunbridge Wells, the Duchess of Kent and Princess Victoria
patronized a 'Fancy Sale', the proceeds of which were to be used in support of
a new school for boys. The Duchess purchased some articles from the bazaar
and made a further donation of £100. A few days later, the Duchess's birthday
was celebrated by the town with a children's 'review' (the students of the
National Schools, Infant and Sunday Schools – 380 in all – paraded past the
assembled royal party) and a public dinner. The *Gazette* reported the affair in
detail and printed the rather obsequious toast given by the dinner's Chairman,
J. Hargraves, Esq., which can serve to illustrate the many such encomiums the
Duchess of Kent received throughout Victoria's girlhood:

> The toast which I next have the honour to propose needs no preface to
> make it acceptable. I feel assured it will be received in the respect, nay,

enthusiasm it merits. Nevertheless, Gentlemen, I never felt my own insufficiency more than at the present moment. . . . But, above all, as Britons, we owe her Royal Highness obligations more deeply sublime, for her maternal and patriotic care, seconded by her own bright example, to form a model in her Royal daughter, which will become the pride, boast, and ornament of this great nation of freemen.[94]

Princess Victoria's health was drunk, three times three.

On this same trip to Tunbridge Wells, Victoria writes a dutiful letter to Uncle Leopold outlining her studies and exaggerating her love of history: 'Reading History is one of my greatest delights . . .'[95] There was no break from studies for the grieving princess. A few of Victoria's written examinations from these years survive: the most complete example is dated from Tunbridge Wells, 1834. These examinations give detailed evidence of the nature of Princess Victoria's education in particular, and girls' education of the Georgian era in general. 'This curriculum was intended to create a literate, cultivated woman who might not necessarily have the proficiency in the classical languages provided by the boys' public schools and the universities, but who would probably have a better knowledge of more recent literature, both English and European, and of history, geography, and natural science.'[96] As the content of middle-class female education moved away from collecting decorative accomplishments and towards developing moral character and intellect – a departure that Hannah More and Maria Edgeworth, among others, heralded – curricular aids such as *Mangnall's Historical Questions* provided examination questions on a wide variety of subjects for the instructor to select. The successful student would require the ability to recall an enormous number of specific details of the dates, people, and events of the past. Causation and analysis of these events were studiously avoided (although a certain ideological scent can be detected), to avoid any 'party prejudices of different historians' (p. iii), as the Preface to *A New Epitome of the British History* (1815) attests.

Among the 'Collection of Promiscuous Questions', students were asked to answer the following questions (and many others) from English history:

❖ Who was Martin Luther? And where was he born?
❖ Who were first called Protestants?

- Whom did Henry marry, after having his wife, Anna Bullen, beheaded?
- Did he appear contented when he married Catherine Howard?
- Why was Sir Thomas More beheaded?
- Who was confessor to Margaret of Richmond, mother to Henry the Seventh?[97]

Victoria's 1834 Tunbridge Wells examination was structured in exactly this format. In this exam Victoria was expected to know facts covering literature, history, science, and scriptural dates. Her corrected answers also survive. There is no 'grade' on the examination, but the corrections are generally minor and few. (Her weakest effort was in horology – the science of measuring time.)[98] Victoria was quite proficient in remembering historical dates and battles. In the 'Questions at Random' section of the test, she had to answer 'Give some account of the following battles, particularly the times when they were fought, the commander & the situation of the places.' There were fifteen battles to be described in all, including Marathon, Philippi, Hastings, Neville's Cross, Shrewsbury and the Boyne. Victoria made no mistakes on this part of the test. She is able to scan correctly a short Latin passage but is confused about the construction of heroic verse. Her knowledge of scriptural dates is accurate and she understands the organization of the planetary system.[99]

The kinds of mathematical question Princess Victoria faced as a girl are familiar in their seeming arbitrariness and initial difficulty. Interestingly, within Victoria's maths book, the context (or 'story') given for solving the problem using different mathematical processes (simple interest, compound interest, fractions, etc.) reflects the class-conscious and male-dominated society in which Princess Victoria was raised. For example,

- A gentleman has an annuity of £896-17s. per annum. I desire to know how much he may spend daily that at the year's end he may lay up 200 gui. and give the poor quarterly £13-10s.
- A younger Brother received £6300 which was 7/9 of his elder brother's fortune. What was the Father worth at his death?[100]

Thus the daily life of the 'pattern' princess progressed. But although Victoria's days were highly organized and monitored, time was allowed for fun and regulated frolic. What Victoria lacked was solitude and a bosom peer. The journal helped to supply an outlet for Victoria's introspection, yet she remained essentially lonely and the object of great scrutiny, both from within Kensington Palace and from without it.

Images of the Princess

Victoria's childhood face and figure were not a mystery to her future subjects. As she grew older and more interesting to the public due to her position with regard to the throne, pictures of the Princess became more desirable. The journals make clear just how much time it took out of a princess's schedule to sit for portraits that would, once engraved, feed the public's appetite for the royal visage and promote the Duchess's aim of attaining widespread approval for her daughter. Perhaps the most significant painting of Princess Victoria from her early teenage years is Sir George Hayter's full-length portrait in oils. Victoria sat for this portrait intended for Leopold when she was fourteen; it was first exhibited in May at Somerset House where Victoria was able to see it, and later displayed at the Royal Academy in the summer of 1833 (ill. 29).[101] The effusive anonymous author of the 1840 *Anecdotes ... of Victoria the First* gives a minute description of this painting for readers who may never have had occasion to view it:

> ... the right hand, in which is a rose, rests on a library table; the left holds negligently at her side a light lace scarf. A beautiful little spaniel, sporting with his mistress's glove, imparts life and spirit to the piece. Windsor Castle is seen towering in the distance, the intervening space presenting a view of the oak trees of the forest, marked with the autumnal hints. . . . The delicacy of the arm and hand, as also of the foot and ancle is exquisite. The face may be pronounced to be an excellent, honest likeness, without any attempt at flattery[102]

The last is an exaggeration – if later photographs of an older Victoria are reliable means of comparison – as Victoria's face is too uniformly pretty and idealized here to be judged free from flattery. This portrait was engraved in

29. After Sir George Hayter, *The Princess (later Queen) Victoria*, engraved by James Bromley.

mezzotint by Bromley and published by Colnaghi and Company in 1834. The extent to which the sittings for the portrait overtook Victoria's life for about seven weeks in early 1833 is made very clear by her journals. Victoria sat for Hayter for two hours at a time (usually from 2.30 until 4.30 in the afternoon). She does not complain about the extent of her commitment, but these awkward, post-prandial sessions must have been uncomfortable indeed. As inspiration, or perhaps preparation, Victoria and the royal retinue had gone to the British Gallery to see the two George Hayter paintings exhibited there. Victoria was also pleased to view the paintings of her drawing master, Richard Westall, on display.[103]

This Hayter painting functions as a narrative of Victoria's life up to that point as well as a projection of her future role. That the portrait was intended for Leopold can be seen in the details of the painting. Leopold felt that it was time for Victoria to become a conventionally pretty and decorous (if not decorative) woman as part of her training as eventual sovereign – hence his concern about her height, eating, and behaviour. The Princess's femininity is highlighted in the painting through her ornate and delicate dress, decorative scarf (rather than a warm shawl), formal gloves, sumptuous jewellery, and elegant hairstyle (Princess Victoria often wore a coronet of braids for formal occasions during this period. This crown of hair neatly prefigures her crown as queen. To her great pride, she began wearing earrings in 1832).[104] The playful King Charles spaniel, Dash, was an appropriate addition to the painting as he was an important companion of Victoria's youth and travelled everywhere with her. This canine glove thief also figures as an 'inside joke' between uncle and niece as he was fond of dogs and Dash's exploits were well known to him through letters and his visits to England.[105] While in the foreground the focus is on a diffident, charming girl and her pet, the immediate background – the shelf of books and globe – underscores the Princess's education and breeding. The volumes behind Victoria include *Life of HRH the Duke of Kent, The History of Saxe Coburg*, and *England*, indicating both the paternal and maternal branches of Victoria's family tree and her role as England's daughter. The rose she fingers, too, iconographically represents Victoria's purity as the 'rose of England'. Blackstone's *Commentaries on the Laws of England*, included in Victoria's curriculum, also appears here as a reminder that serious study of

30. After Sir George Hayter, *The Duchess of Kent and Princess (later Queen) Victoria*, lithographed by Richard James Lane.

her country's legal system was an important aspect of her preparation for queenship.[106] The globe is turned to show Western Europe and Africa, perhaps an allusion to Leopold and Victoria's relatives scattered throughout the royal houses of Europe as well as Belgium's presence in the African Congo. The remote background depicts Windsor Castle, home of England's sovereign since William the Conqueror, which represents Victoria's glorious future. Susan P. Casteras describes this painting as offering 'a majestic glimpse into full-blown adulthood'. By contrast, I read the image of

31. After Beechey, engraving by William Skelton, *The Duchess of Kent and Princess Victoria*, 1820.

Victoria presented here as epitomizing girlhood rather than royalty: as a love-letter to Uncle Leopold reassuring him of Victoria's educational progress, awareness of her lineage and future, love and need of him (especially), and childish interests (the frisking dog), this painting demonstrates that Victoria is a young woman whose destiny is clear, but who as yet remains girlish and dependent.[107] Casteras's reading of the painting may stem, in part, from the persistent misdating of this image. A number of biographies of Victoria – Longford's and Helmut and Alison Gernsheim's

Victoria R., for example – misdate the painting and thus Princess Victoria's age (calling her sixteen years of age). There is an enormous difference between a fourteen-year-old and a sixteen-year-old, a private painting and a propagandistic one. This image of Victoria offers a tantalizing glimpse of the future girl-queen – as a kind of 'pin-up' – but the overriding thematic of the image is flirtatious girlhood rather than 'full-blown womanhood'.

The Hayter study was the first in a series of two paintings featuring Princess Victoria. Its companion piece was a portrait of mother and daughter painted for the Duchess of Kent in 1834 (Ill. 30). In this treatment of the two royals it is interesting to note the painting's flawed perspective, which can be read metaphorically as representing the relative power imbalance between them at this time: the Duchess of Kent is much too large in relation to her fully grown daughter. The Duchess was not a particularly statuesque woman (though taller than Victoria), but in this painting she towers over her daughter, whose disproportionately small size and tiny facial features make her look like a doll or puppet. The Duchess's grasp appears to be holding Victoria up. The Duchess has her eye on Victoria, while the Princess looks sweetly out at the viewer and away from her mother. This painting is reminiscent of an earlier treatment of the same mother/daughter theme. After the death of the Duke of Kent, the Duchess engaged Sir William Beechey to paint a portrait of mother and child (Ill. 31). The devout mother encircles her daughter (here about four years old) with her arm and holds a testament or moral book on her lap. The realistically sized child clutches a miniature of her father (the Beechey portrait in Ill. 3) and displays her English lineage. Although Victoria's subordinate status is emphasized in these paintings, her relationship with her mother was marked by storms and struggles that Victoria not infrequently won. The pressure Victoria was under to be a model girl was certainly intense. The Duchess's advice is really very similar to Leopold's, but Uncle's words were so much easier to hear: to Victoria he had become an exotic stranger who lived far away and was a king himself. Victoria had to live with her mother and her mother's favourite, Conroy, every day without respite. Victoria's reserve with her mother can be found only in subtle clues in her journal such as careting in the word 'dear' before her mother's name as an afterthought while Lehzen is awarded a 'dear' at first writing.[108] Whether

Victoria noticed the omission herself or whether someone else had to remind her, is impossible to say.

Some of the desperation that the Duchess of Kent may have been feeling at the typical emotional gulf that widens as girls grow up occurred just when the Duchess needed Victoria's cooperation the most. Examples of this fear of Victoria's developing maturity can be glimpsed in the rather breathless birthday and New Year's letters that the Duchess was fond of writing to her daughter and slipping under her pillow to be discovered at bedtime. Year after year the Duchess would plead for Victoria to continue her programme of improvement and especially to respect and acknowledge, at least tacitly, the worry that the Duchess had expended on her daughter in the previous year:

> It appears to me a dream, – that you now complete your fifteenth year. – My watchful eye and anxious heart, has observed so many improvements in you, in the course of this year, – that I am confident, I shall have the happiness of making the same remark, next year: – As my dearly beloved child will feel more and more every day the truth, – that to be happy, now and hereafter we must never be stationary in the improvement of our minds, and heart. – God, who knows all our thoughts will give me due credit, for those sincere and anxious ones I feel for your happiness.[109]

Here the Duchess of Kent's sentiments for her daughter are indistinguishable from the prevailing view of the importance of the education of virtues for girls and the necessity for self-reflection and self-improvement. The poem 'A Little Girl's Soliloquy on New Year's Day' included in the 1833 *New Year's Gift; and Juvenile Souvenir* edited by Alaric Watts – given to the Princess by her mother – iterates this ideology of female conduct by using the device of the child speaker who, without any mediation from an authority figure, confesses her faults and resolves to improve her character. The first stanza reads,

> Now the old year's passed away
> And a new one just begun,

Let me, from this very day,
Try all former faults to shun:
First, I am to anger prone,
Therefore I must careful be
To avoid occasions known
When bad temper tempteth me;
I must strive from this day hence,
Not to give or take offence.[110]

A light-hearted ten-stanza poem in this same annual, 'A Little Girl's
Lament for the Fairies', taken in conjunction with the serious and didactic
'Soliloquy', perfectly enacts the conflicted nature of female education in the
Georgian era. On the one hand, and it is the 'upper hand' in this dichotomy,
the confessional verse represents the education of character that adherence
to duty and convention would bring about in the girl, and on the other
hand, the 'elegy' for the fairies, while nostalgic for the innocence of childhood, underscores the adherence to the Enlightenment ideals of rational-
ism and pragmatism in education for the young. The loss of the fairies is
also represented by a turn in literature for the young away from fanciful
fairy tales and toward practical stories such as Edgeworth's or Mrs
Trimmer's. The first and last stanzas of the poem read,

Ah! where are all the fairies flown?
Why ceased their merry reign?
We're all so dull and solemn grown,
I wish they'd come again;
Mid lawns and bowers, when daylight's done,
Once more to dance and play; –
There never has been any fun,
Since fairies went away! . . .

Farewell to all the pretty tales,
Of merry Elfins' dining
On mushroom tables, in the dales,
Lit by the glow-worm's shining;

And tripping to the minstrel gnat,
His jocund measure singing,
While o'er their heads the lazy bat,
A silent flight was winging:
Farewell! like theirs, my song is done;
But yet once more I'll say —
There never has been any fun,
Since fairies went away.'"

Princess Victoria's library did not include collections of fairy tales; as the
lament above explains, 'books — and maps — and lessons'¹¹² were the sum
total of the Evangelical child's education, and fantasy literature's abstract
nature and mythic features were faulted for their alienation from 'truth'.
Victoria had been given, however, a beautiful set of watercolours illustrating the story of Tom Thumb (Ill. 32). These amateur paintings by Miss
Wedderburn may have been intended as a thank you gift for some act of
patronage or favour. The Princess could well have enjoyed looking at these
attractive illustrations, which, taken together, form a picture book about
Tom Thumb, but since they were never bound together or framed in any
way, the gift was probably little used by the child. The Duchess of Kent —
like Georgian parents in general — hoped to inculcate the qualities of
common sense, an appreciation for hard work, modesty, and obedience
through her child's reading, and the fairy tales and fancies of an earlier age
were considered by many to be 'childish things' best put away.

Raising an heir to the British Empire was never an easy job (as Victoria
herself would eventually discover) and at the start of 1835, the Duchess of
Kent wrote a letter to her daughter that tackled the issues of political partisanship (she wanted Victoria to avoid any 'party feeling') and the significance of Victoria's coming majority at the age of eighteen. She also warned
Victoria of the intense scrutiny she would be under as Queen ('… the day
is to come, when you are to take a place: — every eye that rests on you,
endeavours to find out your character, — every word is weighed to ascertain,
your judgement and heart'). This letter is most notable, however, for the
Duchess's bald plea for consideration and her attempted manipulation of
Victoria's feelings by evoking her eventual death: 'This letter I dare say you

32. J. Wedderburn, watercolour illustrating *Tom Thumb*, n.d.

will often read: – perhaps very often, – when the hand that wrote it may be
motionless, – and the heart that dictated it, has ceased to beat.: Your own
heart can now lead you to value it: – And at the later time your happiness
will be encreased if you have followed it.'[113] The Duchess's manipulations
were not confined to epistolary rhetoric about their relationship; the
Duchess also chose her daughter's companions. It is not surprising that
Victoria was not allowed to choose her friends – she had virtually no freedom to meet people beyond those selected for her. This is one reason why
the society of relatives – always sanctioned by the Duchess of Kent (except
in the case of the illegitimate children of King William) – was so dear to
Victoria. In 1831 the Duchess of Northumberland was selected to become
Victoria's 'official' or 'show-governess';[114] although it may have appeared
that Lehzen's star had fallen as she could in no way compete with the glittering social and political stature of Northumberland, but her ascendancy
over Victoria was not diminished. Although not an educator herself, the
Duchess of Northumberland offered advice to Victoria's mother about the

plan of Victoria's reading, based on her knowledge of her niece's educa-tion,[115] and on occasion sat in on Victoria's lessons (the public nature of which often discomfited the Princess).

Victoria and Elizabeth I

While Victoria was growing up in her unique and friendless way, she was often bored, like any young adult. In many of her 1833–34 letters to Feodore or her brother Charles, Victoria refers to Kensington Palace as 'gloomy', 'dull' or 'stupid'.[116] Victoria relished her summer and autumn trips as pleasant disruptions in her normally staid routine. Upon return to Kensington after a delightful three-month trip to Norris Castle in 1833, Victoria grumbles to her journal: 'It is a wretched day here; pouring with rain and *so* foggy. Kensington looks *so gloomy* & the trees are quite bare. What a SAD, SAD change from DEAR Norris!'[117] Even a trip to the theatre a week later does not cheer Victoria up: she complains that the opera – about Gustavus III of Sweden – 'is *heavy* & tedious; the play confused, stupid & *uninteresting*. I was not much pleased.'[118] Victoria appeared to be anxiously waiting for some variety in her life. In fact, her mother supplied this want to a certain extent from 1833 onward as she began to entertain rather lavishly; after showing off her daughter to the country at large through the Royal Progresses, she displayed her locally as well at large dinner parties or assemblies after which Victoria often would list the lumi-naries who had attended, or paste in a column of the 'Court Circular'.[119] Perhaps to encourage the greater contact they began to have with Victoria at this time through drawing rooms and visits, and certainly to display pub-licly their recognition of Victoria as the future sovereign, the King and Queen held a Juvenile Ball at St. James's in honour of Victoria's fourteenth birthday. Victoria was led into the ballroom on the King's arm and was greeted by her dancing mistress, Victoire Conroy and '*many* other children whom I knew'.[120] The first dance was given to George Cambridge, Victoria's cousin. The Princess had a wonderful time at the ball; danced quadrilles with the sons of earls, dukes, and princes, and later sat down to supper between the King and Queen.

This image of the adolescent Princess sandwiched between the reigning monarch and his consort is an important one as it positions her correctly as the acknowledged inheritor of the crown. Another image of Victoria in the presence of royalty is equally significant here: while Victoria's 'promotion' from princess to queen is generally gained in one way only (through the death of her immediate predecessor), of course, the prospect of a young queen recalled for many the glorious reign of Elizabeth I. Certainly, as two of only five queens regnant in English history (the sixth is queen today), comparisons were made between Elizabeth I and Victoria even before her accession to the throne.[121] Indeed, much of the Princess Victoria's education was concerned with memorizing the characters, battles, and politics, that help to construct English history.[122] As part of her lessons, or perhaps as a self-directed continuation of them, Victoria compiled an abecedary of European queens in history: in her brief paragraphs for 'A' she writes about '*Anne*, Queen of Great Britain; *Anne*, Empress of Russia; *Anne*, Boleyn, Queen (Consort) of England', etc.[123] Victoria clearly enjoyed working on this organizational task: she writes to Uncle Leopold in 1834, 'I am very fond of making tables of the Kings and Queens, as I go on, and I have lately finished one of the English Sovereigns and their consorts, as, of course, the history of my own country is one of my first duties.'[124] In these synopses of the lives of her royal predecessors, Victoria would analyse the characters and physical qualities of each woman: among Henry the VIII's wives, Catherine of Aragon is called 'irreproachable', Anne Boleyn is 'extremely beautiful, and accomplished, but inconsiderate', and Anne of Cleves is 'tall & very large & unprepossessing'.[125] Within her abecedaries, Victoria's greatest indulgence in character analysis – as well as her harshest criticism – relates to Elizabeth I, a queen who was 'unable' (and/or unwilling) to combine successfully or gracefully her monarchical with her womanly body: 'Elizabeth was a *great Queen* but a *bad woman*; and even in her royal capacity she erred sometimes; she had a very great idea of her prerogative and was more arbitrary even than her tyrannical father.'[126]

Interestingly, Princess Charlotte who would, of course, have been a queen regnant if she had lived, as a child similarly both recognized her role as future queen and distanced herself from Elizabeth: 'Although on one occasion [Charlotte] is reputed to have said *à propos* of Queen Elizabeth,

"Do not mention that cruel Queen, I cannot bear her," there can be little doubt that she gradually came to model herself on what she knew of the great Tudor.'[127]

Princess Victoria sketches the character and reign of Queen Elizabeth not only in the above-described abecedary, but also in the assessments she made as a younger child of the life of Mary, Queen of Scots, a royal 'victim' with whom she seems to identify. Summarizing her reading in history for Lehzen, in a draft letter (the handwriting appears to be *circa* 1828–30), Victoria writes about Queen Elizabeth in a morally judgemental and superior tone: 'That harshness of character (which she inherited from her father Henry the 8th of England) made her delight at having a rival in her power though every kind heart would pity a poor exiled Queen like Mary.'[128] This connection between the two monarchs was made concrete for the young Victoria in October 1832 when she received a paper book with some embroidery patterns for a coverlet ordered by Lord Essex for Queen Elizabeth, and the next month was shown a Latin exercise book of Elizabeth's written when she was thirteen years old (Victoria's age at the time) and preserved at the Bodleian Library.[129] Victoria's interest in the Queen's 'political body' was surely linked in her mind (even at a young age) to the confines and gestures of her future sovereign self. For everyone else, Victoria represented the hope of a 'new Elizabethan age' and of a female monarch who could equally supply both home virtues and international prominence in commerce, industry, technology, martial strength, and the arts. As suggested above, Victoria's future 'ownership' of the British Isles was symbolically conceived in a number of personal and political ways: through the perceived relationship with factory workers established merely by the sight of the Princess, through the acquisition of souvenirs of British industry and manufacturing, and through a princess's harsh analysis of queenly behaviour through the ages.

Chapter Four

The Importance of Being Victoria

1835

'You see [my diary] is simply a very young girl's record of her own thoughts and impressions, and consequently meant for publication.' (Cecily)

Oscar Wilde, *The Importance of Being Earnest*[1]

'I never travel without my diary. One should always have something sensational to read in the train.' (Gwendolyn)

Oscar Wilde, *The Importance of Being Earnest*[2]

Girlhood Voices

In Oscar Wilde's play *The Importance of Being Earnest* (1895), Act II opens with eighteen-year-old heiress Cecily Cardew's preference for watering the roses instead of taking her German lesson. The elements of Cecily's situation – the garden, the heiress, the German lesson, the watering-can – perhaps coincidentally, perhaps not, come together in the popular nineteenth-century image of the young Princess Victoria, when the Queen's girlhood was but a distant memory. (Ill. 33). However, Wilde's comic character resembles Victoria in another significant respect as well: she is a diary-keeper. Her naive yet wry comment quoted above about the

33. H. H. Emmerson, 'The Princess Gardening' from *The May Blossom: or the Princess and Her People*, by Marion M. Wingrave

dual nature of her diary – girlish thoughts intended for public consumption, and the intersection of the public and private spheres – is Wilde's ironic send-up of the trend in publishing 'meaningless' diaries, as the self-involved Cecily's diary would certainly be. In the nineteenth century, 'the public was eager to read about everyone – not just the famous'.[5] Wilde's witticism delivered in Cecily's voice lampoons the vogue for publishing accounts of 'uneventful' lives, and indicates his belief in the 'unsuitability' of preserving girlhood life writing for posterity. Cecily is so fluffy-headed that her diary functions as the only site of memory for this stereotype of the overgrown country schoolgirl: '"I keep a diary in order to enter the wonderful secrets of my life. If I didn't write them down I would probably forget all about them.'"[4] The nineteenth century was indeed an age of diarists, and certainly large numbers of girls began a life-long habit of journal-keeping as adolescents, just as Princess Victoria did. And as Wilde notes through Cecily's epigrammatic comment, though these diaries were originally conceived as private, many of them were eventually published, often posthumously. The notorious actress Frances Anne Kemble, in her recollections of her girlhood published in 1878, passionately defends the value of the private letter and journal:

> The extraordinary development of the taste for petty details of personal gossip which our present literature bears witness to makes it almost a duty to destroy all letters not written for publication; and yet there is no denying that life is essentially interesting – every life, any life, all lives, if their detailed history could be given with truth and simplicity. For my own part, I confess that the family correspondence, even of people utterly unknown to me, always seems to me full of interest. The vivid interest the writers took in themselves makes their letters better worth reading than many books we read; they are life, as compared with imitations of it – life, that mystery and beauty surpassing every other; they are morsels of that profoundest of all secrets, which baffles alike the man of science, the metaphysician, artist, and poet.[5]

I have selected four published girlhood journals of contemporaries of Princess Victoria to impart some of the 'life' – as Kemble terms it – and flavour of Georgian childhoods and adolescence and to place Princess Victoria's life-writing within the general context of self-representation found in other girlhood diaries of the 1820s and 1830s. Although young Caroline Fox, for one, was among the crowds of people watching the new queen's coronation procession, seemingly separated from her queen by an enormous gulf, what is most surprising about her journal, and the accounts of Emily Shore, Anne Chalmers, and Fanny Kemble alike (all but the last were private individuals and not very widely known when young) is not their differences in situation, station, and character, but the remarkable congruities between their girlhoods.

In fact, Caroline Fox was born on the same day as Princess Victoria – 24 May 1819 – the daughter of Cornwall shipping agent and scientific inventor, Robert Were Fox and Maria (Barclay) Fox. Caroline was the middle child of a large Quaker family of five children. Caroline's diary project was begun at the request of her father, rather than her mother, as was the case for Victoria: 'Journals were in the Quaker tradition; it had been so since George Fox's day. It was natural then that Robert Were Fox should offer his young daughters a guinea if they would keep a diary regularly; Caroline, with typical thoroughness, earned her guinea. . . .'[6] Fox bequeathed the twelve volumes of her diary to her older sister, Anna Maria, before her death from bronchitis at the age of fifty-one. Wendy Monk, a late twentieth-century editor of the journals, believes that Fox had no intention of publishing the journals, but wished them destroyed upon Anna Maria's death. However, Anna Maria only partially obeyed her sister's wishes: in 1882, selections from Caroline's diaries were published by Smith, Elder and Company as *Memories of Old Friends, being Extracts from the Journals and Letters of Caroline Fox, from 1835–1871* edited by Horace N. Pym, a London solicitor and relation. It was believed that the original manuscript journals had been burned, but in 1977 the first manuscript volume of the journal was discovered at Penjerrick, the family's country house.[7]

Margaret Emily Shore (called Emily) was also born in 1819, on Christmas Day, in Suffolk, the eldest of the five children of Margaret Anne (Twopeny) Shore and Thomas S. Shore, an independent clergyman schoolmaster. She began her journal earlier than either Victoria or Caroline, embarking upon it just five months before her twelfth birthday, and filling twelve octavo volumes. Emily was quite as faithful as Victoria in keeping her diary until two weeks before her death. Here the similarities end, however, as Emily Shore died a tragic, early death from tuberculosis in 1839, while her new queen would reign into the next century. Emily became ill in the spring of 1836 and never fully regained her health. The Shore family travelled to London to seek medical advice, and chose a Dr James Clark, probably the same Dr Clark (later Sir James Clark) who was first Prince Leopold's physician and who became physician to the Duchess of Kent and Princess Victoria in 1834.[8] Shore's selected journal was edited by her sisters, the poets Arabella Shore and Louisa Shore, and published in 1891.[9]

Another member of a large family, Anne Chalmers was born in Scotland in May 1813, six years before Princess Victoria, Caroline Fox, and

Emily Shore, the eldest of six girls. Like Princess Victoria after her, Anne Chalmers was singularly unimpressed with the appearance of infant children. At the birth of her youngest sister in 1827, fourteen-year-old Anne wrote, 'It is such a little thing; about the size of Margaret's doll and it has such an old-looking face. They all say it is very pretty but I could never discover beauty in a thing of half an hour old.'[10] Victoria espoused similar sentiments about babies when in her teens and years later when counselling her daughter Vicky about pregnancy — an 'unhappy condition' — and motherhood.[11] Anne Chalmers was the daughter of social reformer Reverend Dr Thomas Chalmers, sometimes called 'the greatest Scottish Churchman of the nineteenth century' and a leader in the establishment of the Free Church of Scotland.[12] Her letters and journals were privately printed by her daughter in 1922, thirty-one years after her death in 1891.

By contrast, the actress Frances (called 'Fanny') Kemble became famous while still very young. She is also the eldest of the girl diarist/memoirists under consideration here. Born in 1809, her three-volume *Record of a Girlhood* (1878) was written as a memoir when Kemble was almost seventy years old. Fanny Kemble had the most actual contact with Princess Victoria (Ill. 34). Kemble's early fame as an actress, and her later notoriety as the author of a somewhat scandalous book about her life in America, piqued Princess Victoria's interest. She was fascinated by this other young woman who was similarly admired for her role-playing abilities, yet who was free to speak 'out of turn'. The actress's triumphant début in 1829 was as Shakespeare's Juliet; by that time, Victoria was already managing the role of future queen of England. Kemble was also an admirer of the handsome 'Mr. Lamb' (later Victoria's first Prime Minister, Lord Melbourne) — 'He was my *beau idéal* of an Epicurean philosopher'[13] — a sentiment Victoria fervently shared once she was queen.

Fanny Kemble's unusual education — she was sent to France for a number of years to attend school there — was unlike the education at home of Princess Victoria, Emily Shore, and Caroline Fox. When Fox was twelve years old, a tutor came to live with the family, and masters of French and drawing would visit regularly. She also went outside the home for Italian lessons. Her brother Barclay's journal noted that Caroline was at times an inattentive scholar, and sent out of class for laughing (the Princess would

34. Princess Victoria, drawing of Fanny Kemble as Lady Macbeth, *c.* 1833.

have been able to empathize with this behaviour).[14] Emily Shore was also educated at home and shared with Princess Victoria a passion for drawing, especially dramatic scenes. '[Emily's] sketches were like little dramas, full of human action; where she had not seen she invented, or took hints from the books she had read.'[15] Some of Princess Victoria's favourite watercolour subjects were the poses and costumes of operas, ballets, and novels.

Emily was fond of concocting imaginary histories of England, like Jane Austen before her. One such imaginary history projected as far into the future as the year 2354. At fourteen, Emily created an entire fictional country 'in the heart of Australia' complete with geography, alphabet, religion, and natural history, and illustrated with pictures of the landscape, flora and fauna, and native people.[16] In her birthday entry of 1832, the thirteen-year-old wrote that she had received Babbage's *Economy of Manufactures*, a gift that she had 'long wished for'.[17] Princess Victoria owned a similar book, but one suited to younger readers: *Scenes of British Wealth, in Produce, Manufactures, and Commerce, for the Amusement and Instruction of Little Tarry-At-Home Travellers* (1823). This instructive and rather charming little book combined factual information, poetry, and a narrative outline supplied by dialogues between a father and son about the different manufactories and products of English towns. After describing 'Geese' as a product of Lincoln Fens, a short poem is appended about the goose's importance to education:

> Yes, genius! For all it has so little brain,
> What learning, and wit it distills;
> But would you this learning and genius obtain,
> Suck it not from its head, but its quills.
>
> So take up its quill, shape it well to a pen,
> And write with it, learning and wit;
> What, can't you? – indeed! – can't you do it? – why then
> It is you are the goose, and not it.[18]

The child writer with quill in hand is an appropriate image for these girl diarists who devoted many hours to composition and orthography. Caroline Fox and her siblings were required to write themes each week that would be read out loud and graded for their proficiency. Some of the topics were abstract qualities such as 'Forgiveness' and 'Curiosity', but the children were also asked to convey their understanding of industrial production such as glass-making, which they had witnessed on an excursion to Bristol.[19]

In Victoria's *Scenes of British Wealth*, one of the child George's dialogues with his father is about whips and the town of Daventry. George does not believe that a whip is an object significant enough to make any town famous for its manufacture. George's father corrects the mistaken child and informs him of the many different kinds of whip there are and the importance of their being well made: "'Now, considering with what force a whip strikes, so that even the smacking it would soon tear it to pieces, if it were not well made, I do think it possible, that some may be a great deal better than others; and if those who make them best live at Daventry, then Daventry may well be a famous town.'"[20]

By the time she was sixteen years old, Princess Victoria had visited a fair amount of England and Wales and was made acquainted with many British industries as part of her training and education. Emily had hoped to receive the same sort of education through books and travel herself. Three years after she had received Babbage's *Economy of Manufactures* as a Christmas gift, she confided to her journal, 'I long exceedingly to become thoroughly acquainted with every manufacture in England. . . . I am very desirous to see all the manufactures with my own eyes, and I should like to travel through Great Britain with that intent.'[21]

Yet Emily Shore never fulfilled her wish to travel through the country seeking manufactories, but spent her entire life at home or in a few healthful spots until in some desperation she was forced to move to a warmer climate in an attempt to save her life. (Shore died in Madeira and was buried in the English cemetery there.) Barbara Timm Gates describes the journal of her last days as a kind of 'holy dying'.[22] But on 21 January 1833, still in health, the young girl described her pleasant and quiet day-to-day home life with her family:

Our daily employments vary but little. As for myself, I rise as soon as I can wake, which is usually as late as half-past seven, and employ myself in doing my Greek and Latin, and learning whatever I have to get by heart. After breakfast I feed the birds with bread-crumbs, and from about that time till twelve o'clock I am usually employed in teaching the children, and in some of my own lessons. At twelve we go out till dinner; after dinner I amuse myself for half an hour; then I read to mamma, and do my needlework; then we go out again for about an hour and a half; then I and Richard finish our Greek or Latin for papa, and I read Fuseli's Lectures to mamma. This employs me till tea, after which I and R do our lesson with papa, and then we amuse ourselves till bedtime.[23]

The unvaried routine of lessons, airings, needlework, and family meals is certainly reminiscent of Princess Victoria's secluded days at Kensington Palace. By contrast, Anne Chalmers began to go to school for part of each day when she was thirteen years old. This day school experience was in addition to the education she received at home with her sisters. On 14 May 1827 she wrote, 'I am in school from eleven till 12 and from ½ past 1 til ½ past 3 except on Mondays and Thursdays when I go at ten in the morning and leave at ½ past 1. Besides I have to practise 2 hours at home and learn my lessons. We are obliged the first Monday of every Month to go to school for fancy work.'[24] The Chalmers sisters had a French governess for home schooling, as well as drawing and dancing masters. Anne Chalmers's girlhood instruction, then, is easily recognizable as the conventional education of accomplishments: some basic knowledge (including French) coupled with dancing, drawing, and decorative arts.

Although Victoria's education included these ornamental aspects as well, her interest in the fine arts – painting, of course, and music especially – went beyond mere appreciation. The same can be said of Emily Shore, and the two girls were ardent admirers of the same popular singers: they each gave Giulia Grisi top honours in their journals and Malibran was next in line.[25] Considering male singers, Victoria's eventual teacher, Luigi Lablache, was favoured by both. Emily wrote after attending a London concert in May 1835 where Victoria was also in attendance, 'Lablache has a stupendous and very excellent voice; I was quite astonished to hear it.'[26] They did not share, however, the same literary taste. As I discuss below, Princess Victoria was passionate about James Fenimore Cooper's romance of Renaissance Venice, *The Bravo* (1831), which she received as an Easter gift in 1835 from her mother, but in 1837 Emily found it uninspiring:

I can hear [*The Bravo*] with a calmness and indifference which I can scarcely realize to myself; the narrative makes no impression on my fancy; I never feel the slightest impatience to begin it, or reluctance to put it down.[27]

Her love for fiction had waned with her declining health, but this alteration gave her some satisfaction: 'I do think, however, that this change in my taste is no bad thing; it gives me a greater enjoyment of soberer and more useful reading.'[28] Natural history, botany, and astronomy (she owned a telescope) excited her imagination; melodrama and pathos left her cold. Victoria was allowed very little fiction that was not moralizing, but novels were forbidden to Anne Chalmers – at least it was suggested by one source that the girls avoid all fanciful literature. Anne, who appears to have been a rather giddy, thoroughly likeable child in her journals and the correspondence she conducted with her girlhood friend, Anne Parker (their correspondence would last sixty years), relates how in 1828 she and her sisters had visited a phrenologist and had their heads examined. Anne was told that 'I have too much romance & that there must be nothing but reality! reality! reality! for us. No fiction but all truth. I don't relish that much, because the chief pleasure in life is living in an ideal world & giving yourself up to your imagination.'[29]

Though Emily Shore's education would include such feminine accomplishments as French and dancing lessons as well as Latin, Greek, and the sciences, from a very young age she was also given free rein to ramble widely in nature, make friends with the birds, and study the insect world. She writes with authority about scientific topics ('clavated feelers', the differences between moths and butterflies, and Latin names for plants, for example). She also enjoyed history, and read classics such as Russell's *Modern Europe* and von Müller's *Universal History*. One comment Shore made in 1835 about the study of history and geography is reminiscent of Victoria's remark to King Leopold about the pre-eminence of history in her curriculum: 'I am convinced that geography and history are among the most useful and interesting of studies.'[30] As she continues to discuss this topic, one significant difference between the two girls' educations is highlighted: 'Besides what I study by myself, I learn a great deal by teaching M [her younger brother Mackworth]; it refreshes my memory, and confirms my knowledge on these subjects.'[31] Emily was responsible for part of her younger siblings' education and she speaks here not only as a student of history, but as a teacher of this subject as well.[32] Princess Victoria never had the opportunity or the benefit of instructing another person, but endured the sometimes uncomfortable or awkward position of pupil in a schoolroom of one, where there were often many others looking on and taking notes (Lehzen, the Duchess of Kent, the Duchess of Northumberland, other visiting ladies or dignitaries).

Victoria's exposure in the schoolroom is just one small aspect of her public life. Although she was not often seen by the public outside of Kensington Gardens when a young girl, her image and doings were widely available through engravings, exhibitions, and newspaper accounts. This high degree of publicity is something that Fanny Kemble shared with her future queen. After her début as Juliet, Kemble was transformed overnight from her position as daughter in the famous Kemble acting family to the toast of London. Society went wild over the 'girl of genius'[33] and treated her to the adoration and objectification that is usually reserved for royalty:

> When I saw the shop-windows full of Laurence's sketch of me, and knew myself the subject of almost daily newspaper notices; when plates and saucers were brought to me with small figures of me as Juliet and Belvidera on them; and finally, when gentlemen showed me lovely buff-coloured neck-handkerchiefs which they had bought, and which had, as I thought, pretty lilac-coloured flowers all over them, which proved on nearer inspection to be minute copies of Laurence's head of me, I not unnaturally, in the fulness of my inexperience, believed in my own success.[34]

Victoria would have well understood the joys and tribulations of becoming a consumer product. This was especially so as she gained her majority at the age of eighteen, and, most significantly, when she became queen. Kemble notes, 'It would be difficult to imagine anything more radical than the change which three weeks had made in the aspect of my whole life. From an insignificant school-girl, I had suddenly become an object of general public interest. I was a little lion in society and the town talk of the day.'[35]

Members of the Royal Family, of course, did not make their début in the same way and were fodder for discussion in every home practically from birth. In an entry for 30 September 1836, when both Caroline Fox and Princess Victoria were seventeen years old, Caroline relates a discussion about Victoria that she found most intriguing. A visitor to their home, Lady George Murray who had been an intimate of the late Queen Charlotte, narrated the story of Princess Victoria learning that she was to become the next ruler of England. In Lady George Murray's version of the story, it is the Duchess of Kent who affirms the truth of the genealogical table, saying,

'"... I am anxious to bring you up as a good woman, then you will be a good queen also"'. Fox then writes about Princess Victoria in her diary. Reading this entry allows access to a limited – yet meaningful – example of what she meant to (some of) her eventual subjects while still a princess, and, more importantly, is evidence of the success of the Duchess of Kent's advertising campaign on behalf of her educational programme for the Princess: 'The care observed in the Princess's education is exemplary, and everything is indeed done to bring about this result. She is a good linguist, an acute foreign politician, and possesses very sound common sense.'[36] Anne Chalmers was also impressed with the Princess. Just before her seventeenth birthday in 1830, Anne and her family went to London for a springtime trip. They visited Somerset House to see the Exhibition of Pictures and Chalmers found the portraits of royalty particularly worth noting in her journal: 'in the upper rooms were a great many portraits, some of which were interesting, such as the King's, Duke of Clarence's, and Princess Victoria's'.[37]

Princess Victoria and the Duchess of Kent also appear in Emily Shore's diary as the subjects of a story she had heard from a staymaker from Hastings named Mrs Howes. When the Shore family was in Hastings in August 1836 for Emily's health, they learned of Mrs Howes's sad history and the following anecdote (which gives another view of the mother/daughter pair):

> When the Duchess of Kent and the Princess Victoria were here, and all the tradespeople in the place sent presents to them, Mrs. Howes, having nothing else to offer, presented to the princess a pair of stays of blue silk, which cost her in making them fourteen pounds. She got nothing in return but a letter of thanks, which, however, did her some good, as it made her known; and now she writes on her cards 'Appointed by their Royal Highnesses' etc. etc.[38]

The Duchess of Kent and Victoria patronized a variety of establishments in London, that, like Mrs Howes, benefited from their patronage. When the Duchess of Kent was selecting a riding master for Princess Victoria in 1829, they visited Captain Fozzard's school and watched a young female pupil having a lesson in keeping her seat under the most difficult circumstances (without reins, without stirrups, arms behind the back, while the horse is kicking and rearing). This rider was Fanny Kemble. Her performance was so impressive that the Duchess of Kent chose Fozzard as Victoria's riding master. A few years later, in December 1831, Kemble was introduced to the Duchess of Kent and Victoria: 'While I was still riding [at Fozzard's], the Duchess of Kent and our little queen that is to be came down into the school; I was presented to them at their desire, and thought Princess Victoria a very unaffected, bright-looking girl.'[39] Reflecting on these early experiences, Fanny ruminates upon the respect that Victoria's character and her position as queen command: 'This was the first time I ever saw the woman who holds the most exalted position in the world, the Queen of England, who has so filled that supreme station that her name is respected wherever it is heard abroad, and that she is regarded by her own people with a loyal love such as no earthly dignity but that of personal worthiness can command.'[40]

Although separated by the wide gulf of class, Princess Victoria and the girl diarists had many points of intersection through shared acquaintances, or places visited at the same time, or brushes with members of the Royal Family, if not Victoria herself. For example, the Shore family visited the summer haunts of the Duchess of Kent and Princess Victoria. In 1831 they were all at Broadstairs and Ramsgate for the health of the children. Emily's view about Broadstairs may well have been shared by Princess Victoria herself: 'Broadstairs is a small town. Mamma describes it by saying that "it has not enough company to make it lively, but it has too much to make it retired"'.[41] In her first trip to London in May 1830, Anne Chalmers met Wilberforce (the family spent quite a lot of time with him), the dramatist Joanna Baillie, the reformer Elizabeth Fry, and the very elderly Hannah More – the last on their trip back to Scotland. On the way, the King died (on 26 June 1830) and Anne felt his loss very keenly. As a younger child she had seen George IV once in Scotland and had been thrilled by this peek at royalty.

Although none of the diaries is especially personal (which is understandable since Kemble's diary – which comes the closest to a confessional document – is properly termed a memoir, and the other published accounts are selections), Emily Shore's journal, in particular, offers the kind of indepth writing that scholars and readers of Princess Victoria's supervised journal envy. When the young Emily was taken to see a printing press and glass-blowing, she describes the event in detail, unlike Princess Victoria who finds such machinery or activity merely 'interesting'.[42] As Estelle C. Jelinek notes, within their diaries, nineteenth-century women writers tended to maintain a core of privacy and distance from highly personal matters 'to protect their vulnerable private lives'.[43] Certainly, Victoria was obliged by good sense and decorum to restrict the degree of private thoughts she confided to the journal. Even as a young girl she knew that safety lay in discretion, and that her diary served a 'public' (her mother and Lehzen) as well as a private function. Emily Shore, too, had always shared her diary with friends and family – though her coterie of readers was by choice and Victoria's by command.

In her *Record of a Girlhood* (3 vols, 1878), Fanny Kemble writes from her position as a member of the most famous English acting family of the nineteenth century, and as an older woman remembering girlhood; her genius for writing as well as acting makes her the most accomplished writer of the five girlhood diarists under discussion here. In her teens, under the literary influence of Byron and Scott, Kemble began to write and 'thus embarked upon the intense literary activity that was to continue throughout her life in the form of plays, poetry, letters, journals, and memoirs, and that entitles her to be considered one of the grandest and most articulate Victorian women of letters'.[44] Her memory of the stage when about seven years old indicates her lively style and sense of the ridiculous:

About this time I was taken for the first time to a real play, and it was to that paradise of juvenile spectators, Artley's, where we saw a Highland horror called 'Meg Murdoch, or the Mountain Hag,' and a mythological after-piece called 'Hyppolita, Queen of the Amazons' in which young ladies in very short and shining tunics, with burnished breastplates, helmets, spears, and shields, performed sundry warlike evolutions around her Majesty Hyppolita, who was mounted on a snow-white *live* charger: in the heat of action some of these fair warriors went so far as to die, which martial heroism left an impression on my imagination so deep and delightful as to have proved hitherto indelible.[45]

The subject matter of this incomparable and compelling drama, performed before Victoria was born, is reminiscent of one of Princess Victoria's earliest preserved drawings – 'Amazons at War' – executed when she was eight years old (Ill. 35). As her interest in artistically capturing the picturesque female warriors attests, the child Victoria would probably also have appreciated this production; her dramatic taste 'improved' as she matured, yet she always retained an appreciation for the slightly absurd and melodramatic.[46] This love for the emotional was fully indulged by Princess Victoria in this period through her writing *beyond* the daily journal. In a short story entitled 'Alice' and in her obsession with James Fenimore Cooper's novel *The Bravo* (1831), Princess Victoria's ardent nature was given an outlet. As I discuss below, Victoria herself would ultimately become a tragic heroine starring in a melodrama worthy of the stage, but before those events of autumn 1835 transpired, she was entertained by reading and writing scenes of tragedy, betrayal, and love.

Poring over Cooper's *The Bravo* – the same novel that Emily Shore had found uninspiring – constituted, for a few weeks from mid-February to early April 1835, Victoria's consuming passion. Although after she had finished reading it, Victoria praised it only lightly in her daily journal – calling it 'a lovely book'[47] – in her reading journal she fully expressed her delight. At first, Victoria confined herself to describing various scenes in the first volume as 'beautiful' (such as a conversation between old Antonio and the hero, Jacopo the Bravo), and then described other books she was reading simultaneously. Soon, however, *The Bravo* takes over almost completely, and all other discussions drop away (Ill. 36). Victoria writes multiple pages of plot summary and transcription – especially from the climactic third volume. The hero is brave, noble, and much-wronged. In one tense scene, Jacopo and his bride Gelsomina, the prison-keeper's daughter, are trapped on the Bridge of Sighs – the doors on either side are locked against them. As the officers of the state seize Jacopo, the trumpets sound, proclaiming Jacopo Frontoni an enemy of the state. Gelsomina, knowing her husband only by an assumed name, carelessly and unwittingly denounces the accused: '"'Tis the officer of the republic, bidding for the head of one who carries a common stiletto," cried the half-breathless Gelsomina, who little heeded the ceremony at that instant; "he merits his fate."'[48] Ultimately,

35. Princess Victoria, drawing of 'Amazons at War', 1833.

tragedy strikes for Jacopo and his loved ones: his imprisoned father dies in his arms; although innocent of any crime, Jacopo is executed in front of a mob; and Gelsomina, who watches her husband's head roll, goes mad.

It was not only the exaggerated pathos of this story that excited Victoria: she was also attracted by the description of the manly hero's character and physical beauty. After she had finished reading the book, she copied out a long description of Jacopo: "'His years were under thirty, though [the] calm gravity of his countenance, imparted to it a character of more mature age. The cheeks were bloodless, but they betrayed rather the pallid hue of mental than bodily disease. The perfect condition of the physical man was

36. Princess Victoria, watercolour of 'The Bravo', 1835.

sufficiently exhibited, in the muscular fulness of a body, which, though light and active, gave every indication of strength. . . ."[49] Jacopo Frontoni was indeed a literary hero to sigh over. In *The Bravo*, Princess Victoria appreciated all elements of melodrama the novel afforded: male and female beauty, victimization, tragedy, and the romantic setting of Venice in the distant past. In her own fiction of this period, dramatic tensions were confined to the domestic sphere: the home and the school.

The last of Victoria's stories preserved in the Royal Archives is entitled 'Alice'. Though others may have been written – especially when she was younger – it is unlikely that many stories existed from this relatively late period in Princess Victoria's girlhood. I date the story as *circa* 1835 (it is likely that Victoria wrote it while travelling and released from her usual rigid lesson schedule as was the case for her 'Sophia and Adolphus' story written in Broadstairs). This lengthy tale was dedicated to the Duchess of Kent: 'To my dear Mamma this my first attempt at composition is affectionately and dutifully inscribed by her affectionate daughter Victoria.'[50] It is doubtful that the story was ever given to the Duchess, however, as it is unfinished and was found among Victoria's things rather than her mother's. The inscription is also misleading since Victoria wrote other stories as a child. 'Alice' is a more mature work than Victoria's other attempts at writing fiction, as it represents an interesting generic mix, combining elements of traditional folk tales in the characters (cruel stepmother, weak father), the school story in the setting (a 'finishing' school for girls) and melodrama (through the retelling of a deathbed scene). The story begins promisingly and dramatically, as twelve-year-old Alice Lascelles begs her father not to send her away. Her story unfolds slowly as the reader learns that Alice is the daughter of Colonel Lascelles, a spineless but good man who is no match for his *'unworthy* and selfish' second wife. The young Mrs Lascelles — only seven years older than Alice — is parent to her own daughter with the Colonel and wants Alice out of the way: 'At first Colonel Lascelles would not hear of parting from his only child, — his pretty, mild, Alice, but when he became the father of a second little girl, and Mrs. Lascelles told him that he neglected both mother and baby for Alice, he weakly consented to send her to school for six years, when she would be of an age to be able to go out in company.'[51] The heart-broken Alice, whose pleas and embraces have gone unheard and unfelt, must resign herself to separation from her home, beloved father, and dear little sister, Rosa. She does not bear this separation with much equanimity, and sobs and cries and is overcome by turns for quite a number of pages. Once her father departs, Alice comforts herself by invoking her dead mother through a display of the first Mrs Lascelles's talismanic last gifts and a recitation of her last words:

'O' said Alice 'it is more valuable to me than all the diamonds and pearls in the world, it contains the *greatest treasure* I possess.' As she said this, she pulled off the red case, and unlocked a little wooden box from which she took a string of hair to which was attached a locket with a lock of hair in it. 'It is my *dear* Mamma's dying gift. But if you should like to hear about it I will tell you.' . . . . 'About two months before my poor Mamma died she cut off a long piece of her beautiful black hair and as she could plait very well she made it into this string and put a lock of her hair into this locket. Well, when she felt her last moment approaching she called me faintly to her bed, and taking this string and locket from her neck said: "This is my work – my hair – and my last gift. Always keep it by you; and remember your dying Mother's last words."[52]

This scene was written to be poignant, and as a child of one parent Victoria may have identified with her character's loss. In Victoria's story, Alice is abandoned first by her mother's death and then by her placement out of the home and into a school as her father capitulates to her stepmother's desire to remove her from the domestic circle. Victoria, similarly, had lost a parent when young, but her extreme youth made the memory of any touching deathbed scenes impossible. Victoria never had an evil step-mother, but she did suffer from Sir John Conroy's involvement in her upbringing with her mother's full approval. As the author of the 'Kensington System', which was predicated on the absolute power of the Duchess of Kent in any and all matters touching Victoria, Conroy was a bad fairy of significant proportions.

Alice's 'revenge' for her abandonment is the reward of her own virtue. Although she had been accused of disobedience and disrespect soon after she arrived (a contraband kitten with her name on it had been discovered in the kitchen and reported to Mrs Dunscombe by the head girl), Alice gains self-control by thinking through her situation: 'Alice went upstairs crying and would have gone on so had not she thought and resoned with herself, and as she knew she was innocent what reason had she to fret and cry? The truth always comes out sooner or later.' In fact, it was the Irish 'wild child' Diana, whose lower-class existence disrupts the staid school, who had hidden the kitten and bribed the cook to write Alice's name on its collar.[53] Some months after Alice's arrival, when everyone prepares to welcome Lady Christina, the first aristocrat in the school, Alice the moralist is ready with platitudes to ease the students' jealousy of Lady Christina's money and rank. '"But Charlotte" said Alice "I do not think Lady Christina is any happier for having fine clothes for did you not observe how anxious she looked when she came through the door lest she should soil her pretty frock; I am sure we are much merrier and happier than she is, in our clean but simple silk or merino frocks with our white aprons; are we not?"'[54]

'Alice' can be located squarely within the tradition of didactic and moral school stories for girls that included Sarah Fielding's *The Governess; or, Little Female Academy* (1749). Here Victoria is writing a story that her mother could approve. The Duchess of Kent continued to give didactic annuals as presents to her daughter, such as *The Christian Keepsake and Missionary Annual*,[55] presented to Victoria as a New Year's gift for 1835, inscribed 'To my dearest Victoria from her sincerely attached Mother.' This volume exists today in such perfect condition that it seems unlikely to have been read with any enthusiasm, if at all. In Sarah Fielding's popular boarding school story, nine female scholars are superintended by Mrs Teachum and her head girl, Jenny Peace. Each of the students has a character fault that must be confessed and reformed in the course of the book. Jenny Peace soothes each girl and helps her to learn that happiness and selfless behaviour are inextricably linked.[56] Victoria, too, lists the students at Mrs Dunscombe's school and their positive and negative traits. For example, the most beautiful girl at school, Charlotte Graves, who appears to resemble Victoria physically – 'not tall but [with] a nice little figure' and who wears her hair rather as Victoria does at the time I believe she wrote this story – is vain and affected. The structure of didactic literature insists that within a fictional moral universe, character flaws must be eradicated or the guilty character must be punished or rejected and removed from that world. Victoria does not finish her tale, but it is not at all clear that she would subscribe to this didactic paradigm, as she had similarly departed from it in writing 'An' and 'Sophia and Adolphus'. Her vision shifts within the story so that the original 'villain' later appears as morally frail, yet humanly so.

In the story, Victoria revisits Lascelles Hall and its inhabitants after a year has passed, leaving a contented Alice at school. Mrs Lascelles had had a difficult time with the birth of her second child, Blanche, yet wilfully and selfishly 'wished nay she forced her husband to take a tour in Italy, France, Switzerland and Germany'. (Whether this trip takes place or not is unclear, as the story ends soon after.) But here the point of view becomes sympathetic to the stepmother, who now is referred to by her first name. The reader learns that Mrs Lascelles's character flaws actually stem from the parenting she received from *her* mother and are therefore not really her fault: 'Her misfortune was that having been an only daughter she had been

dreadfully spoilt by a most indulgent and foolish mother, who lost her husband when Emma [Mrs Lascelles] was only 4 months old and she herself
only eighteen. Emma was consequently the darling of a widowed and
unhappy mother who being rich [Victoria had first written 'poor' and
crossed it out] and without any firmness let her lovely girl run on in all sorts
of bad and foolish habits.' Would Mrs Lascelles be punished through her
own death or that of one of her daughters for her unreasonable desires for
travel? Would the reader's sympathy for her inadequate upbringing con-
tribute to the formulation of a different moral lesson, this one about female
education and training? Obviously, these questions are unanswerable, but
Victoria's unfinished fiction – especially given her *own* perhaps spoiled
upbringing by an obsessive widow, her wide reading in improving literature, her appreciation of romance and dedication to life-writing in her journals – invites these conjectures about the connection between the young
author and the female characters she created.

Consternation and Confirmation

Victoria was fully a young lady in 1835, as H. Collen's flirtatious and pretty
portrait of the sixteen-year-old attests, and it was in this momentous year that
many of the issues of Victoria's childhood – her relationship with her mother,
her role as future queen, her competing desires for independence and
approval – came to a crisis point. Princess Victoria sat to Henry Collen for five
days in August 1835 while at Tunbridge Wells. In December of that year,
Feodore thanks Victoria for the picture by 'Collins' and notes that while he is
the most 'tiresome of painters', he 'paints *beautifully*. Your dear eyes and for-
head I find quite like, the nose is rather too large and the mouth not quite
yours neither, but that is a difficult task, that *dear* mouth of yours; the whole
is *a charming picture*, which makes me *so happy* (Ill. 37).[57] Victoria was growing up: she was allowed greater freedom in her reading, her hairstyle, and her
education (studying Italian and singing was her own idea); her social circle
was enlarged via the enormous parties the Duchess of Kent would throw; and
she became more reflective about her future role and about mortality as a
result of her preparation for her confirmation in the Church of England.

37. After Henry Collen, *Princess Victoria*, 1836, engraved by T. Woolnoth.

This last event, like every other ceremony concerning the Royal Family in which she had played a part, or from which she had been barred (such as her baptism in the former instance and William IV's coronation in the latter), was fraught with tension for the Kents. Preparation for the confirmation, which the Duchess of Kent had wanted to schedule for July 1835 'when the Princess is not called on to mix in company, or to partake of amusements', began in the spring.[58] The Duchess of Kent consulted the authorities on all things relating to the Princess – and then attempted to get her own way. In Princess Charlotte's case, confirmation was delayed until she was seventeen; in a letter to the Archbishop of Canterbury, the Duchess of Kent indicated that she felt that such a postponement would not be beneficial to Victoria, as she preferred the ceremony to be completed when 'Her mind is free' (which was presumably less likely to occur as she became older). In the same letter, the Duchess asked the Archbishop to communicate his requirements for religious instruction to the Dean of Chester, and (with the Bishop of London) to examine Victoria before the ceremony took place.[59] A flurry of correspondence relating to the confirmation flew back and forth between the Duchess of Kent and the Archbishop throughout the spring and early summer of 1835.[60] At issue was the King's approval. King William had his own plans in mind: he wanted to have some say in the date and location of the ceremony; once his commands had been given, the Duchess of Kent could not ignore or disobey them without inviting an unwelcome reprisal. And so the confirmation was to be held at the Chapel Royal at St James's Palace – the King's primary residence.

It did not follow from this acquiescence, however, that the Duchess of Kent became tractable or responsive to the King's every wish. John Conroy and the Duchess of Kent attempted to isolate the Duchess of Northumberland from the confirmation proceedings and the Kensington System in general. As Cecil Woodham-Smith notes, the Duchess of Northumberland, a favourite of the King and Queen, 'had been a disappointment' due to her wish for active involvement, rather than with 'show' only, in Princess Victoria's education and affairs.[61] The Duchess of Kent aggravated the King by asking the Archbishop of Canterbury to be the messenger between Kensington and St James's about this issue. The King desired only the Duchess of Northumberland to act as this conduit. By choosing the Archbishop as her mouthpiece rather than a member of her household (even a very highly placed one), the Duchess of Kent claimed irreproachable authority for her wishes, while at the same time attempting to defy the King. Although it became a sticky issue because the Archbishop was himself a person of authority, Sir Herbert Taylor, the King's confidential secretary, wrote a delicately worded letter explaining his dismissal as messenger and replacement by the Duchess of Northumberland who, the letter avers, had been badly treated by the Duchess of Kent:

... His Majesty had requested the Duchess of Northumberland to be the Bearer of His communications to Her Royal Highness the Duchess of Kent, respecting the period of the Princess Victoria's Confirmation, and ... the manner in which that Communication was met and noticed to the Duchess of Northumberland by Her Royal Highness was very little suited to Her Grace's Station in Society and to the Claim She has so well established to be treated with respect and Courtesy by any and every Branch of the Royal Family.[62]

The King was not about to let the opportunity to demonstrate who was the sovereign pass by without comment: '... it rests with the Sovereign and not with a Subject to determine who shall be the Person employed as a Channel of Communication between them ...'.[63]

The Archbishop of Canterbury's awkwardly scrawled and unsigned letter to the Duchess of Kent (copies were sent to the King and the Duchess of Northumberland) informs her that his attempt to tell the King when the confirmation would take place (in accordance with the Duchess of Kent's desires) was not successful: 'H.M. [His Majesty] having commissioned the Duchess of Northumberland to ascertain Your Royal Highnesses wishes on that subject, His Majesty expects an answer to be returned through the same channel.'[64] Even Queen Adelaide had been pulled into this fray. She wrote gentle pleading letters to the Duchess of Northumberland attempting to explain the King's position and the Duchess of Kent's error in persisting to disobey him.[65] The Duchess of Northumberland's discomfort over this game of wills is evident in a letter she wrote to the Archbishop of Canterbury a few days later. She writes that 'I only hope for the sake of Her to Whom I am so truly devoted, that tomorrow when I pay my Duty as usual, the answer will be delivered.' One assumes that 'the answer' looked for would be directed to the King.[66] Her hope was in vain, as the Duchess did not behave as requested, which prompted the next letter to the Archbishop from Sir Herbert Taylor on 17 July 1835: 'I take this opportunity of mentioning to your Grace that the Duchess of Kent persists in resisting the King's Pleasure respecting the communication through the Duchess of Northumberland, and that His Majesty adheres to it. – Thus the matter stands and I fear that it may have the effect of delaying the

Confirmation of the Princess Victoria.'[67] The ultimate pawn in this game, Victoria, mentions nothing about machinations or manipulations in her journal, but notes her interview on 27 July with the esteemed clerics and the Dean of Chester: '[they were] very well satisfied with me'.[68]

In her letter to the Prime Minister informing him of Victoria's success, the Duchess of Kent linked the Princess's performance to her own maternal satisfaction: 'the result [of the examination] has been most gratifying to every feeling, that should animate a Mother'.[69] But the real reason for this letter to Melbourne was to draw him into the dispute over who should carry messages and who had been wronged. The Duchess of Kent's view is somewhat different from that given by the King's secretary as, for cover, she blames the Archbishop of Canterbury for the confusion:

> The Archbishop of Canterbury took the same opportunity to explain to me that He had inadvertently led to the Duchess of Northumberland being introduced into the communication between the King and me – and, it was to satisfy His Majesty's impatience for an answer and which also led, to His Grace's writing to me, in the King's name, on the 10th instant, – which was a mistake. Under the circumstance in which I am placed by the King, I feel that although I have been treated in a manner, I was quite unprepared to expect, – yet, that, I owe so much to my Child not to delay Her Confirmation and also to avoid making the matter a subject of public observation, which in these times, could not fail to be injurious to the Royal Family. . . .'[70]

This tempest in a teapot concluded when the King himself wrote to the Duchess of Kent triumphing over his victory (he is responding to a communiqué delivered by the Duchess of Northumberland) and avowing his love for Victoria and his assent to the confirmation date: 'His M. will be *most* ready and happy to receive at St. James's Palace on Thursday 30th instant the Mother and his truly beloved Niece the Princess Victoria at Twelve O'Clock in order to compleat the Confirmation of the Princess ascending to the Delights of *that* Church which it is not more the *Duty* than the Inclination of the King to defend.'[71] William then invited the Duchess and Victoria to a dinner at the palace after the ceremony and to stay for the weekend. When the Duchess replied to this letter (the original of her reply was in Sir John Conroy's hand), she turns down his invitation, pleading excessive grief over the death her sister Sophie, Countess Mensdorff.[72] So the Duchess resolved to refuse *something* successfully and to foil the King's plan to see more of Victoria and to claim a greater relationship with her. This struggle over a seemingly minor issue of protocol gives an indication of the uneasy relationship between the King and his sister-in-law. (Their wrangling was aided by Conroy who served to gain if the Duchess was perceived as strong and the King as weak.) This relationship would be damaged even further in the years leading up to Victoria's eighteenth birthday. But for now, because she was Victoria's mother, the Duchess had to be consulted and the King, as 'head of the household', had to be obeyed — eventually. But even then, the Duchess was able to manipulate situations so that she avoided the King and kept Victoria from the court as much as possible.

Taking advantage of the occasion of confirmation, the Duchess wrote one of her holiday letters to her daughter to mark its solemnity. Perhaps the composition of these letters helped the Duchess to formulate her feelings; she may not have been able to express warmth towards her daughter except through missives. Of course, the Duchess was free to be alone with the Princess, but it appears that this seldom occurred. Lehzen was Victoria's intimate; her mother held a more formal role in relationship to her: guardian, politician, coordinator of social activities and education.

The Duchess opens her letter with just such an admission of failure of effective personal communication: 'I must write to you, — as I cannot speak so quietly with you, as I can do, when I write.'[73] The Duchess's letter serves to remind Victoria — yet again — that she is especially privileged. Her confirmation in the Church of England was a momentous occasion as it marked the first adult step towards her eventual vow to 'defend the faith' and stand at the head of the Church: 'For other young persons of your age, [confirmation] may perhaps be less impressive, although the meaning of the act is the same; — but their circumstances and situations are quite different from Your's: — I may say, Providence has singled you out: — much more is required from you, than from other young Ladies of your age. — In making these comparisons, I feel naturally still more anxious for you, my beloved Victoria. . . .'[74] Victoria's continued dependence on her mother until she comes of age 'either eighteen or twenty-one years, according to circumstances' is stressed. Here the Duchess's manipulations are clearly visible since Victoria's age of majority was legally eighteen and never twenty-one (thus a Regency could only take place before she had attained her eighteenth year). As this interesting letter progresses, the Duchess of Kent begins to sound quite like any typical mother offering advice about life and hoping to entice her teenager to confide in her: 'Neither a great Station with all it's [*sic*] luxuries and pleasures; – neither Youth with all it's illusions and charms, can give you *real happiness*, – for all these advantages are not lasting: – But a good, virtuous and well cultivated mind, will give you that happiness which is lasting. – It will enable you to bear up against all those vicissitudes which are inevitable in life, and befall the great and the low; – all must equally submit to them.'[75] She can't help but offer some mild criticism in the midst of her praise: 'You want only reflection, – which is, in our situation, absolutely necessary.'

While all the conflict and criticism raged about her – sometimes touching her directly – how did Victoria feel about her confirmation? She wrote a long journal entry describing her sorrow for her sins and desire for improvement in the ways of obedience and dutifulness:

> I felt that my confirmation was one of the most solemn and important events and acts in my life; and that I trusted that it might have a salutary effect on my mind. I felt deeply repentant for all what I had done which was wrong and trusted in God Almighty to strengthen my heart and mind; and to forsake all that is bad and follow all that is virtuous and right. I went with the firm determination to become a true Christian, to try and comfort my dear Mamma in all her griefs, trials and anxieties, and to become a dutiful and affectionate daughter to her. Also to be obedient to *dear* Lehzen who has done so much for me.[76]

From this comment it is clear that Victoria was sincere in her desire to be good, that she recognized her mother as a bundle of nerves who needed constant 'comforting', and that Lehzen receives the strongest mark of distinction by the italicized 'dear' preceding her name. Victoria described the service in vague terms ('the usual morning service was performed' and 'When the usual address had been read, I [as is usual for all to do] replied "I do"') and claimed to have been 'very much affected indeed when we came home'.[77]

The depth of Princess Victoria's religious feeling is difficult to gauge. Queen Victoria has been called an 'Evangelical' due to her upbringing by 'devout Evangelical parents' and her earnestness and self-righteousness (qualities said to characterize the Evangelicals);[78] certainly George Davys could be called such, and William Wilberforce, at the heart of the early Evangelical Movement in England, was acquainted with the Duchess of Kent. The Duchess helped Victoria to prepare for her confirmation by the presentation of three books relating to this topic. (In her journal Victoria calls them 'all 3 very nice books'.)[79] However, even if Victoria's religious beliefs were Evangelically inflected, the development of such religious fervour cannot be easily discerned in her girlhood writings. Victoria was excited about her confirmation, about the step into adulthood it represented, about the greater notice she was receiving from the King, but she does not appear to be particularly devout or attentive to religious matters (later in the diary she tends to write the text of the Sunday sermon, but she reveals her sometimes desultory attention to this task by leaving blank spaces for the Scriptural passages that – once remembered or reminded of – could be filled in later). In terms of religious devotion, Princess Victoria was much behind her contemporary Emily Shore, whose ill health perhaps developed her piety to a degree unusual in one so young.

On the first Sunday after Victoria's confirmation ceremony, the Duchess again wrote to her daughter, this time as a marker of their 'taking the Sacrament together for the first time'.[80] This letter begins by reflecting on the topic of good intentions and the inevitability of sin. The Duchess goes on to discuss her own preparation for taking the sacrament and its benefits: 'I always feel better and happier after I have taken the holy Sacrament.' These thoughts lead directly to a veiled criticism of Victoria: 'I wish, my beloved Victoria, you may have the same feelings: Your having, or not having that feeling will be the true *test*, of your own conscience, whether you are right with yourself and your God, by your having kept all His commandments towards Him, and your neighbour and yourself. You cannot *escape* your *own feelings*, and *from* the *situation you are born* in, they will be your *best safe* guard and afford you the happiest moments.' The fact that this letter is in the Duchess of Kent's hand but is edited and corrected by Sir John Conroy also helps construct a possible context for the letter's creation and its intended effect. Victoria, of course, would not have read this draft, but a perfect copy in her mother's hand. She is urged to take the good advice offered by unnamed persons as the crucial precursor to that time when she will be autonomous: 'You are for the present not obliged to act upon your own responsibility: Your duties still are not very difficult: You have only to follow the good advice given to you and when the time comes, when you must act for yourself you will know how to make use of it.' Someone – either the Duchess or Conroy – reconsidered the wisdom of communicating the following vaguely threatening and alarming sentiments and crossed them out: 'You will be, it is my duty to tell you more severely observed than any one else in [the world]. You know that very well yourself.'

The letter concludes with an apology and the best clue as to its awkward nature: Victoria had always been a stubborn child, but now she was clearly becoming uncooperative about issues of greater importance than lessons and manners. Victoria and her mother had had some kind of argument, and it seems that the Duchess (and Conroy) hoped to patch things up with this missive that positioned the author as both supplicant and accuser: 'My beloved Child if I in any way but most unintentionally hurt or distressed you, forgive your Mother; as she forgives you, let us follow the example of Him who died for us. Amen.'[81] Victoria's journal never suggests any kind of quarrel, but her entry for this day is notable in that she never mentions her mother's name at all (except as included in the 'we took the sacrament'). She names the other persons who took the sacrament with them as 'Lady Flora, dear Lehzen, & Sir J.C.'[82] It is very unusual for Victoria to use initials to stand for a person, and her hatred for Conroy is made clear by this slight. Victoria's first adult act within the Church does not pass without self-reflection: 'It is a very solemn and impressive ceremony and when one recollects and thinks that we take it in remembrance of the death of our blessed Saviour, one *ought*, nay *must* feel deeply impressed with holy and pious feelings!' Agnes Strickland describes the confirmation scene as one where the Princess was overcome with emotion after the ceremony and, sobbing, laid her head on her mother's shoulder. Although this image is picturesque, '*Not true*' was the Queen's response to it.[83]

Victoria in Crisis

After the drama of the confirmation had concluded, the Duchess attempted to revive the 'Royal Progresses' through the countryside. While his niece appeared, to all intents and purposes, as a 'junior sovereign', and his own health began to fail, King William made known his displeasure with the scope and purposes of these trips. Victoria was in a quandary: she wanted to placate her mother, please the King, and confound Conroy. She fretted and fumed and finally balked. She wouldn't travel and that was that.

Although she was understandably silent about this struggle in her journal, a copy of the Duchess of Kent's letter to Victoria after one of these storms survives. In it, the Duchess attempts to continue their conversation of a few days prior that had been effectively ended when Victoria refused to speak to her mother any further on this topic. The letter of 2 September is so illustrative of the relationship between the Princess and her mother – the combination of criticism, manipulation, hyperbole, back-stabbing, and concern – that it is reprinted in full:

> I must make some more remarks, about the conversation we had together the day before yesterday, – but that must not prevent you to speak to me, – as I wish very much you would always openly and candidly speak out your thoughts to me: But you should give up the idea you have, that I am angry, when I try to convince you, that you have formed an erroneous view of a subject. Now, to the subject.
>
> You may imagine, that I feel very much disappointed and grieved, – that the journey we are to commence tomorrow, is not only disagreeable to you, but that it makes you even unhappy: that the fatigue of it will make you ill, that you dislike it: And that notwithstanding I tried to convince you of the utility of these journies [*sic*], for your future, you will not be convinced. You will not see, that it is of the greatest consequence that you should be seen, – that you should know your Country, – and be acquainted with, and be known by all Classes.
>
> If the King was another man, – and if he *really* loved you, he would, instead of wishing to stop our journey, which he tried every way to do, but which his Ministers told him he could not do, as it would do him

harm: as his jealousy is too well known! Every one else sees the utility and great consequence of these journies: – The K should not only approve of them, but even press one to them.

I must tell you, dearest Love, – if your conversation with me, could be known, – that you had not the sense to see, what all others see, – but you had not energy to undertake the journey, – or that your views were not enlarged enough to grasp the benefits arising from it, – then you would fall in the estimation of the People of this Country. – You must be awake to your Station, – You must have an honourable ambition.

Nothing can be more critical than these present times; – much will depend, on your character, for the future; – if that, could be undervalued, now, my Child, what a price you will pay in that future.

I can have no object, but your welfare: – in a short time, as it flies, I shall be a Spectator; – could I bear to see, my fondest hopes, not realized: – can you be dead, to the Calls your position demands: – Impossible! – reflect, – before it is too late. – Whatever is sown, of that you will reap. – Let the country see you anxious to meet it, – open and cordial in your manners; – shew a promise of character, let the People hope for something, worth having, – free from all the faults of former reigns. – Turn your thoughts and views to your future Station – its duties, – and the claims that exist on you.

Need I assure you, of my Love and Devotion, my dear Angel, – No! – it is not necessary, – and I remain, your ever affectionate Mother.[84]

The Duchess of Kent engages the full force of her persuasive powers in this letter – reminding Victoria perhaps more often than was absolutely necessary that she *will* be queen some day and that she may well fail in this role if her mother's advice is not attended to. This letter is notable also as it illuminates the difference between what was happening outside of the journal and the events actually recorded in the journal. One tiny clue that all was not well between Victoria and her mother occurred on 29 August, four days before the above letter was written. For the first time in the journal, Victoria notes, 'I breakfasted alone.'[85] I assume the 'alone' means 'not with Mamma', as Lehzen would surely have been with her in any case. It seems that the Princess might not have been speaking to her mother just then. But the storms between mother and daughter did not erupt solely at this juncture. In the 1835 Birthday Letter, the Duchess of Kent alludes to earlier troubles: 'But as there is no joy, without pain in this world, so even between us, for moments only, have these feelings been blended, – I advert to the grief I experienced, from some little misunderstandings which clouded our happy intercourses and which never should occur between a beloved child and Her only parent.' She closes the letter in typical manipulative fashion with the mention of a small keepsake she was including with the letter: some hair 'the last perhaps of its natural colour'.[86]

The tensions that Victoria must have felt within herself between her role as the girl who acquiesces and her desire to be the girl who refuses are mirrored in the juxtaposition of two very different books the sixteen-year-old Victoria was reading at this time. Just prior to the disputed trip to York, they had attended the race days at Tunbridge Wells for part of August,[87] and there she began to read *Sully's Memoirs* (sent to her by Uncle Leopold) and Mrs Butler's (Fanny Kemble's) just-published American journal. The two memoirs could not have been more oppositional, and Victoria's responses to them both are revealing of the young woman she had become.[88] *Sully's Memoirs* recounts the long life and political triumphs of Maximilien de Béthune, a French statesman of the late sixteenth, early seventeenth centuries, loyal to Henry IV. This is a man's story of public life and service to the crown, and had the imprimatur of Victoria's only (at this point) political adviser whose advice she sought and respected. Victoria marvels after reading some of Fanny Kemble's *Journal of a Residence in America*, which offers, by contrast, a glimpse into an outspoken young woman's interior life, her passions, and reflections. The *Journal* contained 'some beautiful writing in it though its youthful indiscretions gave much offense at the time'.[89] Harriet Martineau, author of popular works on political economy, was highly censorious of Kemble's 'clever' book: 'I might be, and probably was, narrow and stiff in my judgment of it; but I was sufficiently shocked at certain passages to induce her to cancel some thirty pages.'[90]

Victoria first mentions that she is reading Kemble's memoir on 20 August, yet how she obtained the book is not made clear. Princess Victoria was quite critical of the style and content, but also fascinated: '[Mrs Butler's journal] is very oddly written. There are some fine feelings & descriptions

['& impressions' is crossed out here] expressed in it every now & then; but upon the whole it is pertly & sometimes *even* vulgarly written.'[91] Notwithstanding her apparent disapproval, Victoria spends much time with this book throughout the next month, generally while '[her] hair was doing' both morning and evening.[92] (Victoria was reading other volumes during this time as well, Washington Irving's *The Alhambra* – 'a most delightful book & I litterally devoured it'[93] – and the Bishop of Chester's *Exposition of the Gospel of St. Matthew* – 'It is not one of those learned books in which you have to cavil at almost every paragraph.'[94]) In her discussions of Kemble's journal Victoria again mentions the 'fine feelings' and the amusement she derived from it, but her strongest response continues to be disapproval of its openness. By writing her prim and rather sanctimonious views of Mrs Butler, Victoria reveals her awareness of the threat of exposure within journal-keeping. That is, Fanny Kemble's boldly presented self was alarming to Victoria due to the vulnerability the presentation of such 'impropriety' causes the author, with the threat of social censure. Victoria herself could never risk such publicity, even in a 'private' venue such as her own diary: 'Read in Mrs. Butler's journals. It is a great pity that her style is so inelegant & her expressions so vulgar. If she wrote it only for herself & not for publication it would be all very well, though *I* think that *even* for *oneself* one's expression ought to be delicate & proper, but if she intended to publish it when she wrote it, she is mistaken I think, & I fear it will do her no good.'[95]

Unlike Victoria, Emily Shore believed that although it is natural to censor oneself in life-writing, it is not *necessary* to do so; therefore, she decided to keep a diary that could be the repository of '*all* the secret feelings of my heart', a project Victoria would never have dared to undertake. (Emily's confidential diary has never been found, and may have been destroyed at her death.)[96] Significantly, however, the two writers share the belief in the flawed nature of the diary as an entirely accurate reflection of the writer's thoughts and feelings. Both Victoria and Emily feared embarrassing exposure through their diaries. In a long and thoughtful disquisition on keeping a journal written near the end of her life in 1838, Emily presciently imagined future readers perusing her private journal, and accordingly held her writing in check:

I have written much that I would show only to a very few, and much that I would on no account submit to any human eye. Still, even now, I cannot entirely divest myself of an uncomfortable notion that the whole may some future day, when I am in my grave, be read by some individual, and this notion has, even without my being often aware of it, cramped me, I am sure. I have by no means confessed myself in my journal. . . .[97]

Poignantly, Emily Shore felt the eyes of the future upon her; certainly, Victoria, not afforded the same privacy, avoided confiding personal thoughts to the page.

And yet, even given her fears of revealing too much through the 'permanent' medium of print, Princess Victoria's style in her letters, if not her journal, loosens a bit in 1836, and she even engaged in some 'vulgarities' of her own. In writing to Feodore she cautioned her to take care not to catch cold or 'other nasty things; I ought not to employ so vulgar a word as "nasty"'.[98] In May she had written about attending a 'dandy' dinner-party, composed of some of the 'fashionables'. And the next month she asked the question, 'Are you reconciled to the tight sleeves? I am.'[99] These charming locutions and sentiments highlight the fresh girlishness of the princess revealed in the journal. Notwithstanding timid forays into the 'vulgar', Princess Victoria's journal is primarily the story of her home life. This domestic emphasis can be found in nineteenth-century women's autobiography in general, where the assumption was made about the 'proper modes of women's self-writing' — that this writing would concern relationships and the home. 'One consequence of such assumptions was the rise of the Victorian domestic memoir. Another was the inclusion of domestic patterns — plots of sisterhood, motherhood, conjugal-life — in the autobiography of virtually every major Victorian woman writer'.[100] In reading Mme de Sévigné's letters — or listening to them as Lehzen often read them aloud — Victoria concentrated on the letters between mother and daughter in particular. And although she could not entirely agree with the sentiments about Mme de Sévigné expressed by Sir James Mackintosh, Victoria copied out in her book journal (a discussion and description of the books she had read from 1835 until 1837) a long extract of Mackintosh's she found significant in which he praises the loving relationship between mother and daughter as the most 'bewitching' aspect of the letters.[101] That Princess Victoria – even as she read countless books of history and martial victory, English law, and political intrigue – was most concerned with domestic affairs is not entirely surprising given the strength of middle- and upper-class social expectations about gender and behaviour found in the Georgian and then Victorian eras, and reflected in the journals of Anne Chalmers, Fanny Kemble, Emily Shore, and Caroline Fox. Although she would never really 'work' in the home, Princess Victoria, along with these other girl diarists, grew up with the belief in woman's supremacy in the home sphere, and in the spiritual elevation of women over men. Her sister Princess Feodore espoused the conventional view of male and female roles when she wrote, 'We [women] should be like the purer spirits amongst the other, and try to give everything a pleasing aspect in our homes.'[102] Once Victoria became queen, though she was an unusually placed woman, these expectations of her proper womanly behaviour did not materially alter. For example, in advertisements where the Queen's image was used to sell a variety of domestic products, Lori Anne Loeb argues, '[Queen Victoria's] unique political role is rarely highlighted; instead, advertisers promote the leveling theme of her feminine nature.'[103] The 'leveling' ideology that would eventually link the Queen of Britain and Empress of India with her housewife subjects can also be seen in the essentially domestic life-writing of all the young female diarists under discussion here. For Princess Victoria and her diarist contemporaries, the bonds created by gender and authorship carry greater significance, finally, than their differences in class, religion, and situation.

Tragic Heroine

Regardless of her feelings, Victoria and the royal party embarked upon the much-dreaded autumn trip in early September 1835, travelling north to York to stay at Bishopthorpe, the palace of the Archbishop of York. On 11 September they were still in York and entertained by a series of music festivals at the beautiful York Minster and a fancy-dress ball at the Assembly Rooms. For this event Victoria notes that she wore a 'wreath of white roses round my head like Grisi has in the Puritani'.[104] Victoria was captivated by this costume and performance and executed a number of watercolours depicting Grisi in this role. Though her outward appearance was lovely, and her presence required at a number of pleasant entertainments, all was not well with the Princess. During this trip and in the previous month, Victoria was ill for a few days in the third week of each month – almost certainly suffering symptoms related to her menstrual period. She was tired, uncomfortable, unable to eat ('I *forced* a cup of cocoa down without eating anything'),[105] then dosed with tincture of rhubarb ('nasty stuff'),[106] she began to feel better, but continued somewhat dispirited. Victoria's discomfort, coupled with a negative attitude about the trip in general, probably contributed to the atypical irritability expressed in her journal as they travelled south. Viscount Esher leaves out the following entries from his selections of Victoria's journals, perhaps because of the somewhat unflattering portrait of the Princess that is created by her ungraciousness to her country and people. As they moved through Cambridgeshire, Victoria can find nothing pleasant to say about the scenery and even indulges in mild xenophobia: 'No *hedges* but *ditches*, no *trees* but *willows*, with ugly barren fields, & the whole country as flat as a table. The whole was more like *Holland* than *England*.'[107] When they arrive in Lynn in Norfolk, Victoria is almost beside herself with frustration over their impeded progress and the obstruction of her view caused by the crowds of people who had turned out to welcome them:

Oh! What a business was there, there!! The people, of whom there was a dense mass, insisted upon dragging us through the town & in spite of every effort which was tried to prevent them from so doing, they obstinately persisted in their wish & would dragg us through the town. Not only *through* it, did they dragg us, but *round* it, so, that we were detained exactly *1 hour & a ¼ in Lynn*! I could see nothing of the town; I only saw one living, dense, mass of human beings! We unfortunately drove over a poor man just as we stopped but he is not materially hurt, I hear.[108]

Victoria's anger at the 'mass' of people in her way is so great that her dismay over the injury done to a pedestrian by their carriage is less than it might have otherwise been. And here the difficulty of sustaining the practice of Victoria's 'theory' of 'delicacy' in journal-writing is evident. In fact, the very day after the disaster in Lynn, Victoria finished reading Kemble's journal and decided that, after all, the outspoken work was a worthy piece of writing from a 'poetical mind': 'I must say, that upon the whole I like it very much. There are some vulgar expressions, certainly, but it does not give you the idea of a vulgar mind which I thought at first, on the contrary she must have a very poetical one. Her descriptions of scenery are extremely beautiful & her sentiments very often extremely exalted. The words are very fine with which she ends the book. They are as follows. "I saw Niagara. – Oh, God! Who can describe that sight?"'[109] Regardless of what one thinks of Kemble's powers of description – or of Victoria's literary criticism – it is significant that by the end of the 'scandalous' memoir Victoria is able to look past 'vulgarity' and take pleasure in Kemble's passion and delight in captivating an audience. I believe that this book offered a different kind of education to the Princess, a modelling of the writing life that she could not emulate, but could admire. Some of this admiration comes through in the journal in greater freedom of expression (to be disagreeable, emotional, or frank). Later in the same entry, Victoria mentions that her mother had received an address from the 'Inhabitants' of the port city Wells (in Norfolk). Victoria makes the dutiful comment that these addresses are kindly meant and demonstrate loyalty to the King (she doesn't mention loyalty to her own future reign), but that they are *'ein wenig, sehr langweilig'*, that is, 'a little dull, very dull'.[110] The unusual recourse to the German language here is of course a way to mediate the 'transgressive' resentment the heir to the throne is feeling about displays of devotion from her future subjects.

Princess Victoria's ungenerous feelings did not abate. As they changed horses at Thetford on their way home, Victoria again remarked the ugly scenery and then insulted the townsfolk who ran up to their carriage by calling them 'half drunk, I believe'.[111] Victoria's displeasure and disgust ends only when they return home to Kensington Palace two days later. Unlike her earlier trips about the country, this time Victoria is grateful to spy the gate of Kensington Palace coming into view. Sounding rather like Leopold, she complains about the limitations placed on royalty by their notoriety and social position: 'We cannot travel like other people, quietly & pleasantly, but we go on through towns & crowds & when one arrives at any fine ['fine' is then crossed out] nobleman's seat, one must instantly dress for dinner & consequently I could never rest properly.'[112]

Perhaps this lack of rest, resentment of her mother, and general adolescent malaise contributed to the serious illness to which Victoria succumbed just a few weeks later. Though feeling poorly, Victoria had been heartily cheered by the long-awaited visit of her Uncle Leopold and his new wife, Louise, daughter of Louis Philippe, King of the French, and only seven years Victoria's senior. Here was sororal comfort; here was paternal attention and guidance. Louise was a role model in fashion for Victoria and encouraged her to think of her as an older sister.[113] Leopold's counsel was no longer restricted to brief missives; the uncle and his niece spent long interludes in private, much to Victoria's delight: 'Uncle Leopold came up to my room & sat talking with me till a ¼ to 6. He gave me very valuable & important advice. We talked over many important & serious matters. I look up to him as a Father, with complete confidence, love & affection. He is the best & kindest adviser I have. He has always treated me as his Child & I love him most dearly for it.'[114] In the journal, mentions of Mamma and even Lehzen drop away in favour of these stars in Victoria's heaven. Leopold took her seriously, and, for her part, Victoria listened to Leopold and respected his advice (unlike that given by her mother/Conroy). When the Belgian royals left, Victoria was devastated, and her grief was overwhelming. She had been under Dr Clark's care for a few days prior to their departure, and after the goodbyes were exchanged on 7 October Victoria confided to her journal that she felt 'so ill & wretched'.[115]

At this point the journal stops for about three weeks while Victoria was very sick with what is now believed to have been infected tonsils, or even typhoid fever.[116] Dr Clark determined the illness to be a 'bilious fever'. The drama of this brief interlude and its significance in relation to her later behaviour cannot be underestimated. While Victoria was suffering with fever and other symptoms of the infection, at first the Duchess of Kent and Conroy downplayed the illness and then saw fit to reconsider the issue of a potential Regency and Victoria's future staff once queen. 'Whether the Princess may become, by an event, we must all anxiously hope may be long delayed, her own Mistress at eighteen years of age or be of age at twenty one – as other subjects are – I by this course fit her to enter on her own responsible duties.'[117] The Duchess and Conroy sought to convince Princess Victoria that she was not fit to reign at the age of eighteen, and to influence her eventual choice of a personal secretary; not surprisingly, the person they had in mind was Sir John himself.[118] The Duchess desired her little princess to sign a paper agreeing to such a future appointment – a 'contract' which, of course, would have been morally, rather than legally, binding. Or at least this is what the Duchess of Kent and Conroy assumed. Victoria, sick and harangued, refused to sign time and again. It appears that Victoria's mainstay, Lehzen, with her unflagging loyalty to the Princess and hatred of Conroy, was perceived to be a danger to Sir John Conroy's plans. In March, Feodore felt sufficiently alarmed that Lehzen was in peril of dismissal that she wrote an appeal to the Duchess of Northumberland to use her influence to help maintain Lehzen as Victoria's confidante: 'Dear Duchess we must do everything to preserve Baroness L. . . . I should think the King might well be positive in his wishes if not *orders* on that subject, which is of such importance for the wellfare of our beloved Princess, and I may say for the country; for what sort of person may be put near her, to further the plans of that man.'[119] Harold Albert, in his biography of Feodore, comments, 'Some writers have found it strange that there should be so much planning and contriving for two or three further years of mimic power, but the driving reality was the tangible cash in hand measured against the unreliable prospects of any financial arrangements that Victoria might be pleased to ask of Parliament as Queen.'[120]

For five weeks the Princess was confined to her room. None of the pathos of this intolerable situation with her mother and Conroy was reflected in the journal, certainly, but Victoria – who had a long memory – did not forget this cruel treatment. Victoria's feelings for Conroy were now set for life, and any warmth she may have felt for him as her mother's friend and the father of her childhood companions was now frozen from her heart. The Duchess, too, through her insensitive behaviour and manipulation was irretrievably placed in the enemy's camp as far as Victoria was concerned. She felt that Leopold and Louise, Feodore and Lehzen alone were impartial friends who could be trusted and loved freely.

38. Princess Victoria, self-portrait drawing, 8 November 1835.

And it was Lehzen, not Victoria's mother, who was the ministering angel to Victoria during her long illness. On 31 October, in her first journal entry since becoming sick, Victoria relishes the retelling of her story of weakness, fever, and loss of appetite. Anger at the Duchess never surfaces in the journal except through her conspicuous absence or desultory mention and the continual adulation of Lehzen (and the King and Queen of Belgium) found within its pages.[121] She writes, 'My *dearest best* Lehzen has been, & still is (for I require a great deal of care still) MOST UNCEASING & INDEFATIGABLE in her *great* care of me. I am still VERY weak & am grown VERY *thin*.' In the same entry Victoria lists a number of gifts (mostly china figures and prints) that 'Mamma was so good as to give me during my illness'.[122] The contrast between Lehzen's loving care for Victoria's body and spirit (Victoria reports that Lehzen spent a great deal of time rubbing her feet and reading to her) and her mother's gifts of cold china is quite distinct. It is easy to see how Lehzen had won Victoria's love and the Duchess of Kent had lost it. On 8 November, a very self-pitying princess drew a self-portrait from the 'looking-glass' to capture for ever her forlorn visage (Ill. 38). Victoria wears an adaptation of her favourite current hairstyle of a false crown of braids and sausage curls framing her face, and what appears to be a dressing gown that she might have worn 'while [her] hair was doing'.[123] The drawing, executed in light pencil, emphasizes the Princess's large, widely spaced eyes and tiny mouth (in the drawing rather impossibly shown as about the same size as each eye). But it is the heavy eyelids and wrinkled brows that effectively communicate Victoria's sad and resigned expression. This is a girl who has just heaved a heavy sigh, who doesn't believe that she will ever be quite well again, who *could* smile, but might not be able to find anything to smile about. This sweetly chastened Victoria appears to enjoy her fate (now that she really was out of physical danger), interesting illness and (some of) the attentions it brought.

Concern over Victoria's health did not end with the close of 1835. Dr Clark was in constant attendance upon the Princess into the New Year, and wrote memoranda reflecting his diagnoses and prescriptions for continued good health. Clark's prescription included exercise in the open and 'bracing' air of an 'elevated part of the country' at least three times a week in order to invigorate the system and counteract 'the relaxing effects of the air of Kensington', frequent short walks even within the house to stimulate the circulation, the occasional use of a standing desk, the avoidance of singing or reading aloud after meals, and the 'perfect and deliberate mastication' of food.[124] Sir James was also an advocate of the use of the clubs to strengthen the arms and back, a position that would be shared by any weight-lifting fan today. Although it is difficult to know how often Victoria followed this general advice, her clubs have survived and are stored in Kensington Palace, and her love of open windows (another obsession of Dr Clark's) is well known. By 1835, Victoria had reached her full height of 4 feet 11 inches and was a slender girl, though already tending towards easy weight gain before her illness had slimmed her down. Leopold was ever anxious about the Princess's height, hoping that she would be tall. He wrote in March 1835: '. . . is it true that you are grown so extremely tall? Some people say half an inch less than myself? I understand that is [sic] has created the greatest sensation at the Drawing Room.'[125]

Leopold's visit, her mother's machinations, and her illness combined to give rise in Victoria to a renewed sense of seriousness – sparked earlier by her birthday ('How very old [sixteen years] sounds; but I feel that the two years to come till I attain my 18th are the most important of any almost. I now only begin to appreciate my lessons, and hope from this time on, to make great progress')[126] as she looked towards the inevitable just a few years away. Often this seriousness manifested itself in prim moral judgements and pronouncements. In response to her reading about the court of Louis XIV of France, Victoria remarks, 'How different from now! Where the example of virtue & good behaviour is so well and perfectly set forth in the persons of the King, Queen, & the whole Royal Family. And in the time of Louis XIV, nothing could be more depraved than the Morals were, at Court.'[127] Though Victoria attempts it in her private journal, very few in 1835 could call, without deliberate irony, the Georgian Royal Family and its illegitimate children, great appetites, and petty jealousies, a pack of saints. Leopold's influence – and Victoria's burgeoning morbid sensibility – can be seen in the following pronouncement on Bellini's death and musing about the brevity of life: 'All true lovers of fine Music, (of which I am one of the greatest), must join in lamenting the loss of one whose compositions gave such delight. . . . The one who composed the heart-stirring duet "Il rival" ... now lies still & cold in the grave, never more to move! Alas! How short is life! One ought therefore to employ one's time properly & usefully!'[128] Leopold, for his part, was advising Victoria in a general way through weekly letters, but occasionally committing 'indiscreet' remarks to paper: 'You have another Uncle whose name ends with a "land" who acts on a different prinsciple [sic] [from Leopold's high-minded political purpose], his great delight, is to blow every spark pregnant with strife into flame.'[129] Leopold refers, of course, to the Duke of Cumberland.

Concomitant with this sense of seriousness came the acknowledgement of an independence from her mother that was fast approaching. Victoria begins to write not only about her solemn thoughts, but also about the pleasant times she has privately with Lehzen while they continue to enjoy the relative obscurity and peacefulness of Ramsgate: 'Nous en rimes beaucoup' and 'We laughed a good deal together.'[130] She also began to comment on her reading of the newspapers, a new development for the Princess and one that points up her wider concerns.[131] As the fresh year commenced, Victoria encapsulated her own view of her blessings – not those sent to her by her mother in a New Year's letter, but perhaps inspired by it to reflect on the past year. She is grateful to God for her health and safety and hopes to enjoy many more years with her loved ones. She enumerates her chief joys and sorrows (which concern primarily those beyond her immediate circle at Kensington): 'I have had the happiness of having a little *cousin* born (Aunt Louise's & Uncle Leopold's little son, I mean;) 2dly. I have lost a *dear* & much beloved Aunt; I have had a great deal of anxiety concerning my dearest sister Feodore and great joy at the birth of little Adelaide; and lastly I have had the great happiness of seeing my *dearest* Uncle Leopold again & of making the acquaintance of that *dear beloved* Aunt Louise.'[132]

The watershed year of 1835 certainly brought both pleasure and pain to Princess Victoria. She continued to study, but room was made in her strict schedule to allow for personal taste and the development of proper accomplishments for a young lady. Victoria teasingly responded to Feodore's letter outlining the accomplishments of her two eldest children, 'I am charmed to hear, that Charles makes such progress in writing, and that Eliza is such a clever arithmetician and reader. In work, she begins to resemble her worthy Aunt in England, who *never* works at all.'[133] In the spring before the Ramsgate journey, she enjoyed the many large parties, assemblies, and concerts her mother gave as backlighting to the star her heiress presumptive was becoming.[134] Victoria or Lehzen would clip newspaper accounts of the gatherings and the luminaries who attended and Victoria would insert them into her journal as a record of these notable evenings.[135] Victoria particularly enjoyed the musical events and her admiration for the opera singer

Luigi Lablache, shared by Emily Shore, was perfectly rewarded when she commenced Italian lessons as well as singing lessons taught by none other than Lablache himself.[136] Though the year was fraught with frequent disagreements with her mother, the Duchess of Kent's gift to her daughter of a private concert, featuring Giulia Grisi and other popular singers, reveals her understanding of her daughter's deepest interests. Victoria was in raptures: 'No one could be *more enchanted* than *I* was. I shall never forget it. It was Mamma's birthday present for me!'[137]

Though she did try to please the Princess – and certainly succeeded with the concert – during all of the trials and tribulations, successes and sorrows of 1835, Princess Victoria's education was at the centre of the mother's concerns for her daughter. Accordingly, the Duchess of Kent decided, around the time of her confirmation, that changes needed to be made in Victoria's course of study and that, of course, Parliament (and by extension, the King) would have to be notified of her intentions. In a key memo originally written by Sir John Conroy – scribbled is a more accurate description – to Viscount Melbourne, the Prime Minister, the Duchess/Conroy outlines the new direction that Victoria's education would take. The plan is at the same time both a more enlightened view of education for the heiress to the throne (she is prepared to be educated more like a prince than a princess) and a narrowing of opportunities. Victoria was to become further constricted through the necessity of observing the many proprieties that attend the creation of a personal household, which in this case meant the retitling of some of Victoria's current companions (Lehzen and the Duchess of Northumberland) and the concomitant diminishment of their duties – and the appointment of ladies to her person: 'And the Princess will for the future be waited on, as the other Princesses are by English Ladies, as I have described; so that Her Royal Highness will begin now to acquire those habits and conform to those customs, belonging to Her elevated station.'[138]

In the new plan for educating the Princess, the Duchess was supported by the Dean of Chester. In April 1835 he offered his view of some necessary alterations to the Princess's course of study. The obsequious flattery present in the notes makes one suspect that these ideas for a new system had probably already been discussed and that the Dean was merely giving the Duchess written confirmation of what she wanted to hear: 'In the present case, it is a great relief to consider, that the Princess has the singular advantage of being under the care of her own Mother, under whose direction, and in whose presence, the Princess receives her education, having, at the same time, the full benefit of her Royal Mother's counsel and example, as to the regulation of her conduct, manners, and disposition.'[39] The Dean chooses his words carefully in the memorandum and takes pains to avoid judgement. He notes the fact that to date the Princess's education had been broad rather than in-depth, which *might* give the illusion that 'no great proficiency could be made in *any* of [her subjects]', but that this was due to the natural factors of her busy and unique life. Davys praises the Princess for her 'peculiarly good sense, an excellent judgment and much modesty. . . .' Not wishing to offend, Davys proposes changes – generally enlarging the time period spent on a particular subject such as English literature or Latin – but then takes them back almost immediately – which makes his advice rather useless. For example, in Latin Davys notes that the time spent on this language has not been sufficient to allow the Princess to develop proficiency, yet 'it might scarcely be right to take a greater portion from *other* subjects to give to *this*'. The effect of this noncommittal note is that Victoria is to gain an extra lesson in geography, lose astronomy, suspend the Saturday oral examinations in favour of '*written monthly* questions ... on miscellaneous subjects, to which *written* answers are returned during the course of the month'. Davys gives the 'usual female accomplishments' their due, as well as healthful exercise and duties attendant upon being the next Queen of England. Advice in hand, and mind firmly made up, the Duchess/Conroy addresses the Prime Minister:

> ... If your Lordship will consider the point, to which I have now brought the Princess, by the course before alluded to and which are shewn in the supplementary papers, I also forward – you will find that in all those courses of study on which the Princess is to ground her powers of reasoning and action that she is quite prepared to enter on a course more fitting to the character of a Prince than a Princess. . . . This arrangement will allow the Princess to pass into womanhood, with every advantage to her mind which could rapidly expand under it and

allow Her also to acquire habits of confidence and independence, so essential to her future well doing.[140]

To enter 'her own responsible duties', as her mother concluded this letter, was Victoria's plan as well. No longer a child, her schooldays numbered, her majority looming in two short years, it was time now for Victoria to bloom; it was time for Victoria to fall in love with her people, her position, her power.

Every aspect of Victoria's life underwent a sea change in 1835 when her transformation into the young lady Collen's portrait represents was completed. This portrait is iconographically perfect in its depiction of the backward glance from the future to the past, from the queen she would become, to the girl she had been. Victoria's troubled present girded her well for the trials that would beset her as queen, and trained her in patience and stubbornness. Victoria knew that she was playing a waiting game that she could not fail to win.

Chapter Five

'The Fair White Rose of Perfect Womanhood'

1836–1837

To be NATIONAL is a great thing.

King Leopold I of Belgium[1]

The Rose of England

In the children's book *Victoria's Golden Reign: A Record of Sixty Years as Maid, Mother, and Ruler* (1899), written from the vantage point of sixty years of Victorian rule, A Lady of the Court argues that it was Victoria's sheltered girlhood that ensured her success as queen. And unlike Elizabeth I, that 'pathetic figure of the little motherless Tudor Princess', Victoria received the attentions of a doting mother rather than a 'tyrannical father'. Effective mothering, the book suggests, enabled 'the carefully nurtured bud' to blossom into 'the fair white rose of perfect womanhood'.[2] Over 160 years before Diana, Princess of Wales, was immortalized in song as 'England's rose', this rather more private royal was conceived and articulated as 'the rose of England'.[3] The image was generated by her years as a princess as she entered public life and it then gained political and cultural significance throughout her reign (Ill. 39). Though Princess Victoria rarely wrote about her clothing in specific terms, other accounts of her 'roseate' fashions and accessories survive. As a fifteen-year-old attending the races at Tunbridge Wells, Victoria was picturesque in her 'white muslin pelisse lined with primrose coloured silk; a white chip bonnet, ornamented with a

Victoria

39. Anon., Princess Victoria with autograph.

small bouquet of roses; a wreath of the same flowers encircling her forehead'.[4] In the iconography of Victoria from the 1830s she is often portrayed
holding a rose (as in the George Hayter portrait: see Ill. 29 or even becoming a rose (her face and bust emerging from the blooming flower) (Ill. 40).
This image of the Princess Victoria as 'the rose of England' and a 'flower of
English girlhood' was a significant aspect of the visualization campaign –

waged by the Duchess of Kent and Sir John Conroy as much as by the press – to bring the young princess to the attention of 'the people'. Although the image is a simple one, it packs a powerful ideological punch. This 'blooming' Victoria emphasized her maiden sweetness, purity, and beauty, but also asserted her *Englishness* and claimed for her reign a new Britain that would reflect her youth, innocence, and freshness. In this way, the corrupt and ill-reputed Georgian era would be effectively eclipsed. It was *girlhood*, finally, not martial strength, masculine wisdom, or paternal authority, that was embraced as England's national symbol. Unlike Elizabeth I, whose gender was troubling or even neuter (in her speeches to Parliament she most often referred to herself as a prince),[5] Victoria's femaleness and youth as she acceded to the throne constituted the essence of her sovereign power. As the art historian Susan P. Casteras concludes, 'In the final accumulation of hundreds, if not thousands, of images made of Victoria during her lifetime, it was the metaphor of the child that remained one of the most compelling, conveying as it did the tensions between innocence and experience, private and public, political and personal, that defined not only the persona of the Queen but also the nation she served.'[6] The image of the *young* Victoria, even when she was in old age, functioned also as a 'consumer artefact' for the British people to buy, barter, and exchange (for the actual, ageing, or aged, article), as the proliferation of celebrations of her childhood and young queenhood published in Jubilee years and after her death attest.

The 'national character' of this delightfully childish 'artefact' is perfectly represented in an anecdote of Victoria's childhood referenced in Chapter One. In describing Princess Victoria's 'British spirit', the author asserts that she 'expressed a repugnance to be taken abroad' until she was well acquainted with the country, people, manufacture, and culture of the British Isles, and that 'so far did the youthful heiress carry this patriotic preference, that, although perfectly acquainted with several European languages, and especially French and German, she could never be persuaded to converse in any of them as habit, always observing that "She was a little English girl, and would speak nothing but English."'[7] Although this popular anecdote is false and misleading, it assuaged a kind of general paranoia that Victoria was just another German princess masquerading as a British one, and loitering about the palaces and castles of Old England. In fact,

40. Anon., Queen Victoria as a blooming rose, lithographed by William Clark.

Victoria was able to read, write, and speak French quite well (she practised her French diligently by writing to her Aunt Louise), and although her facility with German was not as great (and with Italian least of all), she enjoyed speaking German with foreign visitors and relations and sprinkling Italian phrases throughout her journal.[8] And rather than expressing a 'repugnance' for travel, within her journal Victoria gave rather histrionic vent to her desires to visit the romantic settings of the novels she was enjoying: 'The descriptions of the country of Granada & of the Alhambra are so beautiful that they make me quite long, that I could see them myself, & wander through the deserted halls and courts of this still splendid pile, & gaze on the fretted architecture wrought with such care ...';[9] 'Oh! Could I once behold *bella Napoli*, with its sunny blue sky, and turquoise bay dotted with islands! That would indeed be delightful. But these are all vain thoughts, all air-castles! of *my ever* seeing Naples, or any part of Italy, *sono senza speranza*.'[10] Victoria's acceptance of the 'impossibility' of this kind of trip was another form of romantic indulgence. The adherence to duty and the repudiation that comes along with it was a means by which Victoria's life began to take on some of the characteristics of romance. After her yearning description of the Alhambra, Victoria takes herself firmly in hand and reminds herself that no one – not even the future Queen of England! – is ever perfectly happy with her life: 'I would give millions to behold but for a day, Brussells [*sic*], Paris, Germany, Italy & Spain & envy all those who do! Perhaps another who was compelled to travel would long to be bound as I am to my native soil! But enough of these reflections, & let me think of what I have and how thoughtful I ought to be for all God has given me.'[11]

God 'gives' Victoria the crown, and the power that this gift would confer was part of her sense of self and duty. For example, when Victoria learned of the death of her old drawing-master, Richard Westall, she lamented to her diary that he died too soon for her to be able to relieve his pecuniary needs: 'I was very much shocked & distressed to hear of his death ... I could now no more, as I had hoped, at a future time make him comfortable & render his old days cheerful & without those worldly cares which, combined with a weak constitution & fragile sickly frame have brought him to the grave.'[12] Victoria's dismay was not relieved when she discovered that Westall had arranged for a letter to be sent to the Duchess of Kent after his death asking for a £100 annuity to be given to his blind sister. Westall wanted the Duchess to know that he had died 'of a broken heart'.[13] As queen, she would have access to very significant amounts of money and could make judgements as to its use; as princess, her purse was light and her charitable efforts thus limited.

As I discuss in Chapter Two, key to Victoria's transformation from the 'little Mayflower', as her German grandmother called her after the month of her birth, to the more culturally significant 'rose of England' were the Royal Progresses throughout the countryside that began when Victoria was

41. Richard Lane, coloured drawing of Queen Victoria, June 1837.

thirteen and continued throughout her teenage years. Of course, the rose is England's national flower, and for the future sovereign to be associated with it made for pleasant, if obvious, patriotic propaganda. In the 'language of flowers' so popular in the nineteenth century, the simplest reading of the rose, according to Frederic Shoberl's *The Language of Flowers; With Illustrative Poetry* (1834), is as 'love' – appropriate in this case as the reciprocal love that exists between the Princess and 'the people'.[14] Richard Lane's rather sentimental 1837 drawing of the young princess features Victoria in profile wearing a crown of roses; this flower fashion translates into 'reward of virtue' (Ill. 41).[15] By the time of her majority, Victoria's image as the sweet-smelling summer flower was firmly inscribed in the popular imagination, as the following song composed by Cornwall Baron Wilson and sung as a serenade to the Princess on the morning of her eighteenth birthday attests:

> … More fragrantly breathing, the flowers we are wreathing,
>   Shall emblem thy virtues and garland thy worth.
>   Like a vision-wrapt sage,
>   Fancy pierces the gloom
>   Of Time's distant page
>   Which thy deeds shall illume!
> And though years may pass ere the tablet of Fame
> Shall be bright with the records that blazon thy name,
> Yet Britannia, prophetic, beholds the proud day
> When the sceptre of freedom Victoria shall sway –
> The vision is bright as her own natal day:
> Awake, Rose of England! and smile on our lay.[16]

In this rather dreadful quasi-pastoral verse, and in the emblem of the 'rose of England' generally, the Princess is invested with the power of the state not by way of the *majesty* or the *masculinity* of the office, but through nature (the flower/figure), feminine delicacy (the virgin wreathed in fragile blooms) and the perfect embodiment of the female Britannia, beloved symbol of the British Isles.

Uncle Leopold was just as cognizant as the Duchess of Kent of the importance of Victoria's acceptance as English by the English people (and by politicians). In his role as mentor (in which he was soon to become eclipsed by Victoria's first Prime Minister, and eventually, Prince Albert), Leopold urged Victoria in his immediately dispatched letter to her after becoming queen, to take responsibility for promoting her national character: 'I should advise [you] to say as often as possible that you are BORN in England. George the 3d *gloried* in this, and as *none* of your cousins are born in England it is your interest "de faire ressortir cela *fortement*".'[17] As a life-long politician himself, Leopold knew how important it was to have loyal employees and companions. He did not want Victoria's 'fair white' reputation to be sullied; even before the momentous change that took place with the King's death just after Victoria's eighteenth birthday, Leopold warned Victoria about the dangers of spies in her household and urged her to take charge of choosing the ladies who would be about her to avoid this possibility. (Victoria was listening carefully here, as the Bedchamber Affair early in her career as queen makes clear.)[18] But Victoria possessed lofty ideals and was not about to be drawn in – so she implied – by petty party quarrels. Feeling very superior and worldly, she wrote to Leopold in early 1837, 'They [the Tories and Whigs] irritate one another so uselessly by calling one another fools, blockheads, liars and so forth, for no purpose. I think violence so bad in everything.'[19]

This attitude of extreme disinterestedness and serenity does credit to the education in comportment provided by the Duchess of Kent (although Victoria would hardly maintain distance from party politics in the early years of her reign: the young queen was overwhelmingly partial to the Whigs). Victoria's education was the greatest concern of the Duchess of Kent's life; its success or failure would be the means by which she would be judged as the parent of the sovereign. As I have discussed elsewhere in this study, the nature of Victoria's education – a combination of the typical female education of general knowledge and 'accomplishments' (dancing, drawing, and singing) with more masculine pursuits such as Latin and English law – helped to determine the queen she would become: thoughtful and careful in political matters, yet thoroughly domestic. Nineteenth-century social standards required from any noblewoman a keen attention to proper feminine conduct above all else – even for one so uniquely situated. A tattered and seemingly well-read book of Victoria's from her girlhood, *The Young Lady's Book: A Manual of Elegant Recreations, Exercises, and Pursuits* (1829), echoes the entirely conventional thought that home is woman's 'empire'.[20] Regardless of the fact that Victoria would one day rule an empire, she was also required to demonstrate the virtues and skills of the domestic empress: 'piety, integrity, fortitude, charity, obedience, consideration, sincerity, prudence, activity, and cheerfulness'.[21] The manual is particularly addressed to the upper class; the 'lady' of the title is not an appellation of courtesy, but an indication of its class-identified audience. The manual argues that the well-born girl can expect to influence and benefit society far beyond the confines of her own home: 'Gently, imperceptibly, but most certainly, will she imbue with her purity and beneficence the atmosphere in which she moves; softening the obdurate, correcting the depraved, and encouraging the timid.'²² This devotion to charitable pursuits is considered a natural part of girlhood: 'The sweet exercise of this virtue seems so congenial to the nature of youth, that I would rather seek to regulate its impulses, than recommend it to an attention, I trust, already attained. A young lady, rich in the possession of friends and fortune, who is devoid of pity, incapable of the offices of humanity, or withholding the aid of charity, appears to me an anomaly in creation.'²³

The form in which 'charity begins at home' is through marriage. Young aristocratic ladies must make up their minds to be married, secure future generations and consolidate property. Future queens were no exception to this rule. And if the nation was prepared to consider Victoria as marriageable for the good of England, it appears that *she* was similarly ready to receive the attentions attendant upon reaching the age of sexual maturity.

Princess Victoria was not the only royal with love on her mind. Although certainly the Duchess of Kent did not want to marry off her younger daughter quite so expeditiously as she had her first daughter, 1836 was not too early to be casting about for matrimonial prospects, if not for love matches. Given the extreme restrictions on suitable marriage partners for monarchs, the pool of potential husbands was a small and select one. But first, Victoria had to be introduced to men – or boys – in general. In her retired lifestyle to date, she had had little opportunity to spend any significant amounts of time with the opposite sex (and when she did have these opportunities – generally with her mother's relations – she very quickly became highly interested in them). This was the case in 1832 when the Mensdorff-Pouilly princes, Hugo and Alphonso, visited, and especially so in 1833 as they received Alexander and Ernst Württemberg). Since her mother was still hostess and in charge of invitations relating to her daughter, the princes on parade through Kensington Palace in the spring of 1836 had a remarkably Germanic cast to them.

Cousins Augustus and Ferdinand (sons of Duke Ferdinand of Saxe-Coburg Kohary) helped to bring fun and frolic to Victoria's life. She mentions spending a lot of time laughing with them during their visit.²⁴ Nineteen-year-old Ferdinand was stopping off in England just prior to setting up house with his bride, young Queen Donna Maria da Gloria, the Queen of Portugal. The Duchess of Kent threw a number of large balls in their honour, and Victoria pasted a two-column newspaper clipping into her diary to commemorate one such occasion: 'Her Royal Highness the Duchess of Kent gave the first of a series of grand entertainments in honour of the arrival of Prince Ferdinand of Portugal, on Saturday evening at Kensington Palace. The invitations comprised the members of the Royal Family, the whole of the *corps diplomatique*, and most of the nobility and gentry in town. . . .'[25] In fact, Ferdinand and Augustus made such a favourable impression on Victoria that she felt she had to revise her opinion of her previous favourites, Alexander and Ernst (sons of the Duchess of Kent's sister, Antoinette). This more mature Victoria takes a dim view of the upbringing and hidden vices of the Württemberg cousins: 'Alas! The two Württembergs Alexander & Ernst who appeared very amiable when they were here, are FAR from *being* what they *appear* to *be*. They lead a *sad* & bad life. They received a shocking education, & had not a father like my Dearest Uncle Ferdinand.'[26] Victoria was pleased to learn that Augustus also kept a journal and 'writes in it every day as I do'.[27] The parties – one of them a costume ball – assemblies, and concerts continued, with Victoria staying up exceedingly late. After Ferdinand's departure for Portugal and then Augustus's later departure, Victoria wrote, 'I shall miss [Augustus] *so* much; he was such a quiet, good companion, nay almost like a play-fellow, if I may so say as we do *not* play.'[28] She is at pains to distinguish her relationship with her cousins from that of children playing together in a mixed group. Victoria was a young lady now and she appeared to enjoy this status enormously.

Other princes appeared, the next group at the invitation of Uncle William, the King, who was most annoyed at the procession of Coburg princes. The Prince of Orange and *his* two sons arrived from Holland hard on the heels of the Coburgs. Princes William and Alexander, as well as George Cambridge (another potential marriage partner for Victoria), were the very eligible young men at King William's ball held at St James's Palace on 13 May 1836. The Prince of Orange had had an earlier connection to the English crown as he had at one time been affianced to Princess Charlotte, before she, for a variety of reasons (one being her terror at leaving England for six months of the year), broke off the engagement. This event left Charlotte free for Leopold to pursue, and he was, of course, successful. But to marry Victoria to a son of the Prince of Orange would again be a means to 'repair' the past. Much to Leopold's satisfaction, Victoria was unimpressed. She wrote: 'The [sons of Orange] are both very plain and have a mixture of Kalmuck and Dutch in their faces, moreover they look heavy, dull and frightened and are not at all prepossessing. So much for the *Oranges*, dear Uncle.'[29]

The loss of her favoured visitors (Augustus, Ferdinand and their father, Victoria's Uncle Ferdinand) prompted Victoria to reflect upon the role of her diary as a confidante and as an appropriate venue for indulging her strong emotions: 'I write much of these dear relations, but when my heart is so full as it is, it is a consolation, & a pleasure for hereafter, to write down my feelings. I wish I could only say more, I cannot praise near enough those two VERY DEAR relations who have just left us & a 3d equally *dear*, who is sailing every day further & further away, from those he loves & who love him!'[30] Victoria's imagination was fired by the romantic – but rather terrifying to contemplate – first meeting between Ferdinand and the young Queen of Portugal (they had been married by proxy on the first of January).[31] Victoria's views on this royal relationship are fascinating, as she takes her cousin's part and confides to her journal that of course Ferdinand will be the ultimate authority both within his marriage and in ruling Portugal (though he, of course, is not Portuguese): 'In fact *Ferdinand* will *govern* though Dona Maria will have the *name* of doing all' (Ill. 42).[32] Victoria's position on this subject was informed by Leopold's three-part manual on king-making, a kind of 'ready and easy way' to become a good ruler. The manual, called *The Directions and Advices*, was highly interesting to Victoria, and she read from the section titled *Affaires politiques* (written in French) to Lehzen.[33]

Victoria would not entirely maintain this view of the consort's limited role once her own reign began and her liking for the job and her deep sense of duty to it overwhelmed her. But Princess Victoria had no real concern for this eventuality, or for the prince who would come to share her life (if not the crown) when cousins Albert and Ernest and their father, Ernest of Saxe-Coburg Gotha (brother to the Duchess of Kent), came to make her acquaintance and to help celebrate her seventeenth birthday.

42. Princess Victoria, drawing of 'Don Fernando', 1836.

At first, Albert, the younger cousin, appeared a very unprepossessing prince, indeed. Though very handsome ('his eyes are large and blue, and he has a beautiful nose and a very sweet mouth with fine teeth'),[34] he looked pallid, frail, and was prone to fits of fainting. At Victoria's birthday ball held at St James's, Victoria reports that Albert retired early after he 'turned as pale as ashes, & we all feared he might faint; he therefore went home'.[35] Still a 'prisoner of his room' the next day, Albert was rather disappointing to the generally vigorous and lively princess. Weintraub argues that 'to Victoria he seemed a child'.[36] On 30 May the Duchess hosted a large ball at Kensington, and here, for the first time, Victoria danced with Albert. The newspaper clipping preserved in the journal highlights the lateness of the hour when mother and daughter left the party (four o'clock) and the general 'brilliance' of the fête, 'marked by the variety of dancing introduced. It was concluded with the mazourka and an English Country dance, which the Princess Victoria led off, and which was danced with great spirit.'[37]

That Victoria had, at this point, an inkling of the matrimonial plots laid by her relatives is relatively clear: she, of course, did not mention any such thing in her journal, yet she did report three rather mysterious conversations with Albert's father, Uncle Ernest, held in her room: '*Uncle Ernest* came up & *talked* to me for a *few minutes!*'[38] Victoria's use of emphasis, exclamation, and circumspection suggests that he was discussing her future and perhaps Albert's place in it.[39] (Ernest, of course, as the elder son, would inherit his father's title and lands, and was therefore not a suitable match.) Victoria gloried in the attention she received from this uncle as she always had with Uncle Leopold. Leopold – never one to pull his punches – was a champion of Albert's cause, certainly, and some of his ire at the way that his nephews were treated by the press emerged not only from his belief in his own persecution by the English newspapers and the Royal Family, but also from his deep desire to see Albert succeed where he had 'failed' (to become consort to the Queen of England), and his need to confound the wishes of William IV. In a letter dismissing the Oranges and the King that is rather surprising for its immoderation and hyperbole, Leopold rants, 'Really and truly I never saw anything like it, and I hope it will *rouse your spirit*; now that slavery is even abolished in the British Colonies, I do not comprehend *why your lot alone should be kept, a white little slavey* in England, for the pleasure of the Court, who never bought you, as I am not aware of their having gone to any expense on that head, or the King's even having *spent a sixpence for your existence*.'[40] As Monica Charlot notes, Leopold's anger at the King is disproportionate to the 'crime' of slavery thus alleged: King William was inviting his relatives to visit *him*. The Prince of Orange's loathing of Leopold is perhaps more easily understood: '"Here is a man who has taken both my wife [Charlotte] and my Kingdom [Belgium]."'[41]

Various matrimonial prospects for the Princess linking her name with George Cumberland, the Duke of Orleans, the Duke of Nemours, one of the Württembergs, King Otho of Greece, and even her own Uncle Leopold, among others, had been bandied about in the press for years in publications such as *The Times*, *The Watchman*, *Morning Post*, *Morning Journal*, *Court Journal*, *Morning Herald*, and *Tait's Magazine*.[42] In the *Sunday Paper* on 6 April 1834 it was opined that '[Princess Victoria] is an English girl, brought up amongst us with an English heart, and English feelings – if she marries, let her call to her affections the descendant of that William of Nassau, upon whom England, in her time of peril, did not rely in vain.'[43] This praise of Victoria's Englishness would have warmed the Duchess of Kent's heart, to be sure, but any advocacy of the Oranges (including the King's, of course), was decidedly *not* to her liking any more than it was to Leopold's.

Certainly, the Duchess of Kent and her brother Leopold were united in their historic distrust of, and feelings of persecution by, the Royal Family. Glimpses of the Duchess of Kent's attitude to William can be seen in some of her letters to Victoria ('if the King was another man, – and if he *really* loved you …'),[44] but Leopold vents his anger in an unusually violent letter (a kind of sequel in tone to the one quoted above), written to Victoria near the end of 1836 in which he castigates not only the present, but also the previous king, for abdicating his financial and affective responsibilities towards Victoria and her mother. He also damns the entire free press:

I give the whole of my income without the reservation of a farthing to the Country, I preserve unity on the Continent [,] have frequently prevented mischief at Paris, and to thank me for all that I get the most scurrilous abuse, in which the good people from *constant practice so much excel*. It cannot be helped that you are my niece, it can now no longer be helped that I did a great deal for my own sister and the dear little daughter, when the King and Country did not think it fit to give you *both a six-pence more* than the pittance of the Royal widow … I said to Lord Liverpool I shall be most happy to do it [support Princess Victoria], but remember that it was not I who grasped at the management of the Princess, but the Princess is by the King in this manner confided to me, and H. Maj. thereby delegates to me a power which belongs to him. . . .

If all the editors of the papers in the countries where the liberty of the press exists were to be assembled we should have a *crew* to which you would *not* confide a dog that you would value, still less your honour and reputation.[45]

This letter must have been very painful for Victoria to read: it makes her role as royal pawn excruciatingly obvious.

Yet, ever mindful of Victoria's place within the Royal Family, whatever her treatment by it (and certainly the reserve and distrust of the Duchess of Kent by the King and company did not spill over to her daughter), the Duchess had decided that the rooms allotted to them in Kensington Palace were entirely unsuitable and required drastic alterations. These renovations were completed without the King's permission while they stayed in Ramsgate in late 1835 and early 1836. Once home again, Victoria went to view her new rooms: 'We instantly went upstairs, that is to say, up *two* stair-cases, to our new sleeping and sitting apartments which are very lofty and handsome. . . . Our bedroom is very large and lofty, and is very nicely fur-nished, then comes a little room for the maid, and a dressing-room for Mamma; then come the old gallery which is partitioned into 3 large, lofty, fine and cheerful rooms. Only one of these (the one near Mamma's dress-ing-room) is ready furnished; it is my sitting-room and is *very* prettily fur-nished indeed.'[46] Victoria was delighted with her new living situation; the King was furious. The Kents were merely guests, after all, and this propri-etary act towards his property constituted a serious breach of respect. The Duchess had plans for her daughter's 'coming out', however, and felt that they had cowered at Kensington long enough. There were grand entertain-ments and balls to put on, and princes were coming to look over Victoria. For the Duchess of Kent, proper preparations for these events and for the eventual accession – the King was now seventy years old – and a possible Regency, naturally included an improvement in their living arrangements in Kensington Palace.

Things went from bad to worse in the relations between sister- and brother-in-law, as the ill-will between the parties became public. The King's seventy-first birthday was celebrated on 21 August 1836 with a grand dinner to which the Kents, of course, were invited. The celebration quickly turned to mortification for both mother and daughter, however, as in front of a hundred people, King William blasted the Duchess for her handling of Victoria's affairs and for exercising poor judgement in choosing advisers. In this speech the King declared,

'I trust in God that my life may be spared for nine months longer, after which period, in the event of my death no regency would take place. I should then have the satisfaction of leaving the royal authority to the personal exercise of that young lady (pointing to the Princess), the heiress presumptive of the Crown, and not in the hands of a person now near me, who is surrounded by evil advisers and who is herself incompetent to act with propriety in the station in which she would be placed. I have no hesitation in saying that I have been insulted – grossly and continually insulted – by that person, but I am determined to endure no longer a course of behaviour so disrespectful to me. . . .'[47]

He went on to command that the Princess Victoria no longer be kept from court and his presence. The gathered company was shocked and horrified; Victoria reportedly burst into tears. Lady Elizabeth Belgrave, who was present, played down the scene in a letter to her mother, writing, 'The Duchess of Kent with Princess Victoria went to Windsor for the King's birthday, … when the King with singular tact took the occasion to tell Princess Victoria at dinner that she was now *quite independent* and under *nobody's control*, which I daresay was tempting to do but must have put the Duchess of Kent in a great rage!'[48] The stress of these continued battles between her mother and the King, Leopold and the King, her mother and herself, Conroy and herself, was intense. In the journal entry for this day, Victoria pens a wish that the King will live many more years, and she remarks, simply, 'At ½ past 7 we *dined*.'[49] Indeed.

King William realized the importance of a girl having her own money and rectified Victoria's relative poverty by sending her a letter a few days before her eighteenth birthday indicating his intention to award her £10,000 in her own name as soon as she was to come of age. This act was highly insulting to the Duchess of Kent, and she forced Victoria to copy out a response to the King (first written by Conroy) in which she acknowledged the money with thanks, but asked, in deference to her youth and inexperience, that it be given to her mother to control instead. The King, after receiving this reply, stated that Victoria had not written it and later wrote to Lord Melbourne stating this. For her part, the Duchess's version of these events was that she and Victoria 'decline[d] the offer made to us' (also written to Melbourne).[50] These struggles further underscored the futility of the Duchess's plans to continue to control Victoria. Time would pass, and soon the King would be dead, making Victoria independent from all interested parties.

Nothing could stop these machinations swirling all around her. But at times Victoria was able to stop worrying about the future and enjoy the here and now. For her part, in the ratings scale of German cousins and itinerant princes, Ernest and Albert come out as clear winners (though it is true that the most recent visitors always receive higher marks than earlier ones): 'My dear Cousins & I were so familiar and *intimate* together, & they were so kind & affectionate to me. Though I wrote more when Uncle Ferdinand, and Augustus went, in my journal about all that, I feel this separation more deeply, though I do not lament, so much as I did then, which came from my nerves not being strong then. I can bear more now. I shall always love dear Ferdinand & dear Augustus very much, but dear Ernest & dear Albert I greatly prefer to the latter (Augustus), they are so much more sensible & grown up, and are so delightful to be with, & to talk to.'[51] It appears that there was less laughing together with the Saxe-Coburgs, but perhaps more serious and improving conversation. Albert was shy, loved painting and literature, and quiet evenings. Though the Duchess of Kent had arranged numerous grand balls with literally hundreds of guests in attendance, Albert wilted under the attention and preferred domestic pursuits to those of the beau monde. The bouncy and healthy Victoria (she had been examined by Dr Clark nearly every day for the entire spring and summer), by contrast, enjoyed every bit of these fashionable gatherings and the dancing, beautiful dresses, long hours, and solicitous guests. In March she had even dismissed with a sniff – 'one of those tiresome Vocal Concerts'[52] – the kind of staid cultural event that had in the past constituted one of her chief

(facing page) 43. Princess Victoria's velvet dress, 1835–37.

pleasures. Victoria was meeting all manner of men, men who would come and go. She was quite taken by three Persian princes who were seeking asylum in England and who had been patronized by the nobility. Victoria wrote a long disquisition in her journal about the history and costume of these men, and her favourable impressions of their royal, soldierly, and handsome bearing. Rather coyly, she then related a bit of delicious flattery too good not to immortalize for later re-reading: 'I must say one thing, which Sir Gore Ouseley [the interpreter] told the Duchess of Northumberland, and which *I* ought not, properly speaking, to mention. They were asked by Sir Gore what struck them most, or what had made the most impression on them in England. The reply was: Windsor Castle, and me.'[53]

Certainly, the heir to the British crown would be worth a second glance, especially as she was so young, tiny, and pleasant-looking. Although the image of fat, severe, matronly Victoria is perhaps the most readily available today, as a girl she was slender and even fashionable, as her surviving clothes from the period attest (Ill. 43). As a long-standing consequence of her illness at Ramsgate, Victoria ate very little at midday, and was pleased with the result: 'As I find my self so much better without [luncheon], I mean to take none for some time to come; I only take a little bread & butter.'[54] So, Victoria was the belle of all the balls: she was old enough to dance with men (as opposed to boys); she was old enough to flirt; old enough to 'know better'. Scandals and intrigues that would have been kept from her as a child are now known and mentioned in the journal or even discussed a little. In February 1836, Victoria notes a change in the household 'Lehzen has a new maid, Charlotte Colson. Anne Mason [Lehzen's previous maid)] had behaved most scandalously & deceitfully and is sent away.'[55] She writes to Feodore about the pregnancies of their relations, whereas when a younger child she would only record the news of a birth.[56] Her brother, Charles Leiningen, provided the means for some juicy gossip between the sisters that Victoria enjoyed recounting: 'A propos about Prince Moscaw do you know, what happened to Charles relative to him? I'll tell you, only don't betray me, and don't say, who told you. Charles dined last winter at Munich, with a large party at Count Pappenheim's (whose wife you know walked off with Prince Pückler) and Charles not knowing this, asked Count Pappenheim if he knew Prince Pückler; the whole party, of course laughed, and the Count stared and those perceiving Charles's unfeigned surprise answered "don't you know, he rid me of my wife?" I think this is too good.'[57]

Victoria's life was not all balls and gaiety, singing lessons and gossip, however. The education of a 'prince' that the Duchess of Kent had suggested as appropriate for Victoria was put into practice in a modest way through an enlarged study of Blackstone's *Commentaries on the Laws of England*. Although Victoria would be advised in all matters by her ministers, she could not afford to be ignorant of the fundamentals of British law. Now no longer reading extracts deemed suitable for her as she had when she was younger, but the complete four-volume work, Victoria noted about the *Commentaries* in February 1836 that 'they are very interesting & of great importance for me'.[58] In 1836 Victoria was also reading *Eikon Basilike* (purported to be the thoughts of Charles I before his beheading in 1649)and Milton's great epic *Paradise Lost* (1667 and 1674).[59] Interestingly, Victoria was thus reading both sides of the revolutionary debate: a defence of Charles I, and the work of the greatest apologist for the Civil Wars, John Milton. Leopold chimed in, of course, to tell Victoria via letter, 'It is so very praiseworthy to have much good intuition about your improvements, a great rule should be to learn *every day something useful.*'[60]

This sage advice came to Victoria after a brief visit from Uncle Leopold in mid-September 1836. The two were closer than ever after this meeting at Claremont, always identified with Leopold in Victoria's mind as it was his English estate and the setting for her happiest childhood days. Victoria seems to have become much more her uncle's niece than her mother's daughter. After private discussions where Uncle Leopold 'talked to [Victoria] about *many important things*',[61] Victoria was once again devastated by the leave-taking of a beloved relation she described in the warmest possible terms: 'It is this firm hope [of another visit from Leopold and Louise the following year] that holds me up in the sad sad, nay terrible, separation from my dearest Uncle, my *father & Protector.* . . . It is dreadful in this life that no happiness comes unsullied with grief, & that one is almost always separated from those one loves dearly, & is encumbered with those one dislikes.'[62] In reflecting on a 'beautiful' sermon which, as she describes it, was seemingly about death and 'the futility of this world' (although the text was actually about the sin of fornication), Victoria is reminded of the general sinfulness of everyone she knows – except for two. 'I know but two human beings whom I can call perfect & they are indeed so; my *inestimable* Lehzen, & my dearest Aunt Louise.'[63] Clearly, mamma (still closely allied with Conroy) couldn't compete with these distant parent figures (in the case of Leopold and Louise) or with the ever-beloved Lehzen. The relative positions of these players would be frozen thus until 'the Rose and Expectancy of the fair State'[64] became queen and the attentive, witty, and distinguished Melbourne would eclipse them all.

Girl No Longer

Victoria's journal is so much a part of her teenage years that its demise at the end of 1836 marks, in a way, the end of her girlhood. The thirteenth manuscript journal is a sad affair, and contains only ten entries before other hands ripped out subsequent pages and ultimately destroyed them. In the year 1837 Victoria became Queen, and although six months of that year were to elapse before this event occurred, Victoria's daughter Princess Beatrice may have believed that Victoria's girlhood concluded with the beginning of 1837, and that therefore Victoria's writing from that time should be protected. In preparing his *Girlhood of Queen Victoria* (2 vols, 1912), Viscount Esher made a transcript of the first fifteen manuscript journals, taking Victoria up to her marriage in 1840.[65] Beatrice did not finish her task of editing all of her mother's journals until nearly a hundred years after this marriage took place. A black-bordered page of note paper containing a brief note by Princess Beatrice to Lord Wigram has been preserved in the thirteenth journal after the entry for 31 December 1836. The note, dated 1940, merely states that Beatrice was sending a half-volume of the diary that had been left in Kensington Palace and not forwarded with 'my finished books on to Lord Wigram'.[66]

Victoria's journals can be accessed through Viscount Esher's transcript, though this typed attempt is at one remove from the original and necessarily introduces errors and flattens the 'unwritten' clues of the manuscript (crossed-out words, additions, blank spaces, handwriting style, etc.). His published selections, of course, do further 'damage' to the record of Victoria's youth, as so much detail is left out.

One obsession of Victoria's thirteenth journal that can only be fully experienced in the original, was her relationship to the poor. In August 1836, Victoria had visited an asylum for vagrant girls and in the spring attended with Albert an event at St Paul's Cathedral celebrating the anniversary of the London Charity Schools.[67] In the last months of 1836 and into 1837, the issue of charity came to occupy Victoria's mind to a greater extent than ever before, in the form of a family of gypsies camped near Claremont where the Kents were spending the winter months. Victoria's devoted patronage of the gypsies also reveals a heightened awareness of her responsibilities to 'her people', of class divisions, of a wider world. She wrote to Feodore, 'I wish, we could go out together, doing good to the poor, and to the poor forlorn gipsies. I should delight in doing so.'[68]

The story of the large Cooper family takes over Victoria's journal — as *The Bravo* had done earlier in her reading journal — her letters (particularly to Feodore), and her leisure reading (she becomes absorbed in James Crabb's *The Gipsies' Advocate*). At first, the gypsy family is merely called '*so picturesc!*' [*sic*][69] by Victoria, and they seem to be no more then curiosities for her even after she has made their acquaintance: 'We saw our gypsy friends peeping out of their frail abode of canvass. They certainly are a "Hard-faring race"' (Ill. 44).[70] She relies upon her painter's eye and her love of romance to help describe the group for the first time:

As we were walking along the road near to the tents, the woman who said she was called Cooper, who is generally the spokeswoman of the party, stepped across the road from the tents, & as we turned & stopped, came up to us with a whole swarm of children, six I think. It was a singular, & yet a pretty & picturesc sight. She herself with nothing on her head, her raven hair hanging untidily about her fine countenance, & a dingy dark green cloak hung on the side of her shoulders, while the set of little *brats* swarming round her, with dark dishevelled hair & dark dresses, all little things and all beautiful children. ... The gipsies are a curious, peculiar & very hardy race, unlike any other!'[71]

44. Princess Victoria, watercolour of gypsy woman and children, 1836.

Princess Victoria's representation of the impoverished gypsy family, seen in her sketches of them, Richard L. Stein suggests, fixes these individuals into set poses that fulfil her expectations about them – as picturesque, as a group identified only by race, as *characters* to be captured by her brush: '[Princess Victoria] has learned her lessons [from Richard Westall, her drawing master] well, and uses her sketches to impose stylized aesthetic form on a reality far different from the world she knows. . . . Her sketching is a way of confirming what she felt she had discovered, a way of turning mere experience into "Art".'[72] In her journal, however, Princess Victoria reveals that although the gypsies function symbolically for her – as worthy, downtrodden subjects — she has also been indelibly touched by them, so that 'Art' turns back into experience and a reminder of her own future power: 'I quite forgot to mention that when on Sunday I walked for the last time on my favourite nice Portsmouth road, that I still beheld the litter of straw which was the only vestige of our poor good Gipsy friends who will *never never* be forgotten. Aunt Sarah, Eliza Cooper, old Mary Cooper, the poor dear little baby, the host of children, and the two other sisters-in-law, are quite present in my mind; I can see and hear them!'[73]

Before the gypsies decamp, as Victoria mentions, a baby is born, and the gypsies' unconcealed pride in this event is displayed to their patrons. Within the paternalistic framework in which she places these needy people (it was wintertime), Victoria finds this pride entertaining: 'I was quite amused by the manner of importance with which [the birth] was announced. I must say they seem very kind to one another …. It is remarkable how well bred & not forward this woman is & what a well-bred manner of speaking she has, with a peculiar accent.'[74] As Victoria finds more evidence of the familiarity of the gypsies, their ability to reflect, even in a limited way (through speech, manners, family relations, children's names — Britannia, Nelson, Francis), Victoria's own life, she takes a greater interest in their fate, and accepts them as objects of pity. She finds the cleanliness of the new baby highly remarkable: '… the neatness & cleanliness of the poor little *boy's* dress, it is quite as clean & neat as you would wish *any* child or infant to be'.[75] With the help of *The Gipsies' Advocate*, and her own experience with the 'model' English gypsies at Claremont, Victoria becomes quite an 'expert' on the supposed virtues and foibles of this 'race' of people: 'They have originally *no* religion, but many have been reformed by kind clergymen & other people. There are societies formed for reforming them. Their conjugal, filial, & paternal affection is *very great*, as also their kindness & attention to their sick, old or infirm. Their morals too are almost always very pure, with an exception of an addiction to petty thefts & fortune-telling.'[76] All was as it should be within this 'natural' relationship between the benevolent (among them, Victoria, Lehzen, and the Duchess of Kent) and the objects of their favour, as Crabb's *The Gipsies' Advocate* encourages. Crabb admonishes the reader by reminding him/her that 'England will have a great deal to answer for in reference to the Gipsies of past generations. For, from a very moderate calculation that [the author] has made, 150,000 of these outcasts must have passed into the eternal world, uninformed, unacquainted with God, since they came to this country. May the present and succeeding generations be wiser than the past!'[77] Stein considers Crabb's book as a screen through which the Princess can see, but remain separate from the gypsies: 'Crabbe [sic] provides [Princess Victoria] with a language that is at once sympathetic and detached; the stress on typical virtues allows Victoria to avoid inquiring too closely into particular conditions, or particular lives.'[78]

In her consideration for the gypsies, Victoria received the satisfaction of fulfilling her duty as a lady and a Christian (as *The Young Lady's Book* outlines), and the gypsies responded appropriately with gratitude and gifts of their own. They offered the ladies the opportunity to rename the baby anything they chose before his christening. The ladies refused this honour, but Victoria was dissatisfied with that decision. She confided to the journal that if she had been '*my own mistress*' she would have named the child Leopold in honour of her uncle on whose birthday the child had been born.[79]

In her letters to Feodore, Victoria defends 'her' Claremont neighbours against the stereotype of gypsies as a heathen, dirty, and dishonest people. She writes, 'They are very much better, than the Gipsies abroad and *much* more civilised; they are Christian here; they are often married at Church, and have their children christened there of which I had a proof, for the old grand-mother told us, the last day, we saw her, that she was going to take the baby to church, for that purpose. . . . I trust, the day will come, when I may be able to do them some *real good*, as many kind ladies have already done.'[80] Victoria reinvents the gypsy outcasts as an English underclass, unrelated, finally, to those others of the race who are not Christian.

Victoria, by her charity to the Cooper family, spreads the word about the plight of the English gypsies. To this end, she sends Feodore a copy of *The Gipsies' Advocate* and informs her of other charities organized in England to help them: 'I got the other day, a very interesting letter from a lady, in Gloucestershire, who, though poor, has herself formed an establishment for poor gipsies' children and which succeeds admirably.'[81] In the journal Victoria has her future power in mind when she writes, '. . . I wish I cld do something to render them comfortable & even to have their children properly instructed.'[82] It is a source of pride to Victoria that her gypsies are grateful and modest; these attitudes attest to their 'desert' of her pity and patronage. Victoria understands some of this behaviour to be racial in character; that is, the Claremont gypsies are 'so quiet, so affectionate to one another, so discreet, not at all forward, or importunate, & *so* grateful; so unlike the gossiping, fortune-telling race-gipsies'.[83] Victoria divests the Claremont gypsies of negative 'racial' characteristics in an effort to reinvent them as insiders and contain them within the boundaries of 'correct' and 'white' English values and manners.[84] The Claremont gypsies became Victoria's first 'subjects', and she indulged herself by imagining what additional good she could do – naming the baby, educating the children – if she were already queen. To be queen seemed pleasant indeed, if it meant giving more assistance to deserving English paupers.

As this picture of Victoria's girlhood has shown, Victoria led a sheltered existence for her entire youth. But some of this control began to crack in 1836 and a wider world became visible to the Princess. She began to read the newspapers regularly and to build up a sustained relationship with some outcasts of English society; she admired the railroad for the first time ('We went to see the Rail road, near Hersham, and saw the steam carriage pass with surprising and startling quickness, striking sparks as it flew along the rail road, enveloped in clouds of smoke and making a loud noise').[85] Victoria viewed herself as 'a terribly modern person'[86] with enlightened ideals (the gypsies are one example of this open-mindedness; her belief that she was above the petty quarrels of the Whigs and Tories is another). Once back in town for the spring, her rapt attention at the Opera (and her long-lived appreciation of the theatre in general) and love of romance show Victoria to be a student of the human passions. Having survived her fifteenth year, Victoria enjoyed 1836 and her long stay at Claremont, her many audiences with the King and Queen, the balls and entertainments, the princes, and the overwhelming fact of her extreme desirability. On her eighteenth birthday she was fêted and petted and celebrated both in royal circles and in the wider world. Sounding like a queen already, Princess Victoria wrote to Feodore about her birthday, 'The demonstration of love, and affection, shown to me, by all classes on that day, was most striking, and gratifying.'[87]

Though there were still tempests to be endured – most notably her Uncle King's outburst at the Duchess of Kent at his birthday party – the crown, and independence were within Victoria's sight. In her letters of 1837 it is readily apparent that Victoria was biding her time until she became queen. She was calm, grateful for the attentions shown her, self-confident, and patient. She wrote to Leopold that the Duchess of Kent would remain her spokesperson, as she could not compose answers to formal addresses 'for the present'.[88] Soon, however, the mute princess would be transformed into a being whose words would magically become commands. Some of this nascent authority can be read in a letter that Princess Victoria wrote to the Duchess of Northumberland in response to birthday greetings. The letter bears an exceedingly light touch, but firm dismissal, and a sense of tying up loose ends, show through the kind sentiments. Victoria seems to be saying that the Duchess of Northumberland is no longer wanted, perhaps had *never* been wanted (by Victoria) and that the Duchess might even have saved herself the trouble of pressing herself upon Victoria during her schoolgirl days: 'Allow me to assure you, how much I prize all the kind expressions of attachment contained in it; and I hope, you will believe that, though you have given up, the situation as my governess, I shall ever entertain the same regard and esteem, I had for you, when you were with me. You are likewise I hope aware my dear Duchess, that I shall always retain a grateful sense of your attendance, which you performed so punctually, even, I fear, often at your own personal inconvenience.'[89] So much for the Duchess of Northumberland.

As the King's terminal illness advanced, Victoria is sombre, but eager, girl no longer. Her lessons continued to the very last; until, when the King was clearly dying, they were stopped for ever.[90] In the final letter to Leopold written while still a princess, it is a very self-assured woman who calls the King, 'Poor old man'. She goes on to write, 'I feel sorry for him, he was always personally kind to me, and I should be ungrateful and devoid of feeling, if I did not remember this.' This is the voice of the child-author who wrote stories of 'girl power' – not the silent rose – here freshly imbued with a confidence hitherto generally concealed within the forms of girlishness. And yet, later in the letter she refers to the meaning of the King's death *for her* in an oblique and modest manner: 'I look forward to the event, which it seems, is likely to occur soon, with calmness and quietness; I am not alarmed at it, and yet, I do not suppose myself equal to all; I trust however, that with *good will*, honesty and courage, I shall not, at all *events fail.*'[91]

Victoria's careful selection of qualities necessary for her success as queen – 'good will', 'honesty', and 'courage' – reflected more than her unassuming and simple nature. In fact, Victoria *returns* herself to the qualities of her girlhood reading and creative writing as she readies herself to become queen. As such, her treatment of the gypsy family and these final thoughts as a princess mark a natural end to this study of Victoria's own words about her early years.

Those who would dismiss didactic children's literature as narrow, boring, and preachy might be interested to learn that as preparation for becoming queen in her final days as a princess, Victoria obsessively read the tales found in her old copy of Edgeworth's *The Parent's Assistant*. As queen, Victoria would eventually fill the role of mother of an empire, but in 1837 she was busy reviewing what it meant to be a good daughter of England. From 4 until 28 March 1837, Victoria reacquainted herself with these old favourites.[92] In referring to the tale 'Simple Susan', considered one of Edgeworth's best,[93] Victoria writes, 'Read in "Simple Susan," which certainly is the most touching pretty story imaginable, and though the Parent's Assistant has been read often by me when a child, I find it far more interesting than many a novel.'[94] In her stories of industrious, honest, and generous lower-class children, Maria Edgeworth constructs a moral world of consequences and justice where the qualities of industry, honesty, and generosity never fail to be rewarded with benefits such as forgiveness, household necessaries, a home to live in, the means to make money. In 'The Basket-Woman', for example, the desperately poor orphans Paul and Anne are scrupulously truthful and sincere in their dealing with all classes of people, and when they return a guinea that was mistakenly given to them for a small service rendered – after being cheated out of it by a cunning servant – this is recognized as an act of heroism. Their reward for their honesty and plain dealing is the receipt of their hearts' desire – a blanket for their adoptive grandmother who suffers from rheumatism – and, significantly, training in the trade of basket-making. Perfidy never goes unpunished in these tales: the dishonest servant loses his position. Edgeworth also outlines the proper response of the poor to the attentions of the rich: in

'The Orphans', the benefactors Isabella and Caroline often gave clothing or materials for sewing and knitting to the orphaned children, however, 'these children did not *expect*, that, because the ladies did something for them, they should do everything: they did not grow idle or wasteful.'[95] Industry, especially for the lower classes, must never be found wanting.

The stories that feature gentlemen's children are similarly concerned with honesty, but these children also practise charity and frugality for, 'It is not only by their superior riches, but it is yet more by their superior knowledge, that persons in the higher ranks of life may assist those in a lower condition.'[96] Upper-class children must be educated to a higher level of thinking than the stark right/wrong available to their less fortunate counterparts. Frivolous and fashionable people come under attack for mean-spiritedness, while the virtuous and good-natured are shown to be both reasonable and happy, and are rewarded for their good conduct. In 'Forgive and Forget', the prejudice 'of a true-born Englishman' against his neighbour, a Scotsman, is exposed as petty, and tolerance is thus advocated: 'It would be well for all the world, if they could be convinced, like Arthur, that to live in friendship is better than to quarrel; it would be well for all the world, if they followed Maurice's maxim of "Forgive and forget," when they receive, or when they imagine that they receive, an injury.'[97] In 'The Mimic', young Frederick learns what it is to be a gentleman – and a man. Publicly confessing his cruelty – against the opposition thrown up by the fashionable and self-serving Mrs Theresa Tattle – Frederick apologizes to the gentle Quaker, Mr Eden, for duping and ridiculing him below stairs. All is forgiven, and although the mishaps also create the opportunity for a thief to steal some of their property, Frederick's parents are grateful for the lesson their son has learned: '"I think the loss of a suit of clothes, and even the disgrace that my son has been brought to this evening, fortunate circumstances in his education."'[98]

Why did Victoria choose Edgeworth's children's tales for her leisure reading during this exciting time in her life? As Mitzi Myers argues, '[Edgeworth's stories] give child readers – boys and girls alike – confidence in themselves and in their abilities to solve problems and to achieve a more satisfying material, intellectual, and emotional life. The characters can think as well as feel, work as well as play.'[99] In re-reading *The Parent's*

45. Henry Tanworth Wells, *Victoria Receiving News of Her Accession*, 1880.

Assistant, Victoria returned to the clear-eyed stories of the past, to girl and boy heroes, to conduct becoming and moral absolutism. Would that being queen was as simple and satisfying as an Edgeworth tale! And yet, for the eighteen-year-old princess, perhaps it was. In Victoria's relationship with the gypsies she is the patron, indeed, a 'father' figure; in reading Edgeworth she is figured as a daughter whose good early training will enable her to make the right choices. In iconography of the moment of her awareness of her change in station, when the inevitable happened on the morning of 20 June and Victoria awoke no longer a princess but a queen, she is most often figured as a 'daughter', a girl in a nightgown (in the dress of repose, helplessness, even infancy: Ill. 45). As Susan P. Casteras argues, 'It was precisely the innocence of childhood that became an essential design in the fabric of mythology produced about the Queen, both in early portraits of her before her accession and in ones towards the close of her long reign.'[100] But this ideological position is imbued with the *frisson* of irony and contradiction. She might have been wearing the garb of inconsequence, but with the King's last breath, Victoria was invested with the power of the constitutional monarchy, its traditions, ceremonies, and majesty.

In her first journal entry as the new sovereign, Victoria described the event thus: 'I was awoke at 6 o'clock by Mamma who told me that the Archbishop of Canterbury and Lord Conyngham were here and wished to see me. I got out of bed and went into my sitting room (only in my dressing gown) and *alone*, and saw them. Lord Conyngham (the Lord Chamberlain) then acquainted me that my poor Uncle, the King, was no more, and had expired at 12 minutes past 2 this morning and consequently that *I* am *Queen*.'[101] Was there ever a greater dramatic moment?'[102]

Much has been written about the young Queen Victoria and the beginning of her reign, including Richard L. Stein's fascinating *Victoria's Year: English Literature and Culture, 1837–1838*, which offers a detailed look at the 'spirit of the age' of Victoria's first year as queen, and Monica Charlot's excellent biography, *Victoria: The Young Queen*. Victoria was free of her mother's interference; she could be *alone*. The fact of her independence comes up over and over again in the journal in the first days after her accession. The novelty of being her own mistress, of meeting ministers and other important men by herself was too great not to warrant repetition.

Lord Melbourne, her Prime Minister, was all the admirer/parent figure/leader she now needed, and the Duchess of Kent lost any influence she may have had over her daughter. A three-day-old queen, Victoria wrote to Uncle Leopold, 'My poor Mother views Lord Melbourne with great jealousy. ....;'[103] and to Feodore, from her new home in Buckingham Palace, she wrote simply, 'I like this life very much.'[104]

Queen Victoria's pleasure aside, however, her accession represented an enormous change for England. In her book *Queen Victoria: Gender and Power*, Dorothy Thompson cites an anonymous pamphleteer who cautioned the new queen that as she was so young, inexperienced, and female, and that the monarchy was under some stress, her reign would be an experiment for the country: '"A new and rude trial of its strength in your person."' And yet, Thompson argues, 'In retrospect both [Queen Victoria's] youth and her sex can be seen as having been great advantages. By contrast with her predecessors and her immediate successor she appeared less threatening and more malleable to politicians, less vicious and more decorative to the wider public.'[105] In her first year she exclaimed to her journal after reviewing the troops: 'The whole went off beautifully; and I felt for the first time like a man, as if I could fight myself at the head of my Troops.'[106] The young Queen was in her glory: playing the part of the martial sovereign with gusto. It hadn't been a year since King Leopold had reminded Victoria that 'high personages are a little like stage actors – they must always make efforts to please their public'.[107]

With the transformation of Princess Victoria into Queen Victoria the First, this book comes to an end. But Victoria's girlhood – any woman's girlhood – cannot be overlooked or separated from the adult she becomes. It is not difficult to discern the girl princess in the young queen. One brief example from among many to be found in Princess Victoria's own words will suffice here: in an early letter to Leopold, written when she was thirteen years old, the pair write back and forth playfully about various subjects, one of them being Leopold's dog, Dächsi, who is personified by Leopold as a great thinker but an imperfect linguist (see Chapter Two). Victoria had ever kept her correspondents abreast of the news surrounding her own beloved pets. Dash, perhaps her favourite dog of the many she owned over the years, was one of the newly crowned queen's first concerns.

On Coronation Day, at the end of all the festivities, Victoria changed out of her robes of state and gave her dog a bath.[108] And even the day before she became queen, when her thoughts might well have been overwhelmed by this interesting event, Victoria sends a few words to Leopold about the death of 'good old faithful Dächsi' who was a 'pleasant souvenir' of 'bella Napoli'.[109]

The girlish image of the 'fair white rose of perfect womanhood' persisted throughout Victoria's reign. As I suggested earlier, for the authors of biographies of Victoria written for children, descriptions of Victoria's girlhood serve a didactic function: to encourage child readers to aspire to her goodness and to emulate her devotion to duty. The popular children's novelist E. Nesbit's attempt in this genre, *Royal Children of English History* (1897), is no exception. Her rosy princess is conventionally sketched: 'In a pleasant palace, surrounded by beautiful gardens, a little girl was brought up by her loving mother. Her teachers instructed her in music and languages, in history and all the things that children learn at school. Her mother taught her goodness and her duty. There she grew up fresh and innocent as the flowers in her own garden, living a secluded life, like a princess in an enchanted palace' (Ill. 46).[110] The reality of Victoria's childhood, as I and her many biographers have shown, was quite different from the sweet portraits offered in children's fare of the late nineteenth century.

My particular purpose in this study of Queen Victoria's girlhood has been to draw upon the rich storehouse of material related to these early years that has been carefully preserved in the Royal Archives. The copybooks, Behaviour Books, 'mundane' elements of the manuscript journals, and stories, have lain, for the most part, quietly undisturbed for over 150 years. And yet, rarely have a childhood and young adulthood been so well documented. The importance of Victoria's girlhood reading to her self-creation has also deserved greater attention than it has hitherto received. Aided and abetted by her reading in 'improving' literature[111] as much as in history, and nuanced by her own strong opinions about seemly — ultimately queenly — behaviour, and developed within an atmosphere of unusual privilege and privation, Queen Victoria's girlhood was defined and produced within narrowly conceived notions of female value but higher expectations of royal conduct. In this study I have attempted to let both Victoria and the

46. M. Bowley, 'The Duchess of Kent and Princess Victoria' from *Royal Children of English History* by E. Nesbit.

children's books of the period speak. Through her stories, journals, lessons, and drawings of the costumed characters who populated the operas and ballets she watched with pleasure, the young Victoria herself coped with her fate as the next queen of England, and composed a Georgian girlhood remarkable both for its surprising conventionality and its singularity. This privileged access to her anxieties, pleasures, and day-to-day life found in these imperfect remains of her thoughts and feelings has enabled me to uncover 'becoming Victoria' and reveal her earliest days to others interested in childhood, Victoriana, and the girl herself.

Notes

Preface

1. 'The Girlhood of Queen Victoria', *The Girl's Own Paper* vol. 1 (1880), p. 5.
2. See the following fascinating studies: Adrienne Munich's *Queen Victoria's Secrets.* (New York: Columbia University Press 1996), Margaret Homans's and Adrienne Munich's edited collection of essays, *Remaking Queen Victoria* (Cambridge: Cambridge University Press, 1997), Margaret Homans's *Royal Representations: Queen Victoria and British Culture, 1837–1876* (Chicago: University of Chicago Press, 1998), and Gail Turley Houston's *Royalties: The Queen and Victorian Writers* (Charlottesville: University of Virginia Press, 1999).
3. Queen Victoria was also depicted as a tutor of womanly virtues to young maidens. The character of the virgin speaking for all female youth in the anonymous pamphlet 'The Queen of Queens' (1897) worships the Queen as an example of a protector of propriety: '"we love you more because you have reigned ever in the hearts of simple English maidens, teaching them to keep Innocency, and shielding them by the strength of your Virtues from sorrow and from harm."' Quoted in Houston, *Royalties*, pp. 7–8.
4. John Darton, *Famous Girls Who Have Become Illustrious Women: Forming Models for Imitation for the Young Women of England* (1864). Repr. Freeport, NY: Books for Libraries Press (1972), p. 182. Mrs Craik concludes her Jubilee publication for youth, *Fifty Golden Years: Incidents in the Queen's Reign* (London: Raphael Tuck and Sons, 1887), by arguing that although the world has since rejected the notion of the Divine Right of kings, Queen Victoria's 'sweet human graces' prove that 'to be a true man or a true woman is the Royalest thing on earth' (p. 62).
5. Adrienne Munich describes Queen Victoria's authority as deriving from her oxymoronic position of 'unique ordinariness': 'Victoria's position, both as representing the period's construction of the middle-class woman and apart from it as resembling no other woman in the world, constructs a queen with open secrets, much of whose

power derives from her unique ordinariness.' Munich, *Queen Victoria's Secrets*, p. 22. Elizabeth Langland, in a chapter of her book *Nobody's Angels* (subtitled 'Her Majesty's a Pretty Nice Girl'), similarly understands Victoria's moral code to be 'middle class' and her primary identification to be domestic; however, she argues that Victoria's position as both queen and mother/wife displayed a 'modern' female role that could accommodate public and private personas: 'In her reliance on Albert, in her professed inaptitude for public rule, Victoria constructed herself through emergent middle-class values; she presented herself through a scrim of domestic virtues emphasizing home, hearth, and heart. That she should, nonetheless, without disabling or disqualifying self-contradiction, take her place as head of the most powerful country in the world bespeaks her own signal role in the construction of a new feminine ideal that endorsed active public management behind a facade of private retirement.' Elizabeth Langland, *Nobody's Angels: Middle-Class Women and Domestic Ideology in Victorian Culture.* Ithaca, NY: Cornell University Press (1995), p. 63.

6.   Linda Wagner-Martin, *Telling Women's Lives.* New Brunswick, NJ: Rutgers University Press (1994), p. 7.

7.   Geraldine DeLuca, 'Lives and Half-Lives: Biographies of Women for Young Adults', *Children's Literature in Education* vol. 7, no. 4 (1986), pp. 241–52, p. 243.

8.   Elizabeth Longford, 'Reflections of a Biographer', in *The Literary Biography: Problems and Solutions*, ed. Dale Salwak. Iowa City: University of Iowa Press (1996), p. 148.

9.   Rupert Holland's *Historic Girlhoods* (Philadelphia: George W. Jacobs, 1910), while obviously written after Victoria's death, rather conventionally celebrates Victoria's youth as queen, emphasizing her childlikeness in the oft-repeated vignette of the new queen receiving the news of Uncle William's death and therefore her accession while dressed in nightclothes, her hair in disarray: 'The two gentlemen were standing talking by a window when a light step in the hall made them turn. Through the doorway came a girl, looking about fifteen years old, clad in a dressing-gown, a shawl over her shoulders, and slippers on her feet. Her long brown hair, falling loose, made a frame for her white and surprised face' (p. 245). Similarly, John Darton's newly made queen in *Famous Girls Who Have Become Illustrious Women* is celebrated for an exaggerated slightness and youth: 'All eyes were riveted upon the fairy form, the pale and pensive countenance of the modest girl, as she appeared before them, graceful and queenly in her child-like loveliness' (Darton, *Famous Girls*, p. 173). This scene is seemingly reprinted from George Pardon's 1861 *Illustrious Women Who Have Distinguished Themselves for Virtue, Piety, and Benevolence*, London: James Blackwood, (n.d. [*c.* 1861]), p. 20. The fantasy of diminishment in regard to Queen Victoria is continued in Nina Auerbach's habitual description of Victoria as the 'little queen' in *Woman and the Demon: The Life of a Victorian Myth* (Cambridge, MA: Harvard University Press, 1982, see pp. 2, 36 and 188).

10.   See Alison Booth's 'Illustrious Company: Victoria among Other Women in Anglo-American Role Model Anthologies' in Munich and Homans, *Remaking Queen Victoria* for a discussion of Victoria's role within this genre. My work on biographies

of Queen Victoria for girls was begun in the late summer/fall of 1997 in a talk delivered at the International Research Society in Children's Literature (IRSCL) in
York, England and one delivered at the Roehampton Institute, London. Booth's
excellent essay, in press at the time of my IRSCL presentation, is not primarily concerned with collective biographies as a form of children's literature.

11.   Royal Archives (RA hereafter) VIC LB16/10, 20 December 1835, letter from
Princess Victoria to Princess Feodore. Princess Victoria's emphasis.

Chapter One: The Baby in the Palace, 1819–1827

1.   J. M. Barrie. *Peter Pan in Kensington Gardens/Peter and Wendy* (1906). Oxford:
Oxford University Press (1991), p. 5.

2.   The Duke of Kent, a happy bachelor who enjoyed the company of a long-standing
mistress, might not have married at all if Charlotte's unexpected death had not
thrown the succession into crisis. Within a very short period, three sons of George
III were married: the Duke of Clarence (William) married the Princess of Saxe-
Meiningen; the Duke of Kent (Edward), the Dowager Duchess of Leiningen; and
the Duke of Cambridge (Adolphus), the Princess of Hesse. Of course, these oppor-
tunistic weddings made easy targets of the Royal Family and were ridiculed in the
popular press. The author and critic Harriet Martineau alludes to this climate of
gossip and conjecture in her autobiography: 'on my return from Bristol in 1819, I
ventured to say what my conscience bade me say, and what I had been led to see by
a dear Aunt, that it was wrong to catch up and believe and spread reports dangerous
to the royal family, who could not reply to slander like other people. . .'
Autobiography. 2 vols (1877). London: Virago (1983), vol. 1, pp. 80–1.

3.   Marquis of Lorne, *V.R.I: Her Life and Empire.* London: Harmsworth Books (*c.* 1901),
p. 7.

4.   RA VIC/M3/1, Duke of Kent to Mr Putnam, 5 April 1819.

5.   In her biography of the young queen, Monica Charlot notes the uncharitable, yet
perhaps understandable antipathy that the future George IV, a disappointed father,
felt towards his younger brother who was racing home to produce a potential heir
to the throne: 'In any case [George IV] was mortified that it was not his own descendants that would sit on the throne of England and this alone made him little
inclined to welcome the newcomers to Kensington Palace.' Monica Charlot,
Victoria: The Young Queen. Oxford: Basil Blackwell (1991), p. 41.

6.   RA Geo. 45501–2 and RA Geo. 45503–4. The three elder brothers of the Duke of
Kent were the future King George IV; Frederick, Duke of York (who died in 1827);
and the future King William IV.

7.   A Lady, *Anecdotes, Personal Traits, and Characteristic Sketches of Victoria the First.*
London: William Bennett (1840), p. 18.

8.   RA VIC/M3/6, translation and transcription of 22 June 1819 letter from Duchess
of Kent to Dowager Duchess of Saxe-Coburg.

9.   *Anecdotes … of Victoria the First*, p. 13. The effusions of this lady author need to be

viewed with some scepticism, however, as her appreciation of Victoria often promulgates misleading stories about the Princess. The author argues, for example, that Prncess Victoria's patriotism was so great that she "'would speak nothing but English'" (106). In fact, Victoria enjoyed learning languages and she became quite fluent in French and was also able to speak and write German with some avidity and Italian with difficulty by the time of her marriage.

10. Charlot, *Victoria: The Young Queen*, p. 98.

11. Dorothy Margaret Stuart suggests, in her biography of the Duchess of Kent, that the Kents chose the name Alexandrina for their baby as a means to send a pretty compliment to the Tsar, with 'whom Kent had been on terms sufficiently cordial to warrant his borrowing money from him'. Dorothy Margaret Stuart, *The Mother of Victoria*. London: Macmillan (1942), p. 79.

12. Victoria denies this story in her marginal comments in her copy of Agnes Strickland's *Queen Victoria: From Birth to Bridal* (London, 1840. Annotated copy in Royal Library). Strickland was so mortified by the Queen's response to this error-riddled biography that the books were recalled. Pneumonia and other diseases cannot, of course, be contracted through dampness of the foot, but Victoria was probably reacting less to a faulty medical diagnosis than to the unwelcome implication in Strickland's story that the Duke was partially to blame for his own death: had he heeded the advice of Conroy (to ignore the baby and change his footwear) he would not have fallen mortally ill.

13. See RA VIC Add./V.1 (translation from the German of RA VIC Z286) for a truly harrowing account of the Duke's illness and death told in letters written by the Duchess of Kent to her friend Pauline von Tubeuf. It is natural to sympathize with the Duchess of Kent's deep distress and grief over her husband's illness. For example, she writes on 19 January 1820, 'Yesterday was the 9th day when the crisis ought to set in and it was a dreadful day for me. The doctors held a consultation quite early in the morning and decided once more to repeat the cupping and the bleeding – this is the sixth time! … My beloved one bears all with an angelic patience. There is hardly a spot on his dear body which has not been touched by cupping, blisters or bleeding.' RA VIC Add./V.1, p. 10.

14. See RA VIC/M3/30.

15. In her letter of 27 January 1820, the Duchess of Kent writes to Pauline von Tubeuf, 'Wetherall and Conroy wanted to get a paper signed by Edward nominating who he wished should act as guardian to our dear little one. As I still did not believe in the hopelessness of his illness, I would not agree to this, dreading the agitating effect it might have upon him.' RA VIC Add./V.1, p. 14. See Katherine Hudson's *A Royal Conflict: Sir John Conroy and the Young Victoria* for an excellent extended discussion of Conroy's relationship with the Kents (London: Hodder & Stoughton, 1994). Much later, the Duchess of Kent would use the Duke of Kent's name to urge Victoria to promise the position of private secretary to Sir John Conroy. See RA VIC M7/46.

16. See *The Letters of Queen Victoria: A Selection from Her Majesty's Correspondence between the Years 1837–1861* where Queen Victoria, writing in 1872, calls her childhood

'rather melancholy'. 3 vols, ed. Arthur Christopher Benson and Viscount Esher. London: John Murray (1907), vol. 1, p. 14.

17.   E. F. Benson, *Queen Victoria*. Abridged. (1935). London: Chatto & Windus (1987), p. 12.

18.   See *The Times* 1828 1 April–30 June. See also, *Anecdotes … of Victoria the First*, p. 109. Written in 1854 to be saved until her death and then delivered to the Queen, Feodore's final missive to her sister was a heartfelt and moving message of love and beyond-the-grave pathos: '… I can never thank you enough for all you have done for me, for your great love and tender affection. These feelings cannot die; they must and will live on with my soul – till we meet again, never more to be separated – and you will not forget.' Quoted in Harold A. Albert, *Queen Victoria's Sister: The Life and Letters of Princess Feodora*. London: Robert Hale (1967), p. 239. Feodore's name is also spelled 'Feodora.' Like many authors, I have decided to use the German spelling.

19.   Quoted in Albert, *Queen Victoria's Sister*, p. 13.

20.   Feodore's biographer Harold Albert similarly notes the lack of portraits showing the sisters together. He comments that 'Princess Feodora has not faded from the pages of history. She was never there.' Ibid., p. 11.

21.   These drawings were published for the first and, to my knowledge, only time in an article by Adeline Edwards in the Diamond Jubilee Number of *The Lady's Realm*. ('A Peep at the Queen in Infancy', *The Lady's Realm* vol. 2, no. 8 [June 1897], pp. 135–8.) My thanks to Miss Jenny Lister of Kensington Palace for this reference.

22.   Victoria's interest in her shell collection never waned, but eventually, the once active child becomes eager to have someone else expend the effort of collecting them. This brief comment illuminates the Princess who became very solicitous of her health as she grew older. The ten-year-old writes to Feodore from Broadstairs in 1829, 'You asked me if I was still fond of looking for shells? I am very fond of having them, but it makes my back ache so to look for them myself.' RA VIC LB1/38, 4 September 1829, letter from Princess Victoria to Princess Feodore.

23.   These toys were put on display in 1903 when Kensington Palace first opened to the public, and have been available for viewing periodically since that time. They became part of a permanent exhibition in the palace in 1998. I would like to thank Miss Lister for making the toys and dolls available to me while they were in storage at Kensington Palace.

24.   RA VIC LB1/24 1829, letter from Princess Victoria to Princess Feodore. The Letterbooks (noted as LB) are a series of copies of many of Princess Victoria's letters from 1828. The earliest examples are in Baroness Lehzen's hand.

25.   Quoted in *Queen Victoria: Her Life and Times, 1819–1861* by Cecil Woodham-Smith. London: Penguin (1972), p. 52.

26.   Sarah A. Tooley, *The Personal Life of Queen Victoria*, 3rd edn. London: Hodder & Stoughton (1901), pp. 18–19.

27.   Alfred E. Knight. *Victoria: Her Life and Reign*, 6th edn. London: S. W. Partridge (1902), p. 21.

28.   See RA VIC A/7/1a, Queen Victoria's Lesson Books.

29. See RA VIC/Z490.

30. RA VIC Y61/2, 11 May 1827, letter from King Leopold to Princess Victoria.

31. RA VIC LB1/5, 23 March 1828, letter from Princess Victoria to King Leopold.

32. RA VIC Y63/5, 7 October 1836, letter from the King Leopold to Princess Victoria.

33. RA VIC Y61/14, 23 January 1832, Letter from King Leopold to Princess Victoria.

34. Dash is somewhat famous as the dirty dog which the young Queen Victoria left Coronation Day festivities in order to bathe. Dash was buried in the grounds of Adelaide Cottage and his headstone epitaph reads: 'Reader, If you would live beloved/And die regretted/Profit by the example of/DASH.' Quoted in Marina Warner, *Queen Victoria's Sketchbooks*. New York: Crown Publishers (1979), p. 28.

35. RA VIC Y33/8, 30 September 1828, letter from Princess Feodore to Princess Victoria. Writing to her aunt, Princess Sophia, two years later, Victoria mourns the death of her pet bird and laments that she had 'teased him at first'. RA VIC/LB1/30.

36. RA VIC Add. A/7/1a, Queen Victoria's Lesson Books.

37. Quoted in Albert, *Queen Victoria's Sister*, p. 62.

38. RA VIC LB1/17, undated letter from Princess Victoria to Princess Feodore. See RA VIC Add. U/171/6, 7 December 1828, letter from Princess Victoria to Princess Feodore.

39. RA VIC LB1/3, 9 March 1828, letter from Princess Victoria to Princess Feodore.

40. RA VIC Add. U/171/11, 5 July 1829, letter from Princess Victoria to Princess Feodore.

41. RA LB1/45, Malvern 1830, letter from Princess Victoria to Princess Feodore.

42. RA VIC/Z119 Frances H. Low, *Queen Victoria's Dolls*. London: George Newnes (1894), n.p.

43. RA VIC Add./V.1, p. 3: 11 January 1820 letter from the Duchess of Kent to Pauline von Tubeuf.

44. *Letters*, vol. 1. ed. Benson and Esher, p. 19.

45. RA VIC Z117, Letters and Drawings by Queen Victoria. A copy of this letter can be found in Queen Victoria's Letterbooks where it is dated 7 December 1828.

46. RA VIC Z117, Letters and Drawings by Queen Victoria.

47. Stuart, *The Mother of Victoria*, p. 7.

48. RA VIC Add./V.1, p. 3, 11 January 1820, letter from the Duchess of Kent to Pauline von Tubeuf.

49. Elizabeth Appleton, *Early Education; or, The Management of Children Considered With a View to Their Future Character*, 2nd edn. London: G. & W. B. Whittaker (1821), p. iv.

50. Ibid., p. 30.

51. Albert, *Queen Victoria's Sister*, p. 55.

52. RA VIC Z122.

53. Victoria's copy of this book and many others of this genre have been saved at Frogmore House in the grounds of Windsor Castle where the Duchess of Kent lived for many years until her death in 1861. Years after Victoria wrote her tale, the children's author Juliana Horatia Ewing's short fantasy, 'Amelia and the Dwarfs' (which first appeared in 1870 in *Aunt Judy's Magazine*) similarly described an unsociable

child spoiled by her mother's indulgence. In Ewing's tale, unlike Princess Victoria's, however, Amelia reforms her disagreeable ways after having been kidnapped by dwarfs and forced to rectify all of her errors (torn frocks, discarded food, broken toys). See 'Amelia and the Dwarfs' in *Forbidden Journeys: Fairy Tales and Fantasies by Victorian Women Writers*, ed. Nina Auerbach and U. C. Knoepflmacher. Chicago: University of Chicago Press (1992), pp. 105–27.

54. *The New Year's Gift and Juvenile Souvenir*, 1829, vi–viii. RL RCIN 1056285.

55. RA VIC Add. A/7/1a, Queen Victoria's Lesson Books.

56. RA VIC Z122, Queen Victoria's prayer book.

57. RA VIC/Y203/79, 6 September 1867, letter from Baroness Lehzen to Queen Victoria.

58. *Letters*, vol. 1. ed. Benson and Esher, p. 19. For information about Baroness Lehzen's early years, see RA VIC Y203/80. Queen Victoria annotated a letter sent to her in 1867 by the long since discarded Lehzen. In this letter, Baroness Lehzen outlines her version of the moment Princess Victoria learned she was one day to become queen. (I discuss this scene in some detail in Chapter Two.) At the end of the letter, Queen Victoria wrote a long comment praising Lehzen's loyalty and selflessness: 'Bass. Lehzen was thoroughly devoted to her charge. She never for the 13 years she was governess to Princess Victoria, *once left* her, for a day, or a night or even for a few hours to pay any visits. She rec'd no visitors, – nor any of her relations – & knew how to amuse & play with the Princess so as to gain her warmest affections ...' RA VIC Y203/81.

59. A. Asenath Smith, *A Brief Life of Queen Victoria for Children*. London, Glasgow and Dublin: Charles and Dibble (1901), pp. 5–6.

60. See RA VIC Add./A7/23, Queen Victoria's Conduct Books.

61. RA VIC Add. A7/23, Queen Victoria's Conduct Books.

62. RA VIC Queen Victoria's Journal (QVJ hereafter), 21 August 1832.

63. RA VIC Add. A7/23, Queen Victoria's Conduct Books.

64. The political nature of the selection process of the Royal Household was argued in the light of day during the 'Bedchamber Plot', one of the first skirmishes the young Queen Victoria waged with her government. Briefly, in 1839, her beloved Lord Melbourne's Whig government failed, and Sir Robert Peel of the Tory Party became Prime Minister. There had not been a queen regnant for many years, since Queen Anne, and Peel thought it only right that the Queen's intimates reflect the politics of the new majority government. The Queen drew herself up, and with an indignation fuelled by moral outrage and appeals to female delicacy, refused to change her Ladies. Victoria won the battle and the Whig government, led by Melbourne, remained shakily in power for two more years.

65. In an anonymous, undated article 'Queen Victoria's Girl Secretary' preserved in the Royal Archives, the author asserts that Queen Victoria appointed Mary Ann Davys to her personal entourage because they were friends: '[the Queen] managed to appoint, for her own pleasure, one girl of her own age who should be permanent and with whom her daily intercourse might be less formal' (RA VIC Add. U336/45). However, there is no evidence from Mary Ann Davys's letters that any such famil-

iarity existed. Davys was to be a kind of personal secretary, but she rarely had any official duties at all, and was often bored while a member of the Royal Household. She was also a very pious and active young woman, who chafed at the inactivity of the Ladies, and fretted over the ornamental nature of their roles about the Queen. For example, she writes from Windsor Castle on 14 April 1838, 'I often wonder how I shall like returning to common life again; all this is very pleasant and I am very much afraid of liking it too well; at the same time I feel that it is *unsatisfying*. I am glad *altogether* that this Windsor visit only lasts a fortnight; it is too delightful, and spoils me for anything else.' (See RA VIC Add. U336 for a transcription of Davys's letters.) Interestingly, Davys shared the Queen's dislike of Sir John Conroy and writes about trying to avoid him. To her aunt from Buckingham Palace, Miss Davys writes thrillingly, 'Did I tell you how nearly I had a recontre with *Sir John* the other day? I was with Lady Mary [Stopford], when he was announced, and I, not feeling disposed for an interview, made my escape into her adjoining bedroom and there remained. Lady Mary cannot *bear* him, but he came to speak to her upon some business' (RA VIC Add. U336, 13 February 1838). Perhaps her father had told unappealing stories about Conroy to his family while he was tutor to Victoria; it seems clear that Davys disliked Conroy and assumed that all of her family would know of and share in this dislike.

Davys spent two years in the Royal Household, and left when her father was named Bishop of Peterborough in 1839. She married Reverend Henry Pratt, later Canon of Peterborough, in 1844, and died in 1888 (see RA VIC Add. U336/44).

66. *Letters*, ed. Benson and Esher, p. 18.
67. RA VIC *V.R.I: Her Life and Empire*, p. 56.
68. Ibid., p. 57.
69. Ibid.
70. *The New Year's Gift and Juvenile Souvenir* (1829), p. vii. See Gail Turley Houston's interesting essay on gender and Princess Victoria's reading, 'Reading and Writing Victoria: the Conduct Book and the Legal Constitution of Female Sovereignty', in *Remaking Queen Victoria*, ed. Munich and Homans, pp. 159–81.
71. Appleton, *Early Education*, p. 353.
72. RA VIC Z121.
73. RA VIC Y203/79, 6 September 1867, letter from Baroness Lehzen to Queen Victoria.
74. RA VIC Add. A/7/1b, *Chronology of the Kings of England* (n.d.), pp. 47 and 69.
75. RA VIC Z112, Progress of Princess Victoria's Education, November 1828–July 1830. See also RA VIC Add. A/7/1, Z111, and Z113.
76. RA VIC Add. A7/1–16, Queen Victoria's Lesson Books. English and Handwriting Copybook.
77. RA VIC Add. A7/1.
78. Alison Plowden, *The Young Victoria*. New York: Stein and Day (1981), p. 55.
79. Stuart, *The Mother of Victoria*, p 133.
80. See RA VIC M7/55.
81. See *Letters of the Princess Charlotte, 1811–1817*, ed. A. Aspinall, London: Home and Van Thal (1949).

82. For example, Victoria writes to Princess Sophia from Tunbridge Wells (the Conroys always accompanied the Duchess of Kent on their trips) in 1828 that 'Victoire Conroy comes every Sunday afternoon and stays till I go to bed, which is generally later than usual for Lady Conroy and all family come to supper, and Victoire goes home with her Mamma.' RA VIC LB1/12, letter from Princess Victoria to Princess Sophia, Tunbridge Wells, 1828.

83. RA VIC Y61/25, 11 March 1834, letter from King Leopold to Princess Victoria.
   In another letter a year later, Leopold returns to the subject of Victoria's height: 'I shall also require some information on the subject of your growth; is it true that you are grown so extremely tall? Some people say half an inch less than myself? I understand that is [*sic*] has created the greatest sensation at the Drawing Room.' RA VIC Y61/42, 9 March 1835.

84. *Anecdotes ... of Victoria the First*, p. 134.

85. RCIN 1056273, *The Juvenile Forget Me Not: A Christmas and New Year's Gift, or Birthday Present for the Year 1829*, ed. Mrs. S. C. Hall. London: N. Hailes (1829). The volume's goal – to aid the moral training of the 'better' class of girls with the help of aristocratic sponsors – is made clear in the last paragraph of the brief preface: 'It will be evident that no expense has been spared to combine taste and elegance with qualities of greater importance; and the Editor refers with confidence to the list of contributors for proof that she has succeeded in her principal object – the production of a volume beneficial to those whose future character must in a great measure depend on their early impressions' (p. iv). As the guiding image of the book, the Princess Victoria lends credibility and approval to the behavioural methods promoted by the tales such as M. J. J.'s 'Recreation and Dissipation; or, the Two Harrys and Lucys' contained within.

86. RA VIC Add. V/84.

87. RA VIC Y61/14, 23 January 1832, letter from King Leopold to Princess Victoria.

88. Feodore wrote in answer to her sister: 'Tell Lehzen, I do not remember that she read Goldsmith's History to me, while lying on the board; I remember that latter disagreeable concern very well, and that she used to read to me, during the time, but I am ashamed to say, not what.' RA VIC Y34/19, 31 December 1834/1 January 1835, letter from Princess Feodore to Princess Victoria.

89. See RA VIC LB 16/10, 20 December 1835, letter from Princess Victoria to Princess Feodore.

90. Quoted in Woodham-Smith, *Queen Victoria*, p. 139.

91. Homans argues that 'Queen Victoria's resemblance to a middle-class wife made her seem ordinary, but its meaning and effectiveness depended on the contrast with her extraordinariness. Her ordinariness was at once genuine and deliberate, that of a unique individual empowered to be exemplary.' Homans, *Royal Representations*, p. 5.

92. J. M. Barrie, *Peter Pan* (1911). Harmondsworth: Puffin (1986), p. 94.

93. Marion M. Wingrave, *The May Blossom; or The Princess and Her People*. London: Frederick Warne and Co. (1881), n.p. My thanks to Miss Bridget Wright, Bibliographer, Royal Library, for first bringing this book to my attention.

94. In a long memorandum, 'Sketch of the Duchess of Kent', written in 1878 by

Frances Conroy, Sir John's daughter-in-law, Mrs Conroy gives an account of the Duke of Cumberland's plot to kill the infant Victoria. Queen Victoria's response is unequivocal: 'utterly false', she writes in the margin. RA VIC Z485/6.

95. See Adrienne Munich's discussion (pp. 73–7) of the recuperation of Victoria's notorious lack of fashion sense in *The Fairies' Favourite*: 'Victoria metamorphoses into a Cinderella in reverse by virtue of no taste at all.' Munich, *Queen Victoria's Secrets*, p. 74.

Chapter Two: The Little Princess Enters Education Land, 1828–1832

1. This is the title of the third chapter of Alice Corkran's *The Life of Queen Victoria for Boys and Girls*, London: T. C. and E. C. Jack (1910), p. 17.

2. Ann Yearsley, the 'milkwoman poetess', was another 'singular' object of More's attention. More's interactions with Yearsley were those of a sometimes unwelcome patron, while her infrequent visits (her selected letters include one such social event) to the young Princess Charlotte were welcome invitations. (See *The Letters of Hannah More*, ed. R. Brimley Johnson. New York: Dial Press (1925), pp. 137–8. For a discussion of Hannah More and Ann Yearsley, see, for example, Patricia Demers, *The World of Hannah More*. Lexington: University Press of Kentucky (1996), pp. 63–75. *Hints* did not fare well in the reviewing press. '*The Edinburgh Review*, always intolerant of what it regarded as cant, tore the *Hints* to pieces, much to the indignation of Miss More'. Dorothy Margaret Stuart, *Daughter of England: A New Study of Princess Charlotte of Wales and Her Family*, London: Macmillan (1951), p. 31.

3. Hannah More, *Hints Towards Forming the Character of a Young Princess*, 2 vols. London: T. Cadell and W. Davies (1805), pp. 13–16. The first edition I am quoting from belonged to Princess Mary, a daughter of George III, who married her cousin the Duke of Gloucester and became Mary, Duchess of Gloucester. Agnes Strickland did her part in promoting the idea that Queen Victoria was more highly educated than was, properly speaking, the case. 'Never' was Victoria's response to Strickland's claim in the recalled *From Birth to Bridal* that the Princess studied Greek (p. 45).

4. More, *Hints*, pp. 68–9.

5. The cautious educator Miss Appleton expressed concern that the abridgements of 'adult' histories were inappropriate reading for a child audience. Her fear of such texts was so great that her own imagination about their improprieties ran rather wild: 'Facts there are, too, of one other kind, but which should studiously be kept from children: history of bloody wars, and massacres, burnings and martyrdoms, with shocking histories of barbarous murders, and images of racks, red hot pincers, engines of torment and cruelty, with mangled limbs, and carcasses all drenched in gore …' (Appleton, *Early Education*, p. 402).

6. See W. Jackson Bate, *John Keats*. Cambridge, MA: Harvard University Press (1963), p. 25.

7. *Catalogue of the Princess Victoria's Books* RL RCIN 1129268.a. This book, the

personal copy of the Duchess of Kent, remains at Frogmore House, her last residence. A copy of this document, although one not annotated in German by the Duchess, and lacking information about the history of Princess Victoria's ownership of the books (who gave each book and, for some of the volumes, to whom it might have later been given, if known), exists at the Royal Archives, RA VIC Z114a. My thanks to Lady de Bellaigue for gathering the Frogmore House volumes for me.

Gail Turley Houston's essay 'Reading and Writing Victoria: The Conduct Book and the Legal Constitution of Female Sovereignty' in *Remaking Queen Victoria*, ed. Munich and Homans, pp. 159–81, reprints the RA document (RA VIC Z114a) in full. See Houston's essay for an extended discussion of Princess Victoria's education via conduct books (Houston includes Edgeworth under this term) and the complications to the gender ideology of these books that arise through the fact of Victoria's ultimate authority as queen: '[t]he possibility of female sovereignty dramatically disrupts the purportedly seamless account of the sexes found in Blackstone and the children's writers Victoria read' (p. 167).

8.   Hannah More, *Hints Towards Forming the Character of a Young Princess*, 5th edn. London: printed for T. Cadell and W. Davies, 1819. Uncatalogued book, Frogmore House, Windsor Castle.

9.   *Anecdotes ... of Victoria the First*, pp. 228–9.

10.   More, *Hints* (1805), p. 29.

11.   RA VIC Z492/4. Copy of 1 March 1830 letter from the Duchess of Kent to the Bishops of London and Lincoln.

12.   Elizabeth Longford, *Queen Victoria: Born to Succeed*. New York: Harper and Row (1964), p. 28. See also Corkran's *The Life of Queen Victoria for Boys and Girls*, p. 19.

Victoria's predecessor, Princess Charlotte, chose another path. In a letter from 1812, the sixteen-year-old noted, 'I have begun to *be false* also ... not false to the good friends that do not forget me, not *false for ever*, not false by nature; but it is the only thing here for defence, to use the same arms as [her relations including her father] do.' Quoted in Stuart, *Daughter of England*, p. 28.

13.   RA VIC M5/8, interview of 10 March 1830.

14.   RA VIC Y203/81, copy of 2 December 1867 letter from Baroness Lehzen to Queen Victoria.

15.   Sarah Tooley's *The Personal Life of Queen Victoria* quotes the Reverend Canon Davys's 'correction' of this story. Davys tells Tooley that his father had given Princess Victoria the task of making a chronology of the monarchs of England (some of these homemade chronologies have been preserved). Victoria ended her chart with 'Uncle William'. When asked why she did not include the future sovereign, Victoria reportedly said, '"I hardly like to put down myself"' (Tooley, *The Personal Life of Queen Victoria*, p. 37).

16.   RA VIC Y203/81.

17.   RA VIC M5/8, interview of 10 March 1830.

18.   Marquis of Lorne, *V.R.I. Her Life and Empire*.

19.   RA VIC M5/2, Distribution of the Day, 1829.

20.   RA VIC Add. A7/1A/1–16, Queen Victoria's Practice Writing Books. The education

of the Fairborne children is the frame surrounding the stories and dialogues of *Evenings at Home*. The older family members and their friends write bits of improving prose and poetry and then put their efforts into a box (or 'budget'). Once an evening, the box would be opened and a paper selected to be read aloud. Natural history, historical drama, and female education are among the topics covered in the first volume.

21. Mary Russell Mitford (1787–1855) was a well-known poet and playwright, but is best known today for her tales of village life. She also collected stories to be included in her numerous anthologies and almanacks; of these, the works for children were among Princess Victoria's books. Once queen, Victoria seemed to forget this author from her childhood. Gail Turley Houston recounts an interesting exchange of letters between Mitford and Elizabeth Barrett Browning on the topic of Queen Victoria's disinclination to visit Mitford. Barrett Browning roundly criticizes the Queen for this slight to her friend. See *Royalties*, pp. 124–7.

22. RL RCIN 1128948. *American Stories for Little Boys and Girls*, ed. Mary Russell Mitford, 3 vols. London: Whittaker, Treacher and Co. (1831), p. 205. 'The Storm', pp. 196–234.

23. Appleton, *Early Education*, p. 397.

24. Ibid., p. 395.

25. See RL RCIN 1129268a, *Catalogue of Princess Victoria's Books*.

26. RA VIC Add. A7/1A 27, Princess Victoria's composition, 13 September 1827.

27. See the pictorial representation of this tour in Lorne, *V.R.I. Her Life and Empire*, p. 47.

28. RA VIC Add. A7/1A/30, Princess Victoria's composition, 11 October 1829. The spelling and other mistakes in this composition have been retained.

29. Other differences between the two versions within the body of the story include additional examples of corrected spelling (although new errors are sometimes introduced), the insertion of an extra minor character, and longer extracts from Goldsmith's poem, 'The Deserted Village', are copied in and credited to him. Otherwise, the stories are exactly the same; Victoria ended the ink version after about four pages of the twenty-page story.

30. As a schoolgirl, Maria Edgeworth was asked by her father to write a 'fable' on 'Generosity' – a topic of his choosing. Catherine Gallagher argues that this task helped set the stage for their later writing relationship: 'In the author's mind, it seemed to link the justification of her fictional tales to their adequate illustration of a prior Idea in her father's mind.' Catherine Gallagher, *Nobody's Story: The Vanishing Acts of Women Writers in the Marketplace, 1670–1820*. Berkeley: University of California Press (1994), p. 268. See also Marilyn Butler, *Maria Edgeworth: A Literary Biography*. Oxford: Clarendon Press (1972), p. 57.

31. Edgeworth's 'Harry and Lucy' stories have a rather complicated history. The first Harry and Lucy story was written in 1779 by Maria's father (and co-author) Richard Lovell Edgeworth and his second wife, Honora. Maria revised this story and it appeared, titled *Harry and Lucy*, as a volume of *Early Lessons* in 1801. *Continuation of Early Lessons* (also about Harry and Lucy, as well as the characters

Frank and Rosamond) was published in two volumes in 1813, while *Harry and Lucy Concluded: Being the Last Part of Early Lessons* (4 vols) appeared in 1825. See Marilyn Butler's biography of Maria Edgeworth for additional bibliographic information.

In the preface to *Harry and Lucy Concluded*, Edgeworth outlines her goals for these final volumes: 'I have endeavoured to pursue, in this Conclusion of Early Lessons, my father's object in their commencement – to exercise the powers of attention, observation, reasoning, and invention, rather than to teach any one science, or to make any advance beyond first principles' (Maria Edgeworth, *Harry and Lucy Concluded*, 3rd edn, 3 vols. London: Baldwin and Cradock (1840), p. ix. In Princess Victoria's well-thumbed copies of the 1825 volumes (some of the pages are stained), the preface 'To Parents' remains uncut (RL RCIN 1082156–9).

The Royal Library also owns the 4th edition (1846) of *Harry and Lucy Concluded* which was presented as a Christmas gift to the Princess Royal from her parents in 1851 (RL RCIN 1082160). This gift attests to the value Victoria must have attached to these books.

32. Butler, *Maria Edgeworth*, p. 63.

33. RA VIC Add. A7/1A/30, Princess Victoria's composition, 11 October 1829.

34. Princess Victoria makes some amusing deviations: in Edgeworth's tale, Harry spends weeks building and rebuilding a masonry bridge over a nearby stream, while Adolphus's plan to build a 'little stone castle with a boat and draw-bridge' is refused because 'his father did not wish to spend usless monney' (ibid.).

35. RA VIC QVJ, 23 June 1833.

36. The 'Harry and Lucy' stories were designed to introduce young readers to scientific knowledge in particular. In the second volume of *Harry and Lucy Concluded*, when the children (and presumably their readers) are fourteen years old, they take a trip to the industrial Midlands. Butler writes, '... most readers are likely to find their attention held by the family's journey on a canal, and Harry's trip down a mine. Some may agree with Lucy, that the great wonders of the industrial landscape tend to become progressively less intriguing as each machine is carefully explained. Others, like Harry, will find the passages of scientific explanation among the best in the book' (*Maria Edgeworth*, p. 167).

It is difficult to tell whether Victoria was a Harry or a Lucy, but worth noting that unlike Sophia and Adolphus, Harry and Lucy actually visit and enjoy the steam engine and cotton manufactory (Edgeworth, 'Cotton Manufactory', *Harry and Lucy Concluded*, vol. 1, p. 159).

37. Carolyn Steedman, *The Tidy House: Little Girls Writing*. London: Virago (1982), p. 62.

38. Elizabeth Kowaleski-Wallace, *Their Father's Daughters: Hannah More, Maria Edgeworth and Patriarchal Complicity*. New York and Oxford: Oxford University Press (1991), p. 104.

39. This interest is later emphasized by Princess Victoria's passion for the theatre and opera.

40. RA VIC LB 1/26, letter dated 1829 with no day or month.

41. RA VIC Add. A7/1A/30, Princess Victoria's composition, 11 October 1829.

42. Ibid.
43. Maria Edgeworth and Richard Lovell Edgeworth, *Practical Education*, 2 vols (1798). New York: Garland Publishing (1974), pp. 332–3.
44. RA VIC Add. A7/1A/30, Princess Victoria's composition, 11 October 1829.
45. Ibid. Victoria originally mentions only one daughter – Mary.
46. Ibid.
47. Mitzi Myers, 'Socializing Rosamond: Educational Ideology and Fictional Form', *Children's Literature Association Quarterly* vol. 14 (1989), p. 52.
48. RA VIC Add. A7/1A/29, Princess Victoria's composition, 11 October 1829.
49. Edgeworth, *Harry and Lucy Concluded* (1840) vol. 3, p. 191.
50. Ibid., p. 192.
51. Ibid., pp. 311–12.
52. RA VIC Y203/79, 6 September 1867, letter from Baroness Lehzen to Queen Victoria.
53. RA VIC Add. A7/1A/33, Princess Victoria's composition, n.d. Princess Victoria's original spelling and punctuation have been retained.
54. Ibid.
55. RA VIC Add. A7/1A/32, Princess Victoria's composition, n.d. Princess Victoria's original spelling and punctuation have been retained.
56. Ibid.
57. Ibid.
58. Ibid.
59. Digby, of course, is the name of Harry and Lucy's hosts.
60. RA VIC Add. A7/1A/32, Princess Victoria's composition, n.d.
61. RA VIC Add./A12/1561, 1888 note to Sir Henry Ponsonby. My thanks to Lady Sheila de Bellaigue for this reference.
62. This image of Victoria's youth continued to be published well into her old age, appearing, for example, in the *English Illustrated Magazine* in the Jubilee year 1897.
63. RA VIC Z492/4. Copy of a letter from the Duchess of Kent to the Bishops of Lincoln and London, 1 March 1830.
64. Ibid.
65. Ibid. Gail Turley Houston's interpretation of this letter emphasizes the conventional superiority afforded to masculinity over femininity (privileging male education over female education): 'Queen Victoria's own mother assumed her daughter's feminine inferiority when she stated categorically that the Princess's education was tailored to her gender' (Houston, 'Reading and Writing Victoria', p. 160). My reading of this letter has a slightly different cast: in this missive, the Duchess is indicating that Victoria's 'large and liberal' education must *combine* seemly 'feminine' areas of study with subjects suited to the future sovereign. It would have been highly unusual for a girl to read *Blackstone's Commentaries on the Laws of England* as Princess Victoria did. This four-volume work was given to Victoria in 1830, significantly, by George Davys. (Cited in 'Catalogue of the Princess Victoria's Books', RCIN 1129268.a).

66. RA VIC Y61/12, 13 December 1831, letter from Leopold to Princess Victoria.

67. RA VIC Y61/3, 15 December 1828, letter from Leopold to Princess Victoria.

68. RA VIC Z492/8, copy of report by Reverend Davys, n.d. Reports on Victoria's progress were made regularly after 1830. See RA VIC M5/29 and RA VIC M5/30.

69. RA VIC Z492/10, copy of report by Reverend Barer, 2 March 1830.

70. RA VIC Z492/11, copy of report by Mr Steward, 2 March 1830.

71. RA VIC Z492/6, copy of letter from Reverend Davys to the Duchess of Kent, 2 March 1830.

72. RA VIC Z492/15, copy of letter from Bishops of London and Lincoln to Duchess of Kent, 23 March 1830.

73. RA VIC Z492/16, letter from Duchess of Kent to the Archbishop of Canterbury, 24 March 1830.

74. RA VIC Z492/18, note by the Archbishop of Canterbury written on the back of a letter from the Duchess of Kent to the Archbishop, 3 April 1830.

75. RA VIC Z492/20, note by the Archbishop of Canterbury written on a letter from the Duchess of Kent to the Archbishop, 27 April 1830. The Archbishop, as requested by the Duchess in a letter (12 May 1830, RA VIC Z492/21) formally gave his opinion on the Princess's abilities and her education in a letter of 13 May 1830 (RA VIC Z492/22).

76. RA VIC Z492/20, note by the Archbishop of Canterbury written on a letter from the Duchess of Kent to the Archbishop, 27 April 1830.

77. See RA VIC Z492/23, 28 June 1830 letter from the Duchess of Kent to the Archbishop of Canterbury in which she asks him to release all of the documents he held pursuant to the Princess's education to 'His Majesty's Ministers'. This letter was composed and sent immediately after George IV's death. In November 1830 she asked the Archbishop please to release these same documents to all the bishops so that they would be informed of the Princess's educational programme (and would also, presumably, communicate it to the people via the pulpit) (RA VIC Z492/24).

78. RA VIC M5/15, copy of letter from the Duchess of Kent to Princess Victoria, 24 May 1830.

79. RA VIC M5/28, letter from the Duchess of Kent to Princess Victoria, 31 December 1831.

80. RA VIC M5/33, letter from the Duchess of Kent to Princess Victoria, 24 May 1832.

81. RA VIC Z117, letters and drawings by Queen Victoria, dated 1 January 1829 in another hand, although the Letterbooks date this letter 17 August 1829 from Broadstairs.

82. Woodham-Smith, *Queen Victoria*, p. 62.

83. See RA VIC M3/39, vol. 2, copy of letter from the Duchess of Kent to Earl Grey, 27 January 1831, where the Duchess's financial history is discussed.

84. RA VIC M3/39, vol. 2, copy of letter from the Duchess of Kent to Earl Grey, 27 January 1831. She had made this point in a letter to the Duke of Wellington in November of the previous year.

85. RA VIC M3/39, vol. 2, copy of letter from the Duchess of Kent to Earl Grey, 27 January 1831. It is interesting to note that this copy was found amongst Sir John

Conroy's papers after his death and given to Prince Albert in 1854. Conroy was certainly the author of this and many other of the Duchess's communications.

86. RA VIC/Y36/128, 17 March 1843, letter from Princess Feodore to Queen Victoria.

87. See Lorne, *V.R.I. Her Life and Empire*, p. 40.

88. Charlot, *Victoria: The Young Queen*, p. 51.

89. RA VIC M5/19, memorandum of the Duchess of Kent, 7 February 1831.

90. Charlot, *Victoria: The Young Queen*, p. 59.

91. Ibid.

92. RA VIC M5/19, memorandum of the Duchess of Kent, 7 February 1831.

93. Strickland, *From Birth to Bridal*, vol. 1, pp. 51–2.

94. Quoted in William Kent, *London in the News Through Three Centuries*. London: Staples Press (1954), p. 175.

95. RA VIC M5/19, memorandum of the Duchess of Kent, 7 February 1831.

Chapter Three: Private and Public Princess, 1832–1834

1. RA VIC Queen Victoria's Journal, 22 October 1832. The manuscript journals will hereafter be referred to as 'QVJ' followed by the entry date. All quotations are from the manuscript journals unless otherwise noted. Princess Victoria's spelling and punctuation have been retained.

   Victoria enjoyed the fireworks at Hardwick Hall (where Mary, Queen of Scots had once lived) which ended with a tribute to the visiting princess's future status: 'The [fireworks] were rockets, wheels, windmills, red & blue lights &c., &c., but towards the end Mamma was taken unwell & was obliged to leave the room, when the prettiest part began. I stayed on and saw a temple & my name in stars & a crown.'

2. RA VIC QVJ, 31 July 1832.

3. See Woodham-Smith, *Queen Victoria*, p. 89.

4. Quoted in Gervas Huxley, *Lady Elizabeth and the Grosvenors: Life in a Whig Family, 1822–1839*. London: Oxford University Press (1965), p. 40.

5. RA VIC QVJ, 1 August 1832.

6. Ibid., 6 August 1832. The Princess has written the word 'singularity' with an unusual – for her – flourish to the 'y'. The Ladies were Lady Eleanor Butler (d. 1829) and Miss Sarah Ponsonby (d. 1831) who, against their families' wishes, set up a lifelong household together in Plâs Newydd.

7. Valerie Sanders, *The Private Lives of Victorian Women: Autobiography in Nineteenth-Century England*. New York: St Martin's Press (1989), p. 12. Sanders goes on to comment, 'Queen Victoria herself sanctioned the practice in 1868, by publishing her *Leaves from the Journal of our Life in the Highlands*' (p. 12).

8. In 1912, Viscount Esher published selections from his transcript of Victoria's journals from 1832 until her marriage to Albert in 1841 as *The Girlhood of Queen Victoria* (the originals of the journals after 31 December 1836 had been destroyed by Victoria's youngest daughter, Princess Beatrice, according to her mother's wishes). Although the annotations make them a very useful source, Esher's published

selections – the only available examples of Victoria's early journal-writing – alter her life-writing to the extent that some of the colour of her youth is blanched out. Esher corrects her at times appalling spelling, omits some interesting, but perhaps not seemly, observations that the Princess made (about drunkenness, for example), and reduces her entries concerning the theatre (thus undervaluing her obsession with performance and display), and (though unavoidable in a published version) is unable to reproduce some of the clues to Victoria's relationships found in little additions she sometimes makes with carets as afterthoughts or perhaps at the bidding of someone reading the journal. Adrienne Munich's negative assessment of the teen journals – that they 'rarely break out of a perfunctory listing of sights and activities, but she allotted herself more space to describing women's dresses' – is probably a result of reading Esher's published selections rather than the entire run of manuscript journals. Although, as I suggest in this chapter, Princess Victoria was not an accomplished stylist, she can be called a lively and emotional writer if the journals are taken as a whole. Victoria rarely describes women's clothing unless it is a costume she admires. Munich, *Queen Victoria's Secrets*, p. 65.

9. Mrs O.F. Walton, *Pictures and Stories from Queen Victoria's Life*. London: Religious Tract Society (1901), p. 21.

10. RA VIC QVJ, 13 October 1852.

11. Ibid., 1 November 1852.

12. Esher fails to include Victoria's rather matter-of-fact description of the dismemberment of her 'prize': 'Then the huntsmen cut off for themselves, the nostrils, ears, & 4 paws; and lastly they threw it to the dogs, who tore it from side to side till there was nothing left.' RA VIC QVJ, 31 October 1852.

13. Ibid., 8 September 1852.

14. Ibid., 28 October 1852.

15. Ibid., 2 August 1852.

16. Ibid.

17. See Maria Edgeworth and Richard Lovell Edgeworth, *Harry and Lucy Concluded*, 3 vols. Baldwin and Cradock (1840), vol. 2, pp. 15–16.

18. RA VIC QVJ, 1 August 1852.

19. Ibid., 13 August 1852.

20. In fact, I believe that this minor illness – characterized by 'sickness' (vomiting), 'weakness', and loss of appetite – was actually caused by Victoria's menstrual period. Although it is impossible to know exactly when Victoria first began to menstruate, she mentions similar symptoms on 16 September, 15 October, and 18 November 1852 as well. Victoria may have begun to menstruate earlier in her thirteenth year, but the fact that she mentions these regular symptoms for a few months running and then stops doing so lends credence to the theory that she was marking her menstrual periods when they were an unpleasant novelty only. Victoria's short stature also suggests that her period began when she was younger than sixteen – the age that historian Joan Jacobs Brumberg places Victoria's first menstruation – as this culmination of puberty generally slows a girl's growth. See Joan Jacobs Brumberg, *The Body Project: An Intimate History of American Girls*. New York: Vintage Books (1998), p. xviii.

21. RA VIC QVJ, 12 August 1832.

22. Ibid., 5 October 1832.

23. Hudson, *A Royal Conflict*, p. 3.

24. RA VIC QVJ, 8 November 1832.

25. Ibid., 25 August 1832.

26. Ibid., 6 September 1832.

27. Ibid., 17 September 1832.

28. Ibid., 25 September 1832.

29. Ibid., 29 September 1832.

30. Ibid., 30 September 1832.

31. Ibid., 4 October 1832.

32. Ibid., 5 October 1832.

33. Ibid., 11 October 1832.

34. Ibid., 14 August 1833. Other games Victoria mentions include Blind Man's Buff 'in a circle with a stick', 'the Key', the game of fans, and 'How Do You Like It'. Ibid., 15 and 16 August 1833. Games such as these were common evening entertainments at country houses such as the Grosvenors' Eaton Hall, where the Kents also visited. See Huxley, *Lady Elizabeth and the Grosvenors*, p. 36.

35. *Youthful Recreations*. Philadelphia. J. Johnson (*c.* 1810), n.p.

36. RA VIC QVJ, 29 September 1832.

37. Ibid., 6 August 1832.

38. Ibid., 21 September 1832.

39. On 26 September 1832, Victoria reports that on a trip aboard the steamer to Puffin Island the weather was quite inclement and many people became very sick, including Victoria and Lehzen (ibid., 26 September 1832). In her annotations to Agnes Strickland's ill-fated *Queen Victoria: From Birth to Bridal*, the Queen denies ever having been seasick.

40. RA VIC QVJ, 10 August 1832.

41. Ibid., 30 August 1832.

42. Ibid., 6 October 1832.

43. Ibid., 21 September 1832.

44. George Rowell, *Queen Victoria Goes to the Theatre*. London: Paul Elek (1978), p. 12.

45. Princess Victoria's appreciation of the gilt, stained glass, and statuary of Lord and Lady Grosvenor's palace Eaton Hall in Cheshire, confided to her journal in 1832, marks a 'childish love of the garish [that] was to remain with her for the rest of her long life,' comments Huxley in *Lady Elizabeth and the Grosvenors*, p. 32.

For an in-depth analysis of the significance of the adult Victoria's use of costume, see Munich's *Queen Victoria's Secrets*, especially Chapter two, 'Genealogies in Her Closet', pp. 23–54. In the 1840s and 1850s, Queen Victoria and Prince Albert hosted a series of costume balls. These fancy-dress occasions, based on eras of English history, gave the royal couple an opportunity to proclaim their British authority and fitness to rule through the performative nature of clothing: '[Victoria and Albert's] costumes constructed nationalistic mythologies, with the couple performing a selective royal genealogy as a way of declaring their sovereignty over the "races" of Britain' (ibid., p. 24).

46. Dash's costume is mentioned in April 1833 journal entries.
47. RA VIC QVJ, 6 January 1833.
48. Ibid., 3 October 1832.
49. Ibid., 9 October 1832.
50. Ibid., 11 December 1832.
51. Ibid., 29 November 1832.
52. Ibid., 5 December 1832.
53. Ibid., 30 November 1832.
54. *Anecdotes … of Victoria the First*, p. 141.
55. RA VIC QVJ, 17 August 1832.
56. Ibid., 17 October 1832.
57. Ibid., 2 November 1832.
58. Later in this entry she learns to spell 'proceeded': a little 'e' is added where lacking. Perhaps Lehzen had corrected her, or she may have asked for the proper spelling.
59. RA VIC QVJ, 17 October 1832.
60. Quoted in Huxley, *Lady Elizabeth and the Grosvenors*, p. 41.
61. RA VIC QVJ, 19 October 1832.
62. Ibid.
63. A typed transcript of this newspaper article has been inserted in the journal for 29 August 1832. This note, written by the Marchioness of Anglesey and mistress of Plâs Newydd almost 150 years after Victoria's visit, was sent to the Royal Archives in April 1978.
64. RA VIC Y63/5, 7 October 1836 letter from King Leopold to Princess Victoria. See Chapter One.
65. 'The Character of Queen Victoria', *The Quarterly Review* vol. 193, no. 386 (1901), pp. 301–37; p.311.
66. RA VIC QVJ, 9 December 1833.
67. Ibid., 24 January 1834.
68. Ibid., 31 January 1833.
69. Ibid., 1 February 1833.
70. Ibid., 27 April 1833.
71. S. C. Hall, 'The Mosspits', in *The Amulet: A Christian and Literary Remembrancer*, ed. S. C. Hall. London: Frederick Westley and A. H. Davis (1832), pp. 91–146. RL RCIN 1056302.
72. See the preface to *The Amulet* (1832), p. iv.
73. Edward Bulwer-Lytton, *Godolphin: A Novel*, 3 vols. London: Richard Bentley (1833), vol. 3, p. 170. RL RCIN 1080802.
74. *The Highland Smugglers*, 3 vols. London: Henry Colburn and Richard Bentley (1832). RL RCIN 1080742. Other novels that Victoria read in the early 1830s include *Ayesha, The Maid of Kars* by James Mosier (London: Richard Bentley, 1834), and Maria Edgeworth's *Helen* (London: Richard Bentley, 1834), which Feodore also read. Feodore called it 'a very useful good novel, which one can not say of every one'.

See RA VIC Y34/17, 17 December 1834, letter from Princess Feodore to Princess Victoria.

75. RA VIC QVJ, 10 August 1832.

76. Ibid., 14 August 1832. See also 23 August and 2 October 1832.

77. For example, Victoria writes that she 'wrote music' multiple times during the day on Monday, 27 August 1832, part of the time 'in Mamma's room downstairs …'.

78. RA VIC QVJ, 16 September 1832.

79. Mrs Hofland, *The Young Northern Traveller, or the Invalid Restored*. London: A. K. Newman (n.d.), p. ii. RL RCIN 1003174

80. RA VIC QVJ, 3 November 1836.

81. RA VIC Y61/34, 4 April 1834, letter from King Leopold to Princess Victoria. This view was shared by George Davys. In the autumn of 1832, after the summer vacation was over, Davys, now Dean of Chester, and the Duchess of Kent conferred about Victoria's education and the Duchess decided that she should spend more time studying with the Dean in order to increase her progress. (In fact, ten months earlier, George Davys had been hinting that Victoria would benefit from extra work time. See RA VIC M5/30, 14 January 1832, letter from George Davys to the Duchess of Kent.) In the extra two hours a day now allotted to study, the Dean suggests that '[m]uch attention should be paid to *History* both *Ancient* and *Modern*: – it would not be well to give much less than an hour, out of the two, every day to this subject' (RA VIC M5/37, 14 November 1832). In a confidential memorandum written to Baroness Lehzen, the Duchess of Kent outlines reasons why Victoria's educational programme needs reforming (some of which are political in nature, as she desires to 'avoid interference in conducting Victoria's education, either as to form, or persons as well to act for Her advantage, and that of the Public, to whom She belongs …' RA VIC M5/40, n.d.). Rather than, or in addition to, her own discussions with Victoria, the Duchess of Kent strongly suggests that the Baroness help Victoria to see the wisdom of this new plan: 'And it will be very desirable for you to engage Victoria, through Her reason, to see the necessity of all this, – and that by cheerfully lending Herself to it, – we may do what is requisite in our present agreeable way' (ibid.).

82. RA VIC Y61/15, 22 May 1832, letter from King Leopold to Princess Victoria. Emphasis in the original.

83. See RA VIC Y61/20, 21 May 1833, letter from King Leopold to Princess Victoria.

84. RA VIC Y61/22, 18 October 1833, letter from King Leopold to Princess Victoria. Emphasis in the original.

85. RA VIC Y61/29, 18 May 1834, letter from King Leopold to Princess Victoria. Emphasis in the original.

86. RA VIC Z493/30, 28 December 1834, letter from Princess Victoria to King Leopold. A disgruntled Victoria wrote to Feodore in 1834 that after her medical examination it was determined that she was 'grown tall, and unhappily very fat'. Princess Victoria was at a loss to explain her weight gain since 'I take so much exercise.' RA VIC LB1/5, 30 October 1834, letter from Princess Victoria to Princess Feodore.

87. RA VIC Y61/38, 22 December 1834, letter from King Leopold to Princess Victoria.

88. RA VIC Y63/11, 18 November 1836, letter from Princess Victoria to Princess Feodore.

89. RA VIC QVJ 24 June 1834.

90. Ibid., July 1834.

91. Ibid., 2 June 1834. Emphasis in the original.

92. Ibid., 26 July 1834.

93. Agnes Strickland, 'Sister's Love', in *Marshall's Christmas Box: A Juvenile Annual.* London: W. Marshall (1831), pp. 157–8.

94. This clipping was slipped into Victoria's fifth manuscript journal.

95. RA VIC Z493/27, 22 October 1834, letter from Princess Victoria to King Leopold.

96. Ellen Jordan, '"Making Good Wives and Mothers"? The Transformation of Middle-Class Girls' Education in Nineteenth-Century Britain', *History of Education Quarterly* vol. 31, no. 4 (Winter 1991), pp. 439–62; p. 451. One of the aims of middle-class girls' education of the period was to mimic upper-class female education as much as possible.

97. [Anon.] *A New Epitome of the British History, To the Present Period. Containing an Account of the Crusades, and the Biography of the Principal Characters that Adorn the British Annals; intended as an Accompaniment to Mangnall's Historical Questions.* London: Minerva Press (1815), p. 376.

98. For example, Victoria was asked, 'On what does the time of day depend?' and she answered, 'The time of day depends on the rising and setting of the Sun', which was corrected to read 'on the *longitude* of that place'. She was similarly incorrect in identifying latitude as the determining factor of the seasons (she again named the sun). Victoria failed to attempt an answer to the question, 'Whence arises the necessity of having accurate time keepers for ascertaining the longitude of any place?' The four exams, tied loosely with a pink ribbon, were placed inside of a copybook. RA VIC Add. A/7/1a, Queen Victoria's Lesson Books.

99. Ibid.

100. RA VIC Add./A/7/1b, Queen Victoria's Account Books and Copy Books, etc.

101. RA VIC QVJ, 3 May 1833.

102. *Anecdotes … of Victoria the First*, p. 476.

103. RA VIC QVJ, 1 February 1833.

104. RA VIC LB3/23 (1831–33).

105. Dash often appears as a character in Victoria's letters to Feodore. On 27 September 1834, writing from the resort town of Tunbridge Wells, Victoria teases Feodore by chiding her: 'Dash, after whom you never enquire, though he was so much attached to you, is greatly improved in beauty; but as for his manners, I fear they are not so, for his voice is shriller than ever, and he hunts the sheep dreadfully.' RA VIC LB6/11 (1834).

106. In a memorandum by the Duchess of Kent that summarized Victoria's daily lessons for a two-week period in the autumn of 1833, she noted that the Princess was reading in Blackstone's *Commentaries* about 'the Rights of Parent and Child, – of Guardian and Ward – of Rights of Persons, of Corporations', and later about the rights of things in general. Rather poignantly, at the end of this document she notes, 'I wish I knew as much, as Victoria knows.' RA VIC M5/44.

107. Susan P. Casteras, 'The Wise Child and Her "Offspring": Some Changing Faces of Queen Victoria', in Munich and Homans, *Remaking Queen Victoria*, p. 189.

108. See RA VIC QVJ, 7 December 1832: 'I gave [dear] Mamma a little writing-box and a nosegay; & she gave me a beautiful broach with little harts, & a pair of lovely gold earrings. Dear Lehzen gave me two lovely china figures.' The exchange of gifts was in remembrance of Feodore's birthday.

109. RA VIC M5/47, 24 May 1834, letter from the Duchess of Kent to Princess Victoria.

110. [Anon.]. 'A Little Girl's Soliloquy on New Year's Day', in *The New Year's Gift; and Juvenile Souvenir*, ed. Alaric Watts. London: Longman, Rees, Orme, Brown, Green, and Longman (1833), pp. 117–18; p. 117. RL RCIN 1056288.

111. [Anon.]. 'A Little Girl's Lament for the Fairies', in *The New Year's Gift*, ed. Watts, pp. 27–30, pp. 27, 30.

112. 'A Little Girl's Lament', p. 29.

113. RA VIC M5/52, 31 December 1834, letter from the Duchess of Kent to Princess Victoria.

114. In her biography of Queen Victoria, *The Youthful Queen Victoria: A Discursive Narrative* (New York, G. P. Putnam's Sons 1952) Dormer Creston gives the Duchess of Northumberland this name, p. 133. Under the Duchess of Kent's patronage, the Duchess of Northumberland saw her social status rise. In a grateful letter acknowledging the confidence the Duchess of Kent had placed in her by appointing her to such an important position in relation to Victoria, the Duchess of Northumberland indicates her excitement at the prospect of her presentation to the King and Queen at an approaching Drawing Room. RA VIC M5/18, 31 January 1831, letter from the Duchess of Northumberland to the Duchess of Kent.

115. Northumberland submitted a 'course of instruction' to the Duchess of Kent in May 1832 that consisted primarily of books to read and topics to cover within the Princess's curriculum. The Duchess of Northumberland focused primarily on religious instruction and history in her lists of recommended texts. Her suggestions are highly conventional except for the inclusion of *Blackstone's Commentaries*. See RA VIC M5/35. See also RA VIC M5/34, 3 June 1832, letter from the Duchess of Northumberland to the Duchess of Kent.

116. See RA VIC LB4 (1833–34).

117. RA VIC QVJ, 7 November 1833.

118. Ibid., 13 November 1833.

119. For example, in May 1833 Victoria mentions four large dinner parties and notes the names of those who attended. Sir John Conroy generally brought up the rear of each list. RA VIC QVJ, 1, 6, 8, 29 May 1833. On 5 May 1834, the Duchess of Kent gave a large 'rout' and Victoria marked the occasion by gluing a clipping into her journal. Ibid., 5 May 1834.

120. Ibid., 24 May 1833.

121. For a discussion of the 'two queens in one isle' see Nicola J. Watson's essay 'Gloriana Victoriana: Victoria and the Cultural Memory of Elizabeth I', in Munich and Homans, *Remaking Queen Victoria*, pp. 79–104. Elizabeth Langland offers a brief discussion of the Victorian connection between the two monarchs in 'Nation and

Nationality: Queen Victoria in the Developing Narrative of Englishness', ibid., pp. 27–30.

In her astute assessment of Victoria's youth and beauty at her coronation as powerfully appealing, Monica Charlot views Victoria as the fourth queen regnant in English history (Mary, Elizabeth, and Anne preceding her): 'None of the three preceding female Sovereigns – Mary, Elizabeth I and Anne – had had the advantages of Victoria. At her Coronation, Victoria was both young and seemly' (p. 116). However, it can be argued that Queen Mary II (of 'William and Mary') was also a 'born' queen, thus making Victoria the fifth.

122. It is interesting to note that Jane Austen, a generation earlier, was also concerned with writing English history, in her case as parody of that schoolroom mainstay, Oliver Goldsmith's four-volume *History of England* (1771). The sixteen-year-old Austen finished her 'The History of England ... By a Partial, *Prejudiced* & Ignorant Historian' in 1791. Jane's history written in defiance of Goldsmith (Princess Victoria was to read him as well) is wickedly humorous and irreverent. See Deirdre LeFaye's introduction to the facsimile edition (London: The British Library, 1993).

123. RA VIC Add. A/7/1A. There are two extant examples of Princess Victoria's books of queens; the longer one begins with the letter 'A' and includes 'C' and one 'E' for 'Elizabeth', the last and longest entry in the book by far. Included in this copybook, however, are numerous slips of paper with letters from 'A' to 'W' with the corresponding queens written below. It appears, then, that Victoria intended to complete her book. Although the books are undated, Victoria writes in ink and with an accomplished hand. I conjecture that the date of the books is probably between 1834 and 1837.

124. RA VIC Z493/27, letter from Princess Victoria to King Leopold, 22 October 1834.

125. RA VIC Add. A/7/1a. In the second book of queens (covering only A-C, and, looking at the script, probably written after the first effort), Catherine of Aragon is called 'a good person but was never liked by Henry who was much younger than she was'; Anne Boleyn's beauty is praised again, but her negative characteristics – 'rather giddy and thoughtless' seem to be rather more significant to Princess Victoria.

126. RA VIC Add. A/7/1a. Victoria's strong position seems to reflect her own opinion (rather than being copied out of a book). Someone (it looks like the hand of her tutor, Reverend George Davys) has pencilled 'amiable as' above the underlined 'bad woman', perhaps to mitigate Victoria's accusation. The Archbishop of Canterbury particularly noted the Princess Victoria's ability to analyse personality strengths and weaknesses after he examined her on various topics on 1 May 1830: 'I asked her opinion on several points, & especially on the character of the English Sovereigns, on which she appeared to have thought for herself, and for a young person her age to have formed a just estimate.' RA VIC Z492/20.

127. Stuart, *Daughter of England*, p. 57.

128. RA VIC Add. A/7/1A.

129. In the first instance, I have assumed that the Princess Victoria is writing about a book of embroidery patterns: it is difficult to determine with absolute certainty the

exact nature of the book she was given as she seems to have left a word or two out of her journal as she was writing it. The entry (like the second half of this first volume of her girlhood journal) is not rewritten in ink, but remains in pencil): 'I received from Mr. Saunderson a paper book with some very extraordinary worked [word missing] which were made for a coverlet by the order of Lord Essex fo[r] Queen Elizabeth when she visited him at Twickenhem.' RA VIC QVJ, 1 October 1832. Regrettably, Princess Victoria's comments about the young Elizabeth's knowledge of Latin do not indicate whether this understanding was greater than her own (although, certainly, the learned Elizabeth, pupil of Roger Ascham, was trained as an intellectual to an extent that Victoria was not). Ibid., 7 November 1832.

Chapter Four: The Importance of Being Victoria, 1835

1. Oscar Wilde, *The Importance of Being Earnest*, ed. Ruth Berggren. New York: Vanguard Press (1987), p. 136.
2. Ibid., pp. 148–9.
3. Estelle C. Jelinek, *The Tradition of Women's Autobiography: From Antiquity to the Present*. Boston: Twayne (1986), p. 41.
4. Wilde, *The Importance of Being Earnest*, p. 101. Cecily goes on to defend her diary-as-memory, noting that 'I believe that memory is responsible for nearly all the three-volume novels that every cultivated woman writes now-a-days, and that no cultivated man ever reads', p. 102.
5. Frances Anne Kemble, *Record of a Girlhood*, 3 vols. London: Richard Bentley and Son (1878), vol. 1, p. 297.
6. Introduction, Caroline Fox, *The Journals of Caroline Fox, 1835–1871*, ed. Wendy Monk. London: Elek Books (1972), p. 13.
7. Robert J. N. Tod, *Caroline Fox: Quaker Blue-Stocking, 1819–1871*. York: William Sessions (1980), p. 9.
8. Dr Clark, who had set up practice in Rome from 1819 to 1826, was the last physician to attend the poet John Keats as he lay dying of advanced tuberculosis in 1821. Although the blood-letting Clark prescribed would not have helped the patient to recover, this was the accepted treatment of the day. In fact, Clark was selected to write an article on tubercular phthisis for the *Cyclopedia of Practical Medicine* which was later reprinted in 1835 as a pamphlet. See Stuart, *The Mother of Victoria*, p. 233.
9. Barbara Timm Gates's introduction to the reprinted first edition of the journal outlines in diary style her search for the missing manuscript journals (only about a sixth of the journal had been published). Despite valiant and repeated efforts, she was unable to track them down. In the last entry to the introductory narrative, however, Gates describes her surprise and delight in the notification that two (of twelve) of the journals had come to light and were to be auctioned on 14 March 1991. This discovery came too late for the volume she had prepared to commemorate the centenary of the 1891 edition. The discovery of a portion of the manuscript diaries also

highlights the expurgated nature of the only Shore diary available to readers. The auction announcement, for example, describes an unpublished conclusion to the seventh volume (from October 1836 until April 1837) that includes Shore's statement that she felt the journal to be her closest companion. This belief may well have disturbed her sister's editing of the journal as it suggests that Shore was somewhat self-absorbed and perhaps constrained in her family's company – a different picture than that of the selfless daughter and sister that the journal proposes (p. xxix). See Barbara Timm Gates, Introduction, *Journal of Emily Shore*. Charlottesville: University Press of Virginia (1991), pp. vii–xxx.

10. Anne Chalmers, *Letters and Journals of Anne Chalmers*, ed. Mrs A. W. Blackie. London: Privately printed by the Curwen Press for the Chelsea Publishing Company (1922), p. 43.

11. Stanley Weintraub, *Victoria: An Intimate Biography*, New York: E. P. Dutton (1987), p. 144. In February 1836 she confided to her journal that 'I for *my* part think all children till 6 months old very ugly.' RA VIC QVJ, 12 February 1836. Some months later she wrote to Feodore, 'I remember when we were at Eaton Hall seeing Lady Robert Grosvenor's little girl, who was not quite a fortnight old, and which was called, & I suppose it was, for *that* age, pretty, but *I* thought it a great fright; it was so red and shapeless.' RA VIC LB 19/1a, 14 October 1836. See also Weintraub, *Victoria*, pp. 150–1.

12. Stewart J. Brown, 'Thomas Chalmers and the Communal Ideal', in *Victorian Values*, ed. T. C. Smout in *Proceedings of the British Academy* 78 (1992), p. 62. See also *The Practical and the Pious: Essays on Thomas Chalmers*, ed. A. C. Cheyne. Edinburgh: Saint Andrew Press, (1985) pp. 9–30.

13. Frances Kemble, *Record of a Girlhood*, 3 vols. London: Richard Bentley and Son (1878), p. 77. Woodham-Smith comments about Queen Victoria's relationship with her first Prime Minister, 'The romantic, childish and innocent admiration of a young inexperienced girl for an older still charming man who is acting as her tutor is a common variety of first love and the young Queen's devotion to Lord Melbourne is a classic example.' Woodham-Smith, *Queen Victoria*, p. 175.

14. Tod, *Caroline Fox*, p. 9.

15. Introduction, *Journal of Emily Shore*. London: Kegan, Paul, Trench, Trübner and Co. (1891), p. xii. All quotations are from this edition unless otherwise noted.

16. Ibid., p. x.

17. *Journal of Emily Shore*, p. 28.

18. Reverend I. Taylor, *Scenes of British Wealth*. London: Harris and Son (1823), p. 160. RL RCIN 1087087.

19. Tod, *Caroline Fox*, p. 10. Tod recounts that once Caroline had cheated a bit in writing a theme on 'humility'. This essay was especially praised by her father, and Caroline guiltily confessed her crime to the page: 'Papa said my theme on humility was the best I had ever written. Extra Private, half of it was copied from the Encyclopedia & the other half from the Bible' (p. 10).

20. Taylor, *Scenes of British Wealth*, p. 162.

21. *Journal of Emily Shore*, p. 130.

22. Gates, Introduction, ibid., p. xxv.

23. Ibid., pp. 31–2.

24. *Letters and Journals of Anne Chalmers*, p. 30.

25. Charlot comments that girlhood crushes such as Princess Victoria's for Giulia Grisi are common 'among children who do not receive sufficient affection' (Charlot, *Victoria: The Young Queen*, p. 74). At the death of Malibran, Princess Victoria's second-favourite singer, Victoria wrote: 'Alas! Poor *Malibran*! Who has *enchanted thousands*, who had the prospect of retiring in 3 years from the stage and living in affluence & comfort, is now cold & immoveable! The iron grasp of Death which spares neither age, sex, nor merit, has been on her & snatched her from her flowery path in one short week!' (RA VIC QVJ, 26 September 1836). Princess Victoria's excitedly morbid ruminations highlight her interest in the tragic.

26. *Journal of Emily Shore*, p. 98. See RA VIC QVJ, 26 May 1835 for Princess Victoria's review of this concert.

27. *Journal of Emily Shore*, Gates edn (1991), p. 184.

28. Ibid.

29. *Letters and Journals of Anne Chalmers*, pp. 51–2. In her Autobiographical Notes written in 1880, Anne (Chalmers) Hanna notes that when she was ten years old in 1823 she had met the famous author, Maria Edgeworth, who was similarly an advocate of 'truth'. Anne had loved her novel *Patronage*, but found Edgeworth the person 'little and plain and elderly', p. 170.

30. *Journal of Emily Shore*, p. 129.

31. Ibid.

32. Emily uses the same texts for Mackworth's lessons that Princess Victoria also read: Mrs Markham's history and Malkins's history of Greece. Ibid.

33. In his *Atlantic Monthly* obituary of Frances Kemble, Henry Lee quotes Christopher North's praise of the actress. *Atlantic Monthly* 71 (January–June 1893), p. 663.

34. Kemble, *Record of a Girlhood*, vol. 2, p. 67. Thackeray had reportedly told Fanny twenty years after her entrance onto the stage, that all the youth of London were in love with her and had displayed the Laurence portrait in their rooms. Henry Lee, 'Frances Anne Kemble.' Ibid.

35. Ibid., pp. 69–70.

36. *Journals of Caroline Fox*, p. 33.

37. Anne Chalmers, *Diary of Anne Chalmers*, p. 84.

38. *Journal of Emily Shore*, p. 146.

39. Kemble, *Record of a Girlhood*, vol. 3, p. 137.

40. Ibid., vol. 2, p. 82.

41. *Journal of Emily Shore*, p. 4.

42. Ibid., pp. 7–9.

43. Jelinek, *Tradition of Women's Autobiography*, p. 41.

44. Introduction by John A. Scott to Frances Anne Kemble, *Journal of a Residence on a Georgian Plantation in 1838–1839*, ed. John A. Scott. Athens, GA: University of Georgia Press (1984), p. xi.

45. Kemble, *Record of a Girlhood*, vol. 1, pp. 63–4.

46. In Louisa May Alcott's novel for adults, *Work* (1873), the heroine, Christie Devon, experiments with a series of different employments available to women. When Christie resolves to try acting, her first role is as an Amazon warrior queen: 'With a clashing of arms and shrill war-cries the rescuers of innocence assailed the sooty fiends who fell before their unscientific blows with a rapidity which inspired in the minds of the beholders a suspicion that the goblins' own voluminous tails tripped them up and gallantry kept them prostrate'. Louisa May Alcott, *Work: A Novel of Experience* (1873). New York: Schocken Books (1977), p. 43. Christie's success in this non-speaking part results in many other engagements, but a serious accident and the eventual realization that acting is a coarsening life for women, convinces her to quit the stage. In thinking about her early life, Fanny Kemble remarks, rather akin to the view presented in Alcott's novel, the dangers for women in acting. As she aged, Kemble espoused primarily negative feelings about her dramatic 'avocation': '... a *business* which is incessant excitement and factitious emotion seems to me unworthy of a man; a business which is public exhibition, unworthy of a woman'. *Record of a Girlhood*, vol. 2, p. 61.

47. RA VIC QVJ, 16 April 1835.

48. RA VIC Z114, entry for 2 April 1835 in Princess Victoria's reading journal.

49. Ibid.

50. RA VIC/Add. A7/31.

51. Ibid.

52. Ibid.

53. Diana, herself an abandoned child (her 'distracted' father left her with a nurse in Ireland for ten years after her mother's death in childbirth), was raised in 'perfect ignorance'. Victoria describes her as animal-like, with dishevelled black hair over her face and back, ill-mannered, badly dressed, and clearly marked by both class and race. She has 'two brawny red arms' and speaks 'in a brogue so unintelligible that [her father] almost started'. This wild child cannot control her temper and screams 'in a most indecorous manner' with alarming frequency.

54. RA VIC/Add. A7/31.

55. RL RCIN 1056459, *The Christian Keepsake and Missionary Annual*, ed. Rev. W. Ellis. London: H. Fisher, R. Fisher and P. Jackson (1835).

56. See my discussion of *The Governess* in *Disciplines of Virtue: Girls' Culture in the Eighteenth and Nineteenth Centuries*. New Haven: Yale University Press (1995), pp. 46–8.

57. RA VIC Y34/38, 12 December 1835, letter from Princess Feodore to Princess Victoria. Victoria responded that she was 'very happy to hear, that the portrait of my ugly face pleased you, and that you find it like; had it not been for your dear sake, I would not have spent so many tedious hours for Collin.' She goes on to mention that her mouth is not 'like' because she kept it shut, especially to please her sister: 'I often shut my mouth now, as it is thought more *becoming*'. RA VIC LB16/10, 20 December 1835, letter from Princess Victoria to Princess Feodore.

There seem to be two Collen paintings: one was sent to Feodore and the other, a miniature, was dated and signed 1836.

58. RA VIC Z492/29, 31 March 1835, letter from the Duchess of Kent to the Archbishop of Canterbury.
59. Ibid.
60. See RA VIC Z492/30 to Z492/33.
61. Woodham-Smith, *Queen Victoria*, p. 98.
62. RA VIC Z492/34, 2 July 1835, letter from Sir Herbert Taylor to the Archbishop of Canterbury.
63. Ibid.
64. RA VIC Z492/36, 10 July 1835.
65. See RA VIC Addl Mss U/72/14 (n.d.) and RA VIC Add Ms U/72/17, 2 July 1835.
66. RA VIC 492/34, 13 July 1835.
67. RA VIC 492/38.
68. RA VIC QVJ, 27 July 1835.
69. RA VIC M5/74, 27 July 1835, letter from the Duchess of Kent to Lord Melbourne.
70. Ibid.
71. RA VIC M5/75, 28 July 1835, letter from King William to the Duchess of Kent.
72. See RA VIC M5/76, 29 July 1835, letter from the Duchess of Kent to King William. In his reply (in Sir Herbert Taylor's hand but signed by William), the King graciously excuses the pair from the pleasure weekend he had planned: 'His Majesty apprises the Duchess of Kent that he enters into Her feelings in the melancholy occasion to which she adverts and that he will not expect her or the Princess Victoria at Kew or to go to Greenwich.' RA M5/77, 29 July 1835, letter from King William to the Duchess of Kent.
73. RA VIC M5/78, 30 July 1835, letter from the Duchess of Kent to Princess Victoria.
74. Ibid.
75. Ibid.
76. RA VIC QVJ, 30 July 1835.
77. Ibid.
78. Ian Bradley, *The Call to Seriousness: The Evangelical Impact on the Victorians.* London: Jonathan Cape (1976), p. 13.
79. RA VIC QVJ, 30 July 1835.
80. RA VIC M5/80, 2 August 1835, letter from the Duchess of Kent to Princess Victoria. Emphasis in original.
81. Ibid.
82. RA VIC QVJ, 2 August 1835.
83. Strickland, *From Birth to Bridal*, p. 82. Victoria also objects to the discussion of a 'cap' that she supposedly wore to her confirmation. In her journal, Victoria describes her attire as 'a white lace dress, with a white crape bonnet with a wreath of white roses round it'. And while a bonnet is not a cap, she also mentions removing the bonnet prior to standing before the altar, as would be proper (RA VIC QVJ, 30 July 1835).
84. RA VIC M5/84, 2 September 1835, letter from the Duchess of Kent to Princess Victoria.
85. RA VIC QVJ, 29 August 1835.

86. RA VIC M5/55, 24 May 1835, letter from the Duchess of Kent to Princess Victoria.

87. Victoria wasn't particularly happy about taking this jaunt either, as the Opera was still on for three more nights. But given the fact of their mourning for Aunt Sophia, they were not able to attend in any case. See RA VIC QVJ, 5 August 1835.

88. One of Princess Victoria's books, *The Juvenile Forget Me Not* for 1835, included a tale 'Country Lodgings in America', satirizing female education superintended by silly mothers. Mrs Pownsey, 'a lady of the Malaprop school', disdains Edgeworth's stories and prefers her daughters to read *Rowland's Ancient History* and *Sully's Memoirs*. However, Mrs Pownsey, who has rejected American history for her American daughters because 'it is never read in England', admires 'Sully' as 'I know Mr. Sully very well. . . . He painted my portrait, and a most delightful man he is, only rather obstinate ...' (p. 201). Thomas Sully (1783–1872) was a well-known American portrait painter. In 1838 he painted a full-length portrait of Queen Victoria for the Society of the Sons of St George in Philadelphia. See RCIN 1056279. *The Juvenile Forget-Me-Not: A Christmas and New Year's Gift, or Birth-Day Present*, ed. Mrs. S. C. Hall. London: Ackermann and Co. (1835).

89. Scott, Introduction to Kemble, *Journal of a Residence on a Georgian Plantation*, p. xv, n.2.

90. In her discussion of Fanny Kemble in her *Autobiography* Martineau calls Fanny a liar and dismisses the entire Kemble family as having 'a green-room cast of mind about them'. Martineau, *Autobiography*, vol. 2 p. 365.

91. RA VIC QVJ, 20 August 1835.

92. Ibid., 16 September 1835.

93. Ibid., 3 September 1835.

94. Ibid., 28 August 1835.

95. Ibid., 7 September 1835.

96. See Gates, Introduction, *Journal of Emily Shore*, 1991 edn, p. xxi.

97. Ibid.

98. RA VIC QVJ, LB 19/1b, 14 October 1836, letter from Princess Victoria to Princess Feodore.

99. Ibid., LB 23/6, 8 May 1836, letter from Princess Victoria to Princess Feodore and LB 25/7 or 8, 21 June 1836, letter from Princess Victoria to Princess Feodore.

100. Linda H. Peterson, 'Institutionalizing Women's Autobiography: Nineteenth-Century Editors and the Shaping of an Autobiographical Tradition', in Robert Folkenflit, *The Culture of Autobiography: Constructions of Self-Representation*. Stanford, CA: Stanford University Press (1993), pp. 80–103; p. 94.

101. See RA VIC Z114, Journal of the Books I Read for 11 January 1837. In the practice of keeping a book journal, Victoria was following her sister, who informed Victoria that she kept such a journal as a record of her opinions and impressions of what she had read. See RA VIC Y34/10, 21 October 1834, letter from Princess Feodore to Princess Victoria.

102. RA VIC Y34/27, 2 June 1835.

103. Lori Anne Loeb, *Consuming Angels: Advertising and Victorian Women*. Oxford: Oxford University Press (1994), p. 85.

104. RA VIC QVJ, 11 September 1835.

105. Ibid., 18 September 1835.

106. Ibid., 21 September 1835.

107. Ibid., 22 September 1835.

108. Ibid.

109. Ibid., 23 September 1835.

110. Ibid. My thanks to Lady de Bellaigue for her translation of the German, and thanks to Robert Shandley for additional help.

111. Ibid., 24 September 1835.

112. Ibid., 25 September 1835.

113. Ibid., 3 October 1835. On 14 November Victoria received with delight two large boxes of 'Parisian millenery' from her aunt.

114. Ibid., 4 October 1835.

115. Ibid., 7 October 1835.

116. See Weintraub, *Victoria*, p. 86 and Woodham-Smith, *Queen Victoria*, pp. 106–7.

117. RA VIC M5/82, 1835 memorandum from the Duchess of Kent to Viscount Melbourne written by Sir John Conroy.

118. In this matter the Duchess of Kent and Sir John Conroy were joined by Princess Victoria's brother, Prince Charles of Leiningen (who would also be dependent upon the future Queen for moneys). Victoria was not persuaded, and Charles, rather guiltily, tried to defend his behaviour in a memorandum written in 1840 at the request of Prince Albert. See RA VIC M7/67, trans. from German in RA VIC Add. V, vol. 2.

119. RA VIC Addl. Mss U/72/15 letter from Princess Feodore to the Duchess of Northumberland, 25 March 1835.

120. Albert, *Queen Victoria's Sister*, p. 86.

121. Cecil Woodham-Smith reminds us that contained within Victoria's adoration there was also a 'tinge of fear': 'Lehzen was a woman of formidable character and in the numerous expressions of love for Lehzen ... scattered through the Princess's Journal there is a hint of propitiation. Lehzen, after all, read the Journal, and passages were written to please her.' Woodham-Smith concedes, however, that Lehzen was the person most responsible for Victoria's success when 'like a butterfly from a chrysalis, the young Queen burst on the world' (*Queen Victoria*, p. 100).

122. RA VIC QVJ, 31 October 1835. She later compares Aunt Louise – whom she had met exactly once – to Lehzen in points of 'sweetness of temper and want of selfishness' (ibid., 18 November 1835). The Duchess of Kent is conspicuous by her absence in this short list of favourites. In fact, in an unusual entry perhaps prompted by Lehzen, Victoria makes a kind of correction to her journal about her mother arranging flowers in the sickroom which she had 'forgotten' to write earlier (ibid., 23 November 1835).

123. Victoria was considering the importance of hair in her lively entry for 25 January 1836. (Viscount Esher leaves this discussion out of his excerpts.) As was still common in the nineteenth century, during a serious illness a woman's long hair would be cut off to cool the head and perhaps interrupt the course of the disease. Victoria had

been very proud of her luxurious hair, now mostly gone: 'I quite forgot to mention that after my illness at Ramsgate I lost my hair frightfully so that I was litterally [sic] now getting *bald*; the comb-tray was full every morning with my hair; as a last & desperate refuge, Lehzen, with Mamma's and my consent, cut off half, and even more, of my back hair, once so thick that she could hardly grasp it in her hand. When I first came to Ramsgate my hair was still *very* thick. There is just enough left to be able to tie it & make a small puff; I wear a false plait of course.' This entry is also significant as it underscores the more intimate relationship Victoria is developing with her journal. Although still not a truly private venue for her, Victoria confides personal details about herself to the journal – such as her hairstyle and illness – that figure it as a friend or confidant.

124. RA VIC M5/86, memorandum dated 29 January 1836.
125. RA VIC Y61/42, 9 March 1835, letter from King Leopold to Princess Victoria. See the discussion of Queen Victoria's height in the *In Royal Fashion* catalogue to the 1997 exhibition of Queen Victoria and Princess Charlotte's clothing (p. 181, n.33). The height of the queen as an adult – before old age – was determined to be 4 feet 11 inches or so, according to the length of the dresses Victoria wore. Kay Staniland, *In Royal Fashion: The Clothes of Princess Charlotte of Wales and Queen Victoria, 1796–1901*. London: Museum of London (1997).
126. RA VIC QVJ, 24 May 1835.
127. Ibid., 2 November 1835.
128. Ibid., 26 September 1835. A few weeks later she also reflected on the death of a young aristocrat and took a lesson from his untimely death: 'Life is short, & this should always be present to the mind of every one! We must strive to do the will of our Heavenly Father while we live so that we may enjoy eternal Bliss & Peace hereafter in a World where all is peace & happiness!' Ibid., 17 November 1835.
129. RA VIC Y62/12 24 December 1835, letter from King Leopold to Princess Victoria.
130. 'We laughed a lot about it.' RA VIC QVJ, 16 and 22 December 1835.
131. Ibid., 29 December 1835.
132. Ibid., 1 January 1836. At the death of her Aunt Sophie, Countess Mensdorff, Victoria had written in her journal – without awareness of any comic irony in her comment – 'They say that a smile was imprinted on her countenance when she died, and that she looked more friendly after her death than she had done some time previous to it.' Ibid., 20 July 1835.
133. RA VIC LB12/12, 6 July 1835.
134. As the author of *Anecdotes … of Victoria the First* comments rather histrionically, the aristocracy saw in Victoria a new Charlotte, and generally approved of the pretty, modest, and shy teenager: '[their hopes] had once already, during the existing generation, been crushed in their budding beauty; but when "the expectancy and rose of the fair state" appeared, the pride and ornament of the high-born throng, many were the earnest prayers put up to Heaven for her preservation …' (p. 315).
135. See, for example, RA VIC QVJ, 10 May and 18 May 1835.
136. These lessons were to continue for twenty years. Rowell, *Queen Victoria Goes to the Theatre*, p. 14.

137. RA VIC QVJ, 18 May 1835.

138. RA VIC M5/82, undated memorandum written by Sir John Conroy (in the Duchess of Kent's name) to Viscount Melbourne.

139. RA VIC M5/53.

140. RA VIC M5/82, 1835 memorandum from the Duchess of Kent to Viscount Melbourne written by Sir John Conroy.

Chapter Five: 'The Fair White Rose of Perfect Womanhood', 1836–1837

1. RA VIC Y63/49, 30 June 1837, letter from King Leopold to Queen Victoria.

2. A Lady of the Court, *Victoria's Golden Reign: A Record of Sixty Years as Maid, Mother, and Ruler*. London: Richard Edward King (1899), p. 2.

3. In an 1838 'Spooner's Transformation' (the optical illusion of two images combining into one when backlit) entitled 'the Rose of England', Queen Victoria and an enormous cabbage rose set in front of Windsor Castle merge. See Homans's *Royal Representations*, p. 12.

4. *Anecdotes ... of Victoria the First*, p. 291.

5. See Janel Mueller, 'Virtue and Virtuality: Gender in the Self-Representations of Queen Elizabeth I', in *Virtual Gender: Fantasies of Subjectivity and Embodiment*, ed. Mary Ann O'Farrell and Lynne Vallone. Ann Arbor: University of Michigan Press (1999), pp. 37–64; p. 42.

6. Susan P. Casteras, 'The Wise Child and Her "Offspring": Some Changing Faces of Queen Victoria', in Munich and Homans, *Remaking Queen Victoria*, pp. 182–99, p. 199.

7. *Anecdotes ... of Victoria the First*, p. 106.

8. For example, when Victoria's brother-in-law Ernest Hohenlohe-Langenburg and his brother Gustav came to England to visit their first cousin, Queen Adelaide, Victoria gleefully wrote to Feodore that she spoke *German* with Gustav during an entire dinner party (Princess Victoria's emphasis). RA VIC LB 42/7, 12 June 1837. In her journal she remarks discussing with Gustav her lack of speaking ability in the German language: 'I have never talked [German] hardly to anybody, much less kept up a long conversation, except with M. Barez. ...' RA VIC QVJ 7 June 1837.

9. RA VIC QVJ, 3 November 1836.

10. Ibid., 6 July 1836.

11. Ibid., 3 November 1836.

12. Ibid., 6 November 1836.

13. Ibid., 13 December 1836.

14. Beverly Seaton's combined vocabulary of flower language (florigraphy) cites Shoberl's rose as 'love'. See *The Language of Flowers: A History*. Charlottesville: University Press of Virginia (1995), p. 191.

15. This image was engraved by F. C. Lewis and published on 24 May 1837 to commemorate Victoria's eighteenth birthday. The flower dictionary quoted from here is Kate Greenaway's illustrated *The Illuminated Language of Flowers* (text by Jean Marsh), London: Macdonald and Jane's (1978), p. 50.

16. *Anecdotes ... of Victoria the First*, p. 448.

17. RA VIC Y63/47, 23 June 1837 letter from King Leopold to Queen Victoria. Later in this letter he also encourages Victoria to capitalize on her relationship to the now long-dead Charlotte for the same purpose of securing the nation's regard: 'Claremont puts me in mind of one thing, which I believe would be agreeable to your feelings and at the same time politic. You recollect the affection which the Nation entertained for Charlotte the hopes which everybody placed on her, I think you might whenever it can be done without "*le tirer par les cheveux*" [forcing the matter] express your hopes, that Providence would permit you to indemnify the Country for the loss which it experienced on that occasion. All rapprochement between you and the great hopes the nation had in Charlotte can only revive a good feeling in the hearts of the people for you, and as it were identify the *Queen that was to have been, even in preference* to your Uncle King William, *with the new Queen that is.*' Emphasis in the original. Some of the advice may come more from wishful thinking that Leopold could keep the memory of his Charlotte – and his own importance to England – alive through Victoria. My thanks to Ralph Schoolcraft for his translation.

   The author of *Anecdotes ... of Victoria the First*, suggests that perhaps Leopold's wish was granted: '... many causes combined to render the Princess an object of peculiar regard; – her sex – her tender age – the excellent education she was known to be receiving under the superintendence of her exemplary Mother – and, above all, the recollection of those hopes and affections which had been so suddenly and sadly blighted, by the untimely death of the still fondly-remembered Princess Charlotte. Victoria, then, was rising as it were from the newly-closed tomb of her "love of millions," which had been so vainly lavished on her predecessor.' *Anecdotes ... of Victoria the First*, p. 441.

18. RA VIC Y63/34 11, April 1837, letter from King Leopold to Princess Victoria.

   It is worth noting that Leopold felt that Victoria's brother Charles was also a spy who needed removing. As his 'Kensington System' document makes clear (see RA VIC M7/67 trans. from German in RA VIC Add. V, vol. 2), Charles was of the same mind as his mother in his promotion of Sir John Conroy. Just after the accession, Leopold wrote to Victoria advising that she send this particular unmasked intercessor away: 'I take this opportunity to insinuate that I think it would be desirable if your brother was to leave England – his conduct towards you, has been something beyond imagination [;] perhaps it was well that it was so at the beginning, it settles the relative positions for the remainders of your lives' (RA VIC Y63/50, 1 July 1837, letter from King Leopold to Queen Victoria).

19. RA VIC LB 37/12. 30 January 1837 letter from Princess Victoria to King Leopold.

20. *The Young Lady's Book: A Manual of Elegant Recreations, Exercises, and Pursuits.* London: Vizetelly, Branston (1829), p. 23. RL RCIN 1056451. Victoria's copy is

inscribed 'To My beloved Victoria from her most affectionate Mother Victoria.' The inscription is not dated.

21. This list is offered in *The Young Lady's Book* as the qualities necessary in the 'daily conduct and habitual deportment of young ladies' (p. 24).

22. Ibid., pp. 23-4.

23. Ibid., p. 27.

24. RA VIC QVJ, 19 March 1836.

25. Ibid.

26. Ibid., 20 March 1836.

27. Ibid., 21 March 1836.

28. Ibid., 2 April 1836.

29. RA VIC LB 24/3. 17 May 1836 letter from Princess Victoria to King Leopold.

30. Ibid. Victoria continues to grieve through the first half of April. Esher leaves out of his selections much of the repetition of Victoria's pain at their departure. This is regrettable because the intensity of her feelings is lost if it appears that she drops this concern. See, for example, 10 April 1836, excerpted in Esher, but missing the beginning of the letter where Victoria expresses her heart-sickness, loneliness, and her need for the journal to be a means for revisiting happy times.

31. See RA VIC QVJ 6 February 1836.

32. Ibid., 10 April 1836. Esher chooses not to include this sentiment.

33. Ibid. Esher notes that 'King Leopold believed that he had reduced the rules of Sovereignty to a science.' Viscount Esher, *The Girlhood of Queen Victoria: A Selection From Her Majesty's Diaries Between the Years of 1832 and 1840*, 2 vols. London: John Murray (1912), vol. 1, p. 154 n.2. In Leopold's opinion, freely expressed to Princess Victoria, England should have been helping him (Belgium) to quell the revolution in Portugal: 'I am very ready to furnish some troops, but we have not means of transporting them [;] that must come from England, and that great country is particularly fond of doing nothing' (RA VIC Y63/5, 7 October 1836, letter from King Leopold to Princess Victoria). The Portuguese monarchy, headed by Manuel II, was overthrown in 1910, and a Portuguese republic was established.

34. RA VIC QVJ, 18 May 1836.

35. Ibid., 24 May 1836.

36. Weintraub, *Victoria*, p. 89.

37. See RA VIC QVJ, 30 May 1836.

38. Ibid., 3 June 1836. See also entries for 6 and 9 June where Uncle Ernest's visit is similarly noted with underlining, and with a suggestive line (noting 'fill in the blank'?) in one entry and in tiny handwriting in another. Clearly, these tête-à-têtes were most exciting to Victoria, so much so that she remarked them in her journal, which had by now become a more private venue for her, in such a way as to protect herself.

39. Certainly Albert's letters to his father after Victoria becomes queen make his own expectations of their future relationship clear. In a 30 July 1837 letter from Bonn, Albert writes about 'the achievement of our aim' (p. 2), 'our purpose' (p. 2) and the 'affair which is so important to my happiness' (p. 3) (RA VIC Addl V translated abstracts of Addl Mss A/14/57). In June, Victoria rather coyly wrote to Uncle

Leopold: '… take care of the health of one, now *so dear* to me, and to take him under *your special* protection. I hope and trust that all will go on prosperously and well on this subject of so much importance to me.' *Letters*, ed. Benson and Esher, vol. 1, p. 62. Emphasis in the original.

The following spring, Albert seems concerned about Victoria's feelings: 'Victoria is said to be very firm and decided about the plan, but she definitely wishes that it should not materialise for a few years yet, which, indeed, is very natural and easy to explain. It is partly that she is still experiencing the first transports of joy at her freedom after the severe repression she suffered throughout her childhood and wants to enjoy it still for some time, partly that she feels herself still too young to think of marriage, and further she wants me to be rather older on the occasion of my first appearance in England, so as not to appear still a child to the English people' (ibid., pp. 4–5). (RA VIC Addl V. translated abstracts of Addl. Mss A/14/66, 6 March 1838, letter from Prince Albert to Ernest I, Duke of Saxe-Coburg-Gotha.)

40. RA VIC Y62/34, 13 May 1836, letter from King Leopold to Princess Victoria.

41. Quoted in Charlot, *Victoria: The Young Queen*, p. 76.

42. See *Anecdotes … of Victoria the First*, pp. 425–40.

43. Quoted ibid., p. 436.

44. See RA VIC M5/84, 2 September 1835, letter from the Duchess of Kent to Princess Victoria.

45. RA VIC Y63/11, 18 November 1836, letter from King Leopold to Princess Victoria. Years earlier, after King George IV refused to grant an allowance for the Princess, insisting that her uncle was rich enough to provide for her, Leopold had supplied additional funds for Victoria's support.

46. RA VIC QVJ, 13 January 1836.

47. Quoted in Charlot, *Victoria: The Young Queen*, p. 68.

48. Quoted in Huxley, *Lady Elizabeth and the Grosvenors*, p. 74. Emphasis in the original.

49. RA VIC QVJ, 21 August 1836. Emphasis in the original.

50. See Charlot, *Victoria: The Young Queen*, p. 69.

51. RA VIC QVJ, 10 June 1836. Victoria was later to write in her journal, 'Today is dearest Albert's birth-day, on which day he completes his 17th year. That every happiness & blessing that this world can bestow, may be his portion, is my most earnest & heartfelt prayer!' (Ibid., 26 August 1836). From this comment it does not appear that Princess Victoria was in love, but she was certainly interested in her cousin.

52. Ibid., 14 March 1836.

53. Ibid., 13 July 1836.

54. Ibid., 19 January 1836. On 3 February she also mentions a diet of bread and butter for lunch, and that she will no long note this in her journal as she always eats such a modest repast for a midday snack.

55. Ibid., 16 February 1836.

56. See, for example, Princess Victoria's letter to Feodore on 26 March 1837 where she discusses pregnancies of the Queen of Portugal (her cousin Ferdinand's wife) and Aunt Louise. RA VIC LB 39/14.

57. RA VIC LB 40/16, 30 April 1837, letter from Princess Victoria to Princess Feodore.
58. RA VIC QVJ, 12 February 1836.
59. Ibid., 6 January 1836 (Milton) and ibid., 31 July 1836 (*Eikon Basilike*). 'Eikon Basilike' means 'royal image'; Milton's response to it, *Eikonoklastes* ('image-breaker'), was also published in 1649.
60. RA VIC Y63/3, 26 September 1836, letter from King Leopold to Princess Victoria.
61. RA VIC QVJ, 15 September 1836. Emphasis in original.
62. Ibid., 21 September 1836. It is interesting to note that Esher leaves out these sentiments in his published selections of the journal. Princess Victoria's obvious preference for her uncle over her mother – contrary to the accepted version of Victoria's life that styled her a devoted daughter – is thereby elided by such excerpting.
63. Ibid., 6 November 1836. Victoria reports that the text for this sermon was St Paul's first epistle to the Corinthians, chapter 5. She writes a blank for the verse number, but does not fill it in. Perhaps the verse was number 11: 'But now I have written unto you not to keep company, if any man that is called a brother be a fornicator, or covetous, or an idolater, or a railer, or a drunkard, or an extortioner; with such an one, no, not to eat' (1 Corinthians 5:11). Such harsh judgements obviously seem just about right to Victoria, and her favourites shine both in comparison with this list of degenerates and with Victoria's other companions.

     Victoria is not always so interested in, or open to, the sermons she hears – or guarded enough to self-censor her negative judgements. Later in the same month, she complains about the 'eternal sermon' she had heard (RA VIC QVJ, 27 November 1836).
64. Princess Victoria is called such by the author of *Anecdotes ... of Victoria the First*, p. 225.
65. These exist in thirteen volumes in the Royal Archives.
66. Clive Wigram, 1st Baron Wigram of Clewer, was the Keeper of the King's Archives from 1931 until 1945.
67. See Queen Victoria's comments on Agnes Strickland's misdating of this outing in the Royal Library copy of *From Birth to Bridal*. Agnes Strickland, *From Birth to Bridal*, p. 54.
68. RA VIC LB 37/14, 5 February 1837, letter from Princess Victoria to Princess Feodore.
69. RA VIC QVJ, 3 December 1836. Even after her romance with the gypsy family at Claremont, Victoria is not able to distance herself completely from the view of the gypsies as aesthetic set pieces or objects of study. When teasing Feodore about her abandonment of drawing, and defending her own consistency in artistic pursuits, Victoria writes, 'You naughty little creature, accuse me of neglecting drawing, when you, yourself, are the culprit; for you owned to me, you had not touched a pencil, for several months, whereas, I have been drawing all year round. Last season, I made quantities of sketches from the Opera; then in the Country, I drew sailors, french boys, Spaniards, Gipsies and illustrated tragedies. . . .' RA VIC LB 39/7, 12 March 1837, letter from Princess Victoria to Princess Feodore.
70. RA VIC QVJ, 11 December 1836.

71. Ibid., 15 December 1836.
72. Richard L. Stein, *Victoria's Year: English Literature and Culture, 1837-1838.* Oxford: Oxford University Press (1987), pp. 26–7. Stein comments that Victoria was unable to see the gypsy family in any way other than as a set piece existing only in relation to her (or others like her): 'Victoria's sketches display no evidence of a sense that there are alternatives to seeing those gypsies in the way she does, no sense that other conditions might await them than the one she depicts' (ibid., p. 35).
73. RA VIC Z431, vol. 3, 14 February 1837.
74. RA VIC QVJ, 16 December 1836. Victoria later claims her own relationship to the infant: 'How I *do long* to be able to do some *real good* for our poor Gipsy friends; to do them spiritually good, and also that dear little *baby* which I may *almost* say I saw born, for I have seen it since it was a *day* old!' RA VIC Z431, vol. 3, 14 January 1837. Emphasis in the original.
75. RA VIC QVJ, 22 December 1836. Emphasis in the original.
76. Ibid., 17 December 1836. Emphasis in the original.
77. James Crabb, *The Gipsies' Advocate*, 3rd edn. London (1832), p. 198.
78. Stein, *Victoria's Year*, p. 26.
79. RA VIC Z430, vol. 3. Esher transcript for 1 January 1837. Emphasis in the original.
80. RA VIC LB 37/5, 22 January 1837, letter from Princess Victoria to Princess Feodore.
81. RA VIC LB 37/14, 5 February 1837, letter from Princess Victoria to Princess Feodore.
82. RA VIC QVJ, 22 December 1836.
83. Ibid., 25 December 1836.
84. Deborah Epstein Nord argues, by contrast, that in mid-nineteenth-century women writers' representations of gypsies (in the work, for example, of Charlotte Brontë, Emily Brontë, and George Eliot) the gypsy 'mark[s] not only cultural difference but a deep sense of unconventional, indeed aberrant, femininity.' '"Marks of Race": Gypsy Figures and Eccentric Femininity in Nineteenth-Century Women's Writing,' *Victorian Studies* vol. 41, no. 2 (Winter 1998), pp. 189–210, p. 190.
85. RA VIC Z430, vol. 3, Esher transcript for 8 February 1837.
86. Ibid., Esher transcript for 18 April 1837. Victoria continued on to discuss music in relationship to this comment (preferring the modern composers Bellini, Rossini, and Donizetti to any others).
87. RA VIC LB 41/19, 28 May 1837, letter from Princess Victoria to Princess Feodore.
88. RA VIC LB 42/1, 30 May 1837, letter from Princess Victoria to King Leopold.
89. RA LB VIC 42/6, 3 June 1837, letter from Princess Victoria to the Duchess of Northumberland.
90. See RA VIC Add./A7/41–5. In an envelope included with books on mathematics, Mr Steward notes that Princess Victoria kept up her algebra lessons until 'a few days before her accession to the Throne'.
91. RA VIC LB 43/1, 19 June 1837, letter from Princess Victoria to King Leopold. Emphasis in the original.
92. In her journal Victoria records reading 'The Birthday Present', 'Simple Susan', 'The Two Bracelets', 'The Little Merchants', 'The Mimic', 'The Basket-Woman', 'The

White Pigeon', 'The Orphans', 'Waste Not Want Not', and 'Forgive and Forget'. See entries (in Esher transcript) from 4 to 28 March 1837.

93. See Mitzi Myers, 'Romancing the Moral Tale: Maria Edgeworth and the Problematics of Pedagogy', in *Romanticism and Children's Literature in Nineteenth-Century England*, ed. James Holt McGavran, Jr. Athens: University of Georgia Press (1991), pp. 96–128, p. 98.

94. RA VIC Z430, vol. 3, 5 March 1837 entry.

95. Maria Edgeworth, 'The Orphans', in *The Parent's Assistant*. 3rd edn (1800). Repr. New York: Garland (1976), vol. 5, p. 92.

96. Ibid., p. 108.

97. Maria Edgeworth, 'Forgive and Forget', ibid., p.220.

98. Maria Edgeworth, 'The Mimic', ibid., pp. 129–30.

99. Mitzi Myers, 'Canonical "Orphans" and Critical *Ennui*: Rereading Edgeworth's Cross-Writing', *Children's Literature* vol. 25 (1997), pp. 116–36, p. 128.

100. Casteras, 'The Wise Child and Her "Offspring": Some Changing Faces of Queen Victoria,' p. 183.

101. RA VIC QVJ, 20 June 1837. Emphasis in the original.

102. See Casteras's essay 'The Wise Child and Her "Offspring"', pp. 195–8 for an excellent discussion of the H. T. Wells painting *Victoria Regina: Victoria Receiving the News of Her Accession* (1880).

103. RA VIC LB 43/18, 23 June 1837, letter from Queen Victoria to King Leopold. Certainly, the Duchess of Kent's life was dramatically altered. Member of the Household Mary Ann Davys notes in a letter to her aunt in 1838 that 'The Duchess of Kent is pretty well and looks very tolerably happy, but I think her life must be a dull one' (RA VIC Add. U336). This estrangement was not to last for ever, however. The passage of time, the dismissal of Sir John Conroy, Albert's influence, all helped to repair the relationship between mother and daughter. By 1867, in a letter from Queen Victoria to Baroness Lehzen, Victoria was able to annotate a letter she received from Lehzen in which the Baroness had commented that Victoria had received many fine qualities from her father. 'More from my dear Mother' was the Queen's note on this letter. See RA VIC Y203/81. Hudson's *A Royal Conflict*, especially Chapters Seven to Nine, explains in detail the triangulated relationship that existed between Victoria, Sir John Conroy, and the Duchess of Kent just prior to and after Victoria's accession.

104. RA VIC LB 44/15, 16 July 1837, letter from Queen Victoria to Princess Feodore.

105. Dorothy Thompson, *Queen Victoria: Gender and Power*. London: Virago (1990), p. 23.

106. Quoted in Charlot, *Victoria: The Young Queen*, p. 106.

107. RA VIC Y61/5, 7 October 1836, letter from King Leopold to Princess Victoria.

108. See Giles St Aubyn, *Queen Victoria: A Portrait*, New York: Atheneum (1992), p. 96 and Longford, *Queen Victoria: Born to Succeed*, p. 83.

109. RA VIC LB 43/1, 19 June 1837, letter from Princess Victoria to King Leopold. Queen Victoria's youth certainly comes through in the second letter she wrote to Feodore once she was queen. Victoria is puffed up with unconstrained pride and officiousness:

'You will, I trust forgive me if I write you but a *very* few lines, as I have SO much to do. I see my Ministers every day, & have a great deal to write & sign & talk & as my duty to my country is my *first* and *greatest* wish & *pleasure*, I trust that you will forgive me if I do not just at present write such a long letter as usual.' RA VIC Add. V/171/81, 29 June 1837, letter from Queen Victoria to Princess Feodore.

110.   E. Nesbit, *Royal Children of English History*. New York: Mershon (1897), p. 103. Nesbit, a member of the socialist Fabian Society, also wrote a children's fantasy, *The Enchanted Castle* (1907), in which the enchanted princess was actually a French governess.

111.   Victoria was also reading a little volume entitled *Female Improvement* by Mrs John Sandford in the winter before her accession. See RA VIC QVJ, 19 February 1837.

Bibliography

Albert, Harold A. *Queen Victoria's Sister: The Life and Letters of Princess Feodora*. London: Robert Hale, 1967.

Alcott, Louisa May. *Work: A Novel of Experience*. 1873. New York: Schocken Books, 1977.

Appleton, Elizabeth. *Early Education; or, The Management of Children Considered With a View to Their Future Character* 2nd edn. London: G. & W. B. Whittaker, 1821.

Aspinall, A., ed. *Letters of the Princess Charlotte, 1811-1817*. London: Home and Van Thal, 1949.

Auerbach, Nina. *Woman and the Demon: The Life of a Victorian Myth*. Cambridge, MA: Harvard University Press, 1982.

Auerbach, Nina and U. C. Knoepflmacher, eds. *Forbidden Journeys: Fairy Tales and Fantasies by Victorian Women Writers*. Chicago: University of Chicago Press, 1992.

Austen, Jane. *The History of England ... By a Partial, Prejudiced & Ignorant Historian*. Ed. Deirdre Le Faye. London: The Folio Society, 1993.

Barrie, J. M. *Peter Pan*. 1911. Puffin, 1986.

———. *Peter Pan in Kensington Gardens/Peter and Wendy*. 1906. Oxford: Oxford University Press, 1991.

Bate, W. Jackson. *John Keats*. Cambridge, MA: Harvard University Press, 1963.

Benson, Arthur Christopher and Viscount Esher, eds. *The Letters of Queen Victoria: A Selection From Her Majesty's Correspondence Between the Years 1837–1861*. 3 vols. London: John Murray, 1907.

Benson, E. F. *Queen Victoria*. Abridged. 1935. London: Chatto & Windus, 1987.

Booth, Alison. 'Illustrious Company: Victoria Among Other Women in Anglo-American Role Model Anthologies'. Homans and Munich, *Remaking Queen Victoria*: 59–78.

Bradley, Ian. *The Call to Seriousness: The Evangelical Impact on the Victorians*. London: Jonathan Cape, 1976.

Brumberg, Joan Jacobs. *The Body Project: An Intimate History of American Girls.* New York: Vintage Books, 1998.

Butler, Marilyn. *Maria Edgeworth: A Literary Biography.* Oxford: Clarendon Press, 1972.

Casteras, Susan P. 'The Wise Child and Her "Offspring": Some Changing Faces of Queen Victoria'. Homans and Munich, *Remaking Queen Victoria*: 182–99.

Chalmers, Anne. *Letters and Journals of Anne Chalmers.* Ed. Mrs. A. W. Blackie. London: Privately printed by the Curwen Press for the Chelsea Publishing Company, 1922.

Charlot, Monica. *Victoria: The Young Queen.* Oxford: Basil Blackwell, 1991.

Cheyne, A. C., ed. *The Practical and the Pious: Essays on Thomas Chalmers.* Edinburgh, 1984: 9–30.

Corkran, Alice. *The Life of Queen Victoria for Boys and Girls.* London: T. C. and E. C. Jack, 1910.

Crabb, James. *The Gipsies' Advocate*, 3rd edn. London, 1832.

Craik, Dinah Mulock. *Fifty Golden Years: Incidents in the Queen's Reign.* London: Raphael Tuck and Sons, 1887.

Darton, John. *Famous Girls Who Have Become Illustrious Women: Forming Models for Imitation for the Young Women of England.* 1864. Freeport, NY: Books for Libraries Press, 1972.

DeLuca, Geraldine. 'Lives and Half-Lives: Biographies of Women for Young Adults'. *Children's Literature in Education*, 17.4 (1986): 241–52.

Demers, Patricia. *The World of Hannah More.* Lexington: University Press of Kentucky, 1996.

Edgeworth, Maria. *Harry and Lucy Concluded*, 3rd edn, 3 vols. London: Baldwin and Cradock, 1840.

——. *The Parent's Assistant.* 3rd edn. 1800. Rpt, New York: Garland, 1976.

Edgeworth, Maria and Richard Lovell Edgeworth. *Practical Education.* 2 vols, 1798. New York: Garland Publishing, 1974.

Esher, Viscount. *The Girlhood of Queen Victoria: A Selection from Her Majesty's Diaries Between the Years of 1832 and 1840.* 2 vols. London: John Murray, 1912.

Fox, Caroline. *The Journals of Caroline Fox, 1835–1871.* Ed. Wendy Monk. London: Elek Books, 1972.

Gallagher, Catherine. *Nobody's Story: The Vanishing Acts of Women Writers in the Marketplace, 1670–1820.* Berkeley: University of California Press, 1994.

Gates, Barbara Timm. Introduction. *Journal of Emily Shore.* Charlottesville: University Press of Virginia (1991): vii–xxx.

'The Girlhood of Queen Victoria', *The Girl's Own Paper*, vol. 1 (1880).

Holland, Rupert. *Historic Girlhoods.* Philadelphia: George W. Jacobs, 1910.

Homans, Margaret. *Royal Representations: Queen Victoria and British Culture, 1837–1876.* Chicago: University of Chicago Press, 1998.

Homans, Margaret and Adrienne Munich, eds. *Remaking Queen Victoria.* Cambridge: Cambridge University Press, 1997.

Houston, Gail Turley. *Royalties: The Queen and Victorian Writers.* Charlottesville: University Press of Virginia, 1999.

———. 'Reading and Writing Victoria: the Conduct Book and the Legal Constitution of Female Sovereignty'. Homans and Munich, *Remaking Queen Victoria*: 159–81.

Hudson, Katherine. *A Royal Conflict: Sir John Conroy and the Young Victoria.* London: Hodder & Stoughton, 1994.

Huxley, Gervas. *Lady Elizabeth and the Grosvenors: Life in a Whig Family, 1822–1839.* London: Oxford University Press, 1965.

Jelinek, Estelle C. *The Tradition of Women's Autobiography: From Antiquity to the Present.* Boston: Twayne, 1986.

Johnson, R. Brimley, ed. *The Letters of Hannah More.* New York: Dial Press, 1925.

Jordan, Ellen. '"Making Good Wives and Mothers"? The Transformation of Middle-Class Girls' Education in Nineteenth-Century Britain'. *History of Education Quarterly*, 31.4 (Winter 1991): 439–62.

Kemble, Frances Anne. *Record of a Girlhood.* 3 vols. London: Richard Bentley and Son, 1878.

Kent, William. *London in the News Through Three Centuries.* London: Staples Press, 1954.

Knight, Alfred E. *Victoria: Her Life and Reign* 6th edn. London: S. W. Partridge, 1902.

Kowaleski-Wallace, Elizabeth. *Their Father's Daughters: Hannah More, Maria Edgeworth and Patriarchal Complicity.* Oxford: Oxford University Press, 1991.

A Lady. *Anecdotes, Personal Traits, and Characteristic Sketches of Victoria the First.* London: William Bennett, 1840.

A Lady of the Court, *Victoria's Golden Reign: A Record of Sixty Years as Maid, Mother, and Ruler.* London: Richard Edward King, 1899.

Langland, Elizabeth. *Nobody's Angels: Middle-Class Women and Domestic Ideology in Victorian Culture.* Ithaca, NY: Cornell University Press, 1995.

———. 'Nation and Nationality: Queen Victoria in the Developing Narrative of Englishness'. Homans and Munich, *Remaking Queen Victoria*: 13–32.

Loeb, Lori Anne. *Consuming Angels: Advertising and Victorian Women.* Oxford: Oxford University Press, 1994.

Longford, Elizabeth. 'Reflections of a Biographer'. *The Literary Biography: Problems and Solutions.* Ed. Dale Salwak. Iowa City: University of Iowa Press, 1996.

———. *Queen Victoria: Born to Succeed.* New York: Harper and Row, 1964.

Lorne, Marquis of. *V.R. I: Her Life and Empire.* London: Harmsworth Books, 1901.

Low, Frances H. *Queen Victoria's Dolls.* London: George Newnes, 1894.

Martineau, Harriet. *Autobiography.* 2 vols. 1877. London: Virago, 1983.

More, Hannah. *Hints Towards Forming the Character of a Young Princess.* 2 vols. London: T. Cadell and W. Davies, 1805.

Mueller, Janel. 'Virtue and Virtuality: Gender in the Self-Representations of Queen Elizabeth I'. *Virtual Gender: Fantasies of Subjectivity and Embodiment.* Ed. Mary Ann O'Farrell and Lynne Vallone. Ann Arbor: University of Michigan Press (1999): 37–64.

Munich, Adrienne. *Queen Victoria's Secrets.* New York: Columbia University Press, 1996.

Myers, Mitzi. 'Romancing the Moral Tale: Maria Edgeworth and the Problematics of Pedagogy'. *Romanticism and Children's Literature in Nineteenth-Century England.* Ed. James Holt McGavran, Jr. Athens, GA: University of Georgia Press (1991): 96–128

——. 'Socializing Rosamond: Educational Ideology and Fictional Form'. *Children's Literature Association Quarterly* 14 (1989): 52–8.

——. 'Canonical "Orphans" and Critical *Ennui*: Rereading Edgeworth's Cross-Writing'. *Children's Literature* 25 (1997): 116–36

Nesbit, E., *Royal Children of English History.* New York: Mershon Company, 1897.

Pardon, George. *Illustrious Women Who Have Distinguished Themselves for Virtue, Piety, and Benevolence,* London: James Blackwood, n.d. [*c.* 1861].

Peterson, Linda H. 'Institionalizing Women's Autobiography: Nineteenth-Century Editors and the Shaping of an Autobiographical Tradition'. *The Culture of Autobiography: Constructions of Self-Representation.* Ed. Robert Folkenflit. Stanford: Stanford University Press (1993): 80–103.

Plowden, Alison. *The Young Victoria.* New York: Stein and Day, 1981.

Rowell, George. *Queen Victoria Goes to the Theatre.* London: Paul Elek, 1978.

St Aubyn, Giles. *Queen Victoria: A Portrait.* New York: Atheneum, 1992.

Sanders, Valerie. *The Private Lives of Victorian Women: Autobiography in Nineteenth-Century England.* New York: St. Martin's Press, 1989.

Scott, John A. Introduction. Frances Anne Kemble, *Journal of a Residence on a Georgian Plantation in 1838–1839.* Athens, GA: University of Georgia Press (1984): ix–lxi.

Seaton, Beverly. *The Language of Flowers: A History.* Charlottesville: University Press of Virginia, 1995.

Smith, A. Asenath. *A Brief Life of Queen Victoria for Children.* London, Glasgow and Dublin: Charles and Dibble, 1901.

Staniland, Kay. *In Royal Fashion: The Clothes of Princess Charlotte of Wales and Queen Victoria, 1796–1901.* London: Museum of London, 1997.

Stein, Richard L. *Victoria's Year: English Literature and Culture, 1837-1838.* Oxford: Oxford University Press, 1987.

Strickland, Agnes. *Queen Victoria: From Birth to Bridal.* London, 1840.

Steedman, Carolyn. *The Tidy House: Little Girls Writing*. London: Virago, 1982.

Stuart, Dorothy Margaret. *Daughter of England: A New Study of Princess Charlotte of Wales and Her Family*. London: Macmillan, 1951.

———. *The Mother of Victoria*. London: Macmillan, 1942.

Thompson, Dorothy. *Queen Victoria: Gender and Power*. London: Virago, 1990.

Tod, Robert J. N., ed. *Caroline Fox: Quaker Blue-Stocking, 1819–1871*. York, England: William Sessions, 1980.

Tooley, Sarah A. *The Personal Life of Queen Victoria* 3rd edn. London: Hodder & Stoughton, 1901.

Vallone, Lynne. *Disciplines of Virtue: Girls' Culture in the Eighteenth and Nineteenth Centuries*. New Haven and London: Yale University Press, 1995.

Wagner-Martin, Linda. *Telling Women's Lives*. New Brunswick, NJ: Rutgers University Press, 1994.

Walton, Mrs O.F. *Pictures and Stories from Queen Victoria's Life*. London: Religious Tract Society, 1901.

Warner, Marina. *Queen Victoria's Sketchbooks*. New York: Crown Publishers, 1979.

Watson, Nicola J. 'Gloriana Victoriana: Victoria and the Cultural Memory of Elizabeth I'. Homans and Munich, *Remaking Queen Victoria*: 79–104.

Weintraub, Stanley. *Victoria: An Intimate Biography*. New York: E. P. Dutton, 1987.

Wilde, Oscar. *The Importance of Being Earnest*. Ed. Ruth Berggren. New York: Vanguard Press, 1987.

Wingrave, Marion M. *The May Blossom; or The Princess and Her People*. London: Frederick Warne and Co., 1881.

Woodham-Smith, Cecil. *Queen Victoria: Her Life and Times, 1819–1861*. London: Penguin, 1972.

Youthful Recreations. Philadelphia. Published by J. Johnson, *c.* 1810.

Index

Adelaide, Queen of William IV (*earlier*
    Duchess of Clarence):
children, 2, 6
in dispute over Victoria's confirmation,
    145
marriage, 204n.2
relations with Victoria's mother, 8
and Victoria's juvenile ball, 119–20
Adolphus Frederick, Prince *see*
    Cambridge, Prince Adolphus
    Frederick, Duke of
Aikin, John, 27
Aikins's nursery classics, 46
Albert, Harold, 160
Albert, Prince of Saxe-Coburg-Gotha
    (*later* Prince Consort):
annotates Duchess of Kent's
    memorandum on Victoria's behaviour,
    45
charitable interests, 189
and Charles of Leiningen's supposed
    spying, 231n.118
criticized in English press, 3
and Fischer's portrait of infant Victoria,
    6
hosts costume balls, 219n.45
temperament, 184
Victoria favours as suitor, 184
and Victoria's knowledge of German,
    12

on Victoria's strong will, 31
visits Victoria, 178–80
Alcott, Louisa May: *Work*, 228n.46
Alexander, Prince of Orange, 177–8
Alexander, Prince of Württemberg, 176–7
*Amulet, The: A Christian and Literary
    Remembrancer*, 97
*Anecdotes, Personal Traits, and
    Characteristic Sketches of Victoria the
    First* (anon), 5, 109
Anglesey, Henry William Paget, 1st Earl
    of, 98
Appleton, Elizabeth: *Early Education*, 20,
    27, 47–8, 211n.5
Argyll, 9th Duke of *see* Lorne, John
    Campbell, Marquis of
Augusta, Dowager Duchess of Saxe-
    Coburg-Saalfeld (Victoria's
    grandmother), 26
Augustus, Prince of Saxe-Coburg Kohary,
    176–8, 184
Austen, Jane, 127, 224n.122
    Mansfield Park, 87

Babbage, Charles: *Economy of
    Manufactures*, 128–9
Baillie, Joanna, 134
Barbauld, Anna Letitia, 27
Barrie, Sir James Matthew:
    Peter Pan, 37

Peter Pan in Kensington Gardens, 1–2, 39

Beatrice, Princess (Victoria's daughter), 188, 217n.8

Bedchamber Affair (1839), 175, 208n.64

Beechey, Sir William, 114

Behnes, William, 31

Belgrave, Lady Elizabeth, 76, 91, 183

Bellini, Vincenzo, 163, 238n.86

Benson, Edward Frederic, 8

Blackstone, Sir William: *Commentaries on the Laws of England*, 187

Blomfield, Charles James, Bishop of London, 43–4, 61–2, 64, 66, 144

Booth, Alison, xviii

Broadstairs, Kent, 18, 134, 138

Brock, Mrs (Victoria's nurse), 28

Bromley, William (engraver), 111

Brontë, Charlotte and Emily, 238n.84

Browning, Elizabeth Barrett, 213n.21

Bulkeley, Sir Richard, 91

Bulwer-Lytton, Edward *see* Lytton, 1st Baron

Butler, Lady Eleanor, 217n.6

Butler, Marilyn, 51

Butler, Mrs Pierce *see* Kemble, Frances Anne

Butler, Weeden, 79, 86

Byron, George Gordon, 6th Baron, 135

Cambridge, Prince Adolphus Frederick, Duke of (Victoria's uncle), 49, 204n.2

Cambridge, Augusta, Duchess of, 6

Cambridge, Prince George William, Duke of (Victoria's cousin), 6, 119, 177

Canterbury, Archbishop of *see* Howley, William

Carlota, Empress of Mexico (*earlier* Charlotte), 71

Caroline, Queen of George I, 2

Casteras, Susan P., 112–13, 170, 198

Chalmers, Anne: journal, 124–6, 130–2, 134, 156

Chalmers, Revd Dr Thomas, 126

Charles I, King: *Eikon Basilike*, 187

Charles, Prince of Leiningen (Victoria's half-brother), 8, 52–3, 119, 186–7, 231n.118, 234n.18

Charles the 12th of Sweden (play), 53, 57

Charlot, Monica, 7, 71–2, 180

Victoria: The Young Queen, 198

Charlotte, Princess (Duke of Clarence's daughter), 6, 12

Charlotte, Princess (George IV's daughter), 2, 41–3, 61, 120, 144, 177–8, 212n.12, 234n.17

Charlotte, Queen of George III, 30

Chatsworth House, Derbyshire, 87, 98

Chester, 91, 98

Chester, Bishop of *see* Sumner, John Bird

Chester, Dean of *see* Davys, George

Choveaux, Mr: gives *Secret Dramas* to Victoria, 42

Christian Keepsake and Missionary Annual, The, 141

Chronology of the Kings of England, 28

Claremont, near Esher, 12, 189, 191–3

Clarence, Prince William, Duke of *see* William IV, King

Clark, Dr (Sir) James, 125, 159, 162–3, 184

Collen, Henry, 33, 142, 167

Colnaghi and Company, 111

Colson, Charlotte, 186

Conroy family:
    accompanies Duchess of Kent on travels, 210n.82
    Victoria's dislike of, 52, 85

Conroy, Elizabeth, Lady, 85

Conroy, Jane, 30, 88

Conroy, (Sir) John:
    attends dinner parties, 223n.119
    Charles of Leiningen favours, 234n.18
    dismissed, 239n.103
    and Duchess of Kent's regency, 72
    gives books to Victoria, 47
    honoured in Oxford, 84–5
    influence on Duchess of Kent, 8, 60–1, 70, 114, 188

interferes in Victoria's upbringing, 140

'Kensington System', 8, 140

Mary Ann Davys dislikes, 209n.65

promotes image of Victoria, 170

proposed as Victoria's private secretary,
160

and Victoria's 1835 illness, 159

and Victoria's education, 61–2, 64, 66,
70–2, 140

in Victoria's family circle, 6, 8

Victoria's hatred of, 18, 30, 52, 150–1,
160

in Victoria's journal, 84

and Victoria's progresses throughout
Britain, 74, 82, 89–90

on Victoria's taking after Queen
Charlotte, 30

and William IV's conflicts with Duchess
of Kent, 147

writes and edits letters for Duchess of
Kent, 147, 150

writes to Melbourne on Victoria's
education, 165–6

Conroy, Victoire:

attends Victoria's juvenile ball, 119

dolls, 17

painting with Victoria, 100

relations with Victoria, 30, 46, 84–5

Victoria dresses up in costume, 87–8

Conyngham, Francis, 2nd Marquis, 198

Cooper family (gypsies), 189–92

Cooper, James Fenimore: *The Bravo*, 130,
136–8, 189

Cowper, William, 28

Crabb, James: *The Gipsies' Advocate*, 189,
191–2

Cumberland, Prince Ernest, Duke of
(Victoria's uncle), 39, 74, 164

Cumberland, Frederica, Duchess of, 6

Darton, John: *Famous Girls Who Have
Become Illustrious Women*, xvi

Dash (Victoria's dog), 15, 88, 111, 199–200,
207n.34

Davys, Revd George, Dean of Chester
(*later* Bishop of Peterborough):

advises on revision of Victoria's studies
as Evangelical, 149

amends Victoria's note on Elizabeth I,
224n.126

dislikes Conroy, 209n.65

examines Victoria for confirmation, 144,
146, 165–6

tutors Victoria, 23, 26–7, 29, 45–6,
212n.15, 221n.81

Davys, Revd Canon (George's son), 45

Davys, Mary Ann (*later* Pratt), 26,
239n.103

DeLuca, Geraldine, xvii

Diana, Princess of Wales, 168

'Distribution of the Day 1829', 45

Donizetti, Gaetano, 238n.86

Eaton Hall, Cheshire, 219nn.34, 45,
226n.11

Edgeworth, Maria, 27, 42, 49–50, 107, 116,
227n.29, 230n.88

'The Basket-Woman', 195

'Forgive and Forget', 196

'Harry and Lucy' tales, 50–6, 81

'The Orphans', 196

The Parent's Assistant, 194, 196, 198

Practical Education (with Richard
Lovell Edgeworth), 54

'Simple Susan', 195

Eliot, George, 238n.84

Elizabeth I, Queen, 10, 28, 120–1, 168

Elizabeth, Princess (Duke of Clarence's
daughter), 6

Ellis, T. Mullett: *The Fairies' Favourite, or
the Story of Queen Victoria told for
Children*, 39

Elphinstone, Margaret Mercer (comtesse
de Flahault), 30

Emerald (yacht), 87

Emmerson, H.H., 37

Ernest I, Duke of Saxe-Coburg-Gotha
(Albert's father), 178, 180

Ernest II, Duke of Saxe-Coburg-Gotha
(Albert's brother), 178, 180, 184
Ernest Christian Charles, Prince of
Hohenlohe-Langenburg, 9, 104,
233n.8
Ernst, Prince of Württemberg, 176–7
Esher, Reginald Baliol Brett, 2nd Viscount:
selections and transcriptions of
Victoria's journals (*The Girlhood of
Queen Victoria*), 157, 188–9, 217n.8,
231n.123, 235n.30, 237n.62
Esterhazy, Prince, 71
Evangelical Movement, 149

Feodore, Princess of Leiningen (*later*
Hohenlohe-Langenburg; Victoria's
half-sister):
attempts to straighten spine, 33
and Collen portrait of Victoria, 33, 142
defends Lehzen against possible
dismissal, 160
final letter to Victoria, 206n.18
gives up drawing, 237n.69
marriage and children, 9, 20, 70, 104,
164, 176
public interest in, 11–12
relations with mother, 6
Victoria misses after departure, 62, 70
Victoria sends children's books to, 47
Victoria writes to, 53, 57, 70, 104, 119,
155, 186, 189, 192–3, 199
and Victoria's concern for poor, 189, 192
and Victoria's dolls, 16–18
and Victoria's pleasure at accession, 199
Victoria's relations with, 9, 11–12, 19,
30, 49, 104–5
on Victoria's tormenting canaries, 16
on women's role, 156
Ferdinand (of Saxe-Coburg Kohary), King
of Portugal, 176–8, 236n.56
Ferdinand, Prince of Saxe-Coburg
(Duchess of Kent's brother), 104, 178,
184
Fielding, Sarah: *The Governess*, 141

Fischer, Paul Johann Georg: portrait of
infant Victoria, 6
Fitzalan, Henry Grenville Fitzalan-
Howard, Lord (*later* 14th Duke of
Norfolk), 71
FitzClarence, Adolphus and Sophia
(William IV's illegitimate children), 49
Flahault, comtesse de *see* Elphinstone,
Margaret Mercer
Fox, Anna Maria, 125
Fox, Barclay, 126
Fox, Caroline: journal, 124, 126, 128,
132–3, 156
Fox, Maria (*née* Barclay), 125
Fox, Robert Were, 125
Fozzard, Captain: Riding School, 25,
133–4
Frederick, Prince *see* York, Prince
Frederick, Duke of
Fry, Elizabeth, 134

Gates, Barbara Timm, 129
Gay, John, 28
Gazelle (yacht), 87
George III, King, 2
George IV, King (*earlier* Prince Regent):
confers title on Louise Lehzen, 23
death and succession, 18–19, 61, 67, 134,
204n.5
denies financial allowance for Victoria,
236n.45
and Duchess of Kent's finances, 68–9
marriage and child, 2
and Victoria's baptism, 7
in Victoria's childhood book, 28–9
George, Prince of Cumberland (*later* King
George V of Hanover), 6, 181
George William, Prince *see* Cambridge,
Prince George William, Duke of
Gernsheim, Helmut and Alison: *Victoria R*,
113–14
Girl's Own Paper, xvi, xviii
Gloucester, Princess Mary, Duchess of,
211n.3

Goldsmith, Oliver, 224n.122
Grandineau, M. (Victoria's French tutor), 29
Great Malvern, Worcestershire, 49
Greville, Charles, 33
Grey, Charles, 2nd Earl, 69–70
Grisi, Giulia, 93, 130, 157, 165
Gustav, Prince of Hohenlohe-Langenburg, 233n.8

Hall, Mrs S.C.: 'The Mosspits', 97
Harcourt, Edward Venables Vernon, Archbishop of York, 156
Hardwick Hall, Derbyshire, 217n.1
Hargraves, J. (of Tunbridge Wells), 106
Hastings, Lady Flora, 150
Hastings, Sussex, 133
Hayter, Sir George, 16, 109, 111–14, 169
Hazledine, Mr (foundry owner), 91
Heathcote, Elizabeth Anne, 9
Heathcote, Lady Elizabeth Keith, 9, 11
Highland Smugglers, The (novel), 98
Hofland, Barbara: *The Young Northern Traveller, or the Invalid Restored*, 100
Hohenlohe-Langenburg, Charles, Prince of (Feodore's son), 104
Hohenlohe-Langenburg, Eliza, Princess of (Feodore's daughter), 104
Hohenlohe-Langenburg, Prince Ernest Christian Charles *see* Ernest Christian Charles, Prince of Hohenlohe-Langenburg
Hohenlohe-Langenburg, Prince Gustav *see* Gustav, Prince of Hohenlohe-Langenburg
Honey, Mrs (dancer), 93
Howes, Mrs (staymaker of Hastings), 133
Howley, William, Archbishop of Canterbury, 1, 7, 62, 64–5, 67, 144–6, 198, 224n.126
Hudson, Katherine, 84

Innkeeper's Daughter, The (melodrama), 93

Irving, Washington: *The Alhambra*, 154
Italy: Victoria wishes to travel in, 171–2

Jelinek, Estelle C., 135
Jordan, Dorothea, 73
Juvenile Forget Me Not, The (annual), 31, 230n.88

Kaye, John, Bishop of Lincoln, 43–4, 61–2, 64, 66
Keats, John, 225n.8
Kemble, Frances Anne (Fanny):
riding, 134
Journal of a Residence in America, 153–4, 153–4
Record of a Girlhood (diary), 124–6, 132, 134–5, 156
Kennedy, William, 31
Kensington Palace:
animals and pets at, 16
Duchess of Kent renovates, 81, 182
Victoria's childhood in, 1–3, 6, 11, 17, 85, 119
'Kensington System', 8, 140
Kent, Edward, Duke of (Victoria's father), 2–3, 6–8, 34
Kent, Victoire, Duchess of, Princess of Leiningen (Victoria's mother):
advises Victoria against political partisanship, 117, 175
background, 3
and birth of Victoria, 4, 6
birthday celebrations (1832), 91
breastfeeds baby Victoria, 4–5
concern for Victoria's status as heir, 73–4
confides in Conroy, 8
Conroy's influence on, 60–1, 114, 140, 160
devotion to Victoria's upbringing, 12, 19–20, 25, 67–8, 71–2, 117–18, 132–3, 148
disapproves of novels, 46
dispute with William IV over Victoria's confirmation, 143–7

finances, 61, 68–70
gives concert for Victoria, 165
gives educational and improving books
    to Victoria, 42–3, 97, 141, 149
holidays and travels with Victoria, 14,
    18, 106
and husband's death, 7–8
jealousy of Melbourne, 199
Leopold helps to support, 12
limited English, 8, 12, 26
loses influence with Victoria on
    accession, 199
marriage to Edward, 204n.2
named sole Regent for Victoria, 19, 61,
    72–3
in Norfolk with Victoria, 158
organizes Victoria's progresses, 75–6,
    78, 84, 89–92, 119
parties and balls, 142, 164, 177, 180, 184,
    223n.119
patronizes shops and establishments, 133
portrait with Victoria, 114
Princess Sophia supports, 52
promotes image of Victoria, 170
receives loyal addresses on travels, 78,
    84, 91, 158
relations with royal family, 73, 81, 147,
    181–2
religious practices, 149
seeks approbation for Victoria's
    upbringing, 61
in Tunbridge Wells, 106
Victoria dedicates story to, 138–9
and Victoria's 1835 illness, 159–60, 162
and Victoria's dressing up, 88–9
and Victoria's education, 26–7, 60–2,
    64, 118–19, 131–2, 165–6, 175, 187,
    221n.81, 222n.106
on Victoria's honesty, 43–5
and Victoria's interest in gypsies, 191
and Victoria's marriage prospects,
    176–7, 180–1
and Victoria's refusal to resume
    progresses, 151–2

Victoria's relations with, 67–8, 82, 84,
    114–18, 147–53, 160, 162, 164, 188,
    239n.103
as Victoria's spokesperson, 194
and Victoria's tantrums, 19
Westall requests annuity from for blind
    sister, 172
William IV rebukes, 183, 194
and William IV's promise of financial
    aid to Victoria, 183–4
Kent, William, 3
King's Lynn, Norfolk, 157–8
Knutsford, 91
Kowaleski-Wallace, Elizabeth, 53
Kuper, Revd Dr William, 20

Lablache, Luigi, 130, 165
Lamb, Charles, 27
Lane, Richard, 35, 37, 173
Laurence, Samuel, 132
Leamington, Warwickshire, 90
Lehzen, Louise, Baroness:
    encourages Victoria's journal keeping,
        75
    gives miniature album to Victoria, 15
    hostility to Conroy, 160
    influence on Victoria, 231n.121
    inks over Victoria's pencillings, 78
    nurses Victoria during 1835 illness,
        161–2
    reads aloud to Victoria, 155
    reads Victoria's journal, 135, 231n.121
    replaces maid, 186
    status in Victoria's household, 165
    takes sacrament with Victoria, 150
    travels with Victoria, 85
    Victoria confides in, 23
    Victoria dedicates story to, 49
    Victoria reads to from Leopold's
        Directions and Advices, 178
    and Victoria's awareness of station, 44–5
    and Victoria's behaviour, 43
    Victoria's devotion to, 23, 30, 49, 70, 82,
        114, 147–8, 161–2, 164, 188, 208n.58

and Victoria's dolls, 16–18, 82, 88
in Victoria's family circle, 6
as Victoria's governess, 6, 12, 23–5,
    28–30, 33, 98, 131
and Victoria's interest in gypsies, 191
on Victoria's story-telling, 56–7
Leiningen, Prince Charles of *see* Charles,
    Prince of Leiningen
Leopold, King of the Belgians (Prince of
    Leiningen):
as Belgian King, 69
castigates William IV and George IV,
    181, 183
correspondence and relations with
    Victoria, 12, 14, 63, 70–1, 100, 102–3,
    107, 120, 159, 160–1, 175, 187, 194,
    199–200
departs from England (1831), 70
English pension, 12
financial support for sister (Duchess of
    Kent) in England, 69
gives financial aid to Victoria, 236n.45
and Hayter's portrait of Victoria, 109,
    111–13
influence on Victoria, 14–15, 102, 114,
    163, 178, 187
marriage to Princess Charlotte, 123, 178
preoccupation with health, 103–4
on role and demands of royalty, 92,
    102–4, 158
second marriage (to Louise), 70
sends book to Victoria, 153
son born, 164
supports Albert as suitor for Victoria, 180
Victoria confesses wish to travel on
    continent to, 100
on Victoria's eating habits, 32
and Victoria's education, 65, 131
on Victoria's popular acceptance as
    English, 174
on Victoria's small stature, 31, 111, 163
visits Victoria in England, 159, 163, 187
warns of spies in household, 175
The Directions and Advices (manual), 178

Lincoln, Bishop of *see* Kaye, John
'Little Girl's Lament for the Fairies, A'
    (poem), 116
'Little Girl's Soliloquy on New Year's Day,
    A' (poem), 115
Liverpool, Charles Jenkinson, 3rd Earl of,
    181
Loeb, Lori Anne, 156
London, Bishop of *see* Blomfield, Charles
    James
Longford, Elizabeth, Countess of, xvii, 113
Lorne, John Campbell, Marquis of (*later*
    9th Duke of Argyll): *V.R.I: Her Life
    and Empire*, 27, 45
Louis XIV, King of France, 163
Louise, Queen of the Belgians (Leopold's
    wife), 14, 70, 159–61, 164, 171, 187–9,
    231n.122, 236n.56
Low, Frances H., 18
Lytton, Edward George Earle Bulwer-, 1st
    Baron: *Godolphin*, 97–8

Mackintosh, Sir James, 155
Malibran, Marie Félicité, 130
Malvern Hills, Worcestershire, 18
Mangnall's Historical Questions, 107
Maria da Gloria, Queen of Portugal, 71,
    177–8, 236n.56
Martineau, Harriet, 153, 204n.2
Mary II, Queen, 224n.121
Mary, Princess *see* Gloucester, Princess
    Mary, Duchess of
Mary, Queen of Scots, 121
Mason, Anne, 186
Melbourne, William Lamb, 2nd Viscount:
    Fanny Kemble admires, 126
    and government changes, 208n.64
    and Victoria's education, 165–6
    Victoria's relations with, 7, 23, 174, 188,
        199, 226n.13
    and William IV's disclaiming Victoria's
        declining financial aid, 184
Mensdorff-Pouilly, Hugo and Alphonso
    (Victoria's cousins), 84, 176

Mensdorff-Pouilly, Countess Sophia
(Duchess of Kent's sister; Victoria's
aunt), 84, 147, 230n.87, 232n.132
Milton, John: *Paradise Lost*, 187
Mitford, Mary Russell: 'The Storm', 46
Monk, Wendy, 125
More, Hannah, 12, 42, 47, 107, 134
*Hints Towards Forming the Character of
a Young Princess*, 40–3, 71
The Search for Happiness (play), 87
Müller, Johannes von: *Universal History*,
131
Murray, Lady George, 132
Myers, Mitzi, 54, 196

Nemours, Duke of, 181
Nesbit, E.: *Royal Children of English
History*, 200
New Epitome of the British History, A,
107
New Year's Gift and Juvenile Souvenir, The,
21–2, 27, 115
Norris Castle, Isle of Wight, 119
North Wales Chronicle, 92
Northumberland, Charlotte Florentia,
Duchess of:
duties and title redefined, 165
Feodore seeks help to prevent Lehzen's
dismissal, 160
gives Hannah More book to Victoria,
42
and Persian princes' flattery of Victoria,
186
and Victoria's confirmation into Church,
144–6
Victoria's letter of dismissal to, 194
as Victoria's state governess, 42, 70–1,
118, 131
Norwich, 91

Orleans, Ferdinand Philip Louis Charles,
Duke of, 181
Otho, King of Greece, 181
Ouseley, Sir Gore, 186

Oxford:
confers honours on Conroy, 84–5
Victoria visits, 84, 98

Pappenheim, Count, 186–7
Parker, Anne, 131
Peel, Sir Robert, 208n.64
*Pictures and Stories from Queen Victoria's
Life*, 78
Plâs Newydd, Anglesey, 98
Plowden, Alison, 30
Poetry Without Fiction; by a Mother, 28
Ponsonby, Sir Henry, 60
Ponsonby, Sarah, 217n.6
Portugal: revolutions in, 235n.33
Pückler-Muskau, Prince Hermann von,
186–7
Pym, Horace N., 125

Ramsgate, Kent, 14, 16, 18, 21, 134, 164,
182, 186
Regency Bill (1831), 72
Rossini, Gioachino Antonio: *The Barber of
Seville*, 93, 238n.86
Rowell, George: *Queen Victoria Goes to the
Theatre*, 87
Rowley, George, 84
Russell, William: *History of Modern
Europe*, 42, 131

St Laurent, Julie de, 7
Sanders, Valerie: *The Private Lives of
Victorian Women*, 78
Saxe-Coburg Kohary, Prince Augustus of
see Augustus, Prince of Saxe-Coburg
Kohary
Saxe-Coburg, Prince Ferdinand of *see*
Ferdinand, Prince of Saxe-Coburg
Saxe-Coburg-Gotha *see* Albert, Prince;
Ernest I, Duke; Ernest II, Duke
Saxe-Coburg-Saalfeld, Dowager Duchess
Augusta of *see* Augusta, Dowager
Duchess of Saxe-Coburg-Saalfeld
Saxe-Weimar, Prince William of, 71

Scenes of British Wealth, 128
Scott, Sir Walter, 135
Sévigné, Marie de Rabutin-Chantal,
    marquise de, 155
Shoberl, Frederic: *The Language of*
    Flowers, 173
Shore, Arabella, 125
Shore, Emily:
    journal, 124–32, 134–6, 154–6, 165
    religious devotion, 149
Shore, Louisa, 125
Shore, Mackworth, 131
Shore, Margaret Anne (*née* Twopenny), 125
Shore, Thomas S., 125
Smith, Elder and Company (publishers),
    125
Smith, Thomas Assheton, 87
Sophia, Countess Mensdorff *see*
    Mensdorff-Pouilly, Countess Sophia
Sophia, Princess (Victoria's aunt), 6, 30,
    52
Steedman, Carolyn, 53
Stein, Richard L., 190, 192
    Victoria's Year: English Literature and
    Culture, 1837–1838, 198
Steward, Mr (Victoria's tutor), 29, 63
Stopford, Lady Mary, 209n.65
Strickland, Agnes, 73, 150
    'Sister's Love', 105–6
Stuart, Dorothy Margaret, 19, 30
Sully, Maxmilien de Béthune, duc de:
    Memoirs, 153
Sully, Thomas, 230n.88
Sumner, John Bird, Bishop of Chester:
    Exposition of the Gospel of St
    Matthew, 154
Sussex, Augustus Frederick, Duke of
    (Victoria's uncle), 14

Taglioni, Marie, 93
Taylor, Sir Herbert, 144–5
Thackeray, William Makepeace, 227n.34
Thompson, Dorothy: *Queen Victoria:*
    Gender and Power, 199

Times, The: reports royal births, 6
Trimmer, Sarah, 27, 116
Tubeuf, Pauline von, 8, 19–20
Tunbridge Wells, Kent, 106–8, 142, 153,
    168, 222n.105

Vanity Fair (magazine), 9
Victoria, Queen:
    absent from William IV's coronation,
        73
    accession, 188, 198–9, 203n.9
    achieves majority at age eighteen, 72,
        132, 148, 193
    advised against political partisanship,
        117, 175
    appearance, 31–5, 109, 157, 162, 186,
        221n.86, 224n.121
    artistic imagination, 56
    attends juvenile balls, 71, 119
    attitude to babies, 126
    aversion to bishops, 12
    baptized (Alexandrina Victoria), 7, 143
    becomes aware of station, 44–5
    'Behaviour Books', 15, 24–6, 29, 44, 49
    birth, 3
    boisterousness, 85–6, 184
    boredom, 119
    in Caroline Fox's diary, 133
    collects objects on travels, 80
    concern for poor and gypsies, 189–93,
        195
    confirmation into Church of England,
        142–8, 150
    Conroy's influence on upbringing, 8
    coronation, 224n.121
    court and household as Queen, 26
    daily routine, 45–6, 98
    'Daily State' books, 29
    dancing, 71, 87
    and death of father, 6, 8
    on decline and death of William IV,
        194
    develops taste for gossip, 186–7
    on display to people, 89–92

dolls, 16–18, 30, 82, 87–8

drawing and painting, 15, 27, 50, 98, 100, 127, 136, 190, 201, 237n.69

dress and clothing, 10–11, 168

dressing up and love of costume, 87–9

early education, 23–4, 26–30, 39

eating habits, 32–3, 186

emotional attachment to family, 104–6

emotionalism, 15

exercises and health regime, 162–3

Fanny Kemble praises, 134

fictional family life, 51–4, 60

fondness for animals and pets, 15–16, 111, 199–200

formal educational training, 40–2, 60–3, 70, 98, 107–8, 118–19, 130–2, 165–6, 175, 221n.81, 222n.106, 238n.90

genealogy and family background, 2

growing seriousness, 163–4

hair loss, 232n.123

handwriting, 63, 78

as heiress presumptive, 19, 37, 65, 73, 120

honesty and truth-telling, 43–4

hostility to Conroy, 30, 52, 150–1, 160

hosts fancy-dress balls, 219n.45

illnesses: (1832), 82; (1835), 159–63

journal, 25, 75–85, 88, 92–5, 97–8, 109, 124, 134–5, 142, 154–5, 157–8, 178, 186, 188, 190, 201

juvenile writings and stories, 21–2, 48–60, 138–42, 201

keeps account books, 100

knowledge of royal predecessors, 120–1

lacks close childhood friends, 30, 109

language studies and proficiency, 12, 41, 45, 63, 142, 165, 170–1, 233n.8

Leopold's influence on, 14–15, 102–4

letter-writing, 155

in line of succession, 3–4, 29, 44, 132

marriage prospects, 176–81, 184, 186

meets Albert, 179–80

menstrual period pains, 91, 157, 218n.20

morbid sensibilities, 163

mother breastfeeds, 4–6

musical education and interests, 98, 100, 130, 142, 165, 238n.86

name modified, 74

partiality to Whigs, 175

performance as princess and queen, 14–15

popular image of as girl, 37–9, 132, 168–70, 172–3, 200

portraits and sketches of, 6, 9–11, 33–5, 37, 60, 109, 111–14, 133, 142, 169, 173

progresses throughout Britain, 74, 75–80, 84–5, 89–92, 98, 100, 106–8, 119, 129, 172

puts on weight, 221n.86

reading and books, 27–8, 46–7, 97–8, 117, 128, 130–1, 136, 142, 153–6, 158, 187, 195–6, 198, 200

refuses to resume progresses, 151–2

relations with Louise Lehzen, 23, 30, 49, 70, 82, 114, 147–8, 161–2, 164, 188, 208n.58

relations with mother, 67–8, 82, 84, 114–18, 147–53, 160, 162, 164, 188, 231n.122, 239n.103

religious education and beliefs, 20–1, 149, 237n.63

riding, 25, 86, 134

rumoured illness, 73–4

sailing, 87

sculptures of, 31

shell collection, 206n.22

small stature, 31, 111, 163

strong will, 31, 64

tested by outside (ecclesiastical) examiners, 62, 64–7

theatre-going and love of drama, 27, 53, 88, 92–3, 97, 193, 201

toys, 11

travels, 18, 48–9, 156–7

upbringing, 20, 71–2

vaccinated against smallpox, 6

wilfulness and tantrums, 18–20, 23, 27, 150

William IV offers financial support for, 183–4

wish to travel abroad, 100, 171–2
witnesses William IV's public rebuke of
    mother, 183
and women's role, 156, 175
writing style, 48
Leaves from Our Life in the Highlands,
    60
*More Leaves from . . . a Life in the
    Highlands*, 60
Victoria, Crown Princess (Queen Victoria's
    daughter; *later* Empress of Germany),
    126
'Victorian': as term, 2
*Victoria's Golden Reign: a Record of Sixty
    Years as Maid, Mother, and Ruler* (by
    A Lady of the Court), 168

Wagner-Martin, Linda: *Telling Women's
    Lives*, xvi
Wales: Victoria visits, 75, 78–9, 86, 89,
    91–2, 98
Washington, George, 44
Watts, Alaric, 115
Wedderburn, Miss J. (illustrator), 117
Weintraub, Stanley, 180
Wells, Norfolk, 158
Westall, Richard, 15, 60, 100, 111, 190
    death, 172
Wigram, Clive, 1st Baron Wigram of
    Clewer, 188
Wilberforce, William, 12, 134, 149
Wilde, Oscar: *The Importance of Being
    Earnest*, 122–4
William III (of Orange), King, 3
William IV, King (*earlier* Duke of
    Clarence):
    children, 2, 6, 72–3, 118
    coronation, 73, 143
    death, 175, 198, 203n.9
    disapproves of Duchess of Kent's
        renovations at Kensington Palace, 81,
        182

and Duchess of Kent's Regency, 61
    gives juvenile ball for Victoria, 119
    health decline, 194
    improves Duchess of Kent's finances,
        69–70
    Leopold on Victoria's succession to,
        234n.17
    marriage, 204n.2
    opposes Victoria's progresses, 75–6, 78,
        151–2
    promises financial aid to Victoria on
        coming-of-age, 183
    publicly rebukes Duchess of Kent, 183,
        194
    relations with Duchess of Kent, 73, 147,
        181–2
    succession to, 18, 37, 102, 182
    and Victoria's confirmation, 144–6, 149
    and Victoria's marriage prospects, 177,
        180
    and Victoria's name, 74
William, Hereditary Prince of Orange
    (*later* King William II), 177, 180
William, Prince of Saxe-Weimar *see* Saxe-
    Weimar, Prince William of
Wilson, Cornwall Baron, 174
Wingrave, Marion: *The May Blossom; or
    The Princess and Her People*, 37
Woodham-Smith, Cecil, 68
Wren, Sir Christopher, 3
Württemberg *see* Alexander, Prince of
    Württemberg; Ernest, Prince of
    Württemberg

Yearsley, Ann ('milkwoman poetess'),
    211n.2
York, 156
York, Archbishop of *see* Harcourt, Edward
    Venables Vernon
York, Prince Frederick, Duke of, 204n.6
Young Lady's Book, The, 175, 192
Youthful Recreations, 86